Rethinking Progress

Rethinking Progress

MOVEMENTS, FORCES, AND IDEAS
AT THE END OF THE
20th CENTURY

Edited by

JEFFREY C. ALEXANDER

and

PIOTR SZTOMPKA

Boston
UNWIN HYMAN
London   Sydney   Wellington

Unwin Hyman Inc.,
8 Winchester Place, Winchester, Mass. 01890, USA

Published by the Academic Division of
Unwin Hyman Ltd
15/17 Broadwick Street, London W1V 1FP, UK

Allen & Unwin (Australia) Ltd,
8 Napier Street, North Sydney, NSW 2060, Australia

Allen & Unwin (New Zealand) Ltd in association with the
Port Nicholson Press Ltd,
Compusales Building, 75 Ghuznee Street, Wellington 1, New Zealand

First published in 1990

Library of Congress Cataloging in Publication Data is available

British Library Cataloguing in Publication Data

Rethinking progress: movements, forces and ideas at the end of the 20th
century.
1. Progress
I, Alexander, Jeffrey C. II. Sztompka, Piotr
303.44
ISBN 0-04-445753-7

Typeset in 10/12 point Palatino by Fotographics (Bedford) Ltd
and printed in Great Britain by Cambridge University Press

Contents

vii

Notes on contributors

Jeffrey Alexander is Professor and Chair in the Department of Sociology at the University of California. He is the author of *Theoretical Logic in Sociology, Twenty Lectures: Sociological Theory Since World War II, Structure and Meaning* and *Action and Its Environments*. He has also edited several books of essays. He is currently studying the cultural dynamics of democratic societies.

Klaus Eder is Professor of Sociology at the European University Institute in Florence, Italy. His most recent publication is *Die Vergesellschaftung der Natur. Studien zur sozialen Evolution der praktischen Vernunft*. His main sociological interests are the sociology of social movements, political communication and legal sociology.

Eva Etzioni-Halevy is Professor in the Department of Sociology and Anthropology, Bar-Ilan University, Israel. She is the author of *Social Change, Bureaucracy and Democracy, The Knowledge Elite and the Failure of Prophecy, National Broadcasting Under Siege* and *Fragile Democracy*. Her areas of interest include political sociology, bureaucracy and social theory.

Ron Eyerman is a Senior Lecturer in the Department of Sociology, University of Lund, Sweden. His recent publications include *Reading Social Movements* and *The Emerging Environmental Consciousness: A Comparative Study of the Environmental Movements in Sweden, Denmark and the Netherlands*, both with Andrew Jamison. He is currently researching a comparative historical study of intellectuals.

Bob Holton is Associate Professor of Sociology at Flinders University of South Australia. Publications include *The Transition from Feudalism to Capitalism, Cities, Capitalism and Civilisation* and (with Bryan Turner) *Talcott Parsons on Economy and Society*. His research interests include theories of economy and society, and processes of immigration, ethnic relations and cultural pluralism.

Hans Joas is Professor of Sociology and North American studies at the Free University of Berlin. Recent publications include *Social Action and Human Nature* and "Institutionalization as a Creative Process" in American Journal of Sociology 94. His main sociological interests are the sociological theory and history of sociology and the sociology of peace and war.

David Kettler is a Professor in the Department of Political Studies at Trent University, Canada. His recent publications include " 'Sancho Panza as Governor'. Max Weber and the quest for substantive justice in law" in Heinze Zipprian and Gerhard Wagner (eds), *Reader zu Max Webers Wissenschaftslehre* and "Unionization and labour regimes in Canada and the United States: considerations for comparative research" in *Labour/Le Travail*, 25 (Spring 1990). His interests revolve around varieties of politically consequential and institutionalized knowledge forms.

Volka Meja is Professor of Sociology at the Memorial University of Newfoundland, Canada. His recent publications include *Modern German Sociology* and *Politisches Wissen*. His current research focuses on the sociology of knowledge and on political ideologies and social movements in the present-day West.

Carlo Mongardini is Professor of Sociology at the University of Rome. His recent publications include *Il magico e il modern, Saggio sul gioco*, and *Profili storici per la sociologia contemporanea*. His research interests are in the history of sociology, sociological theory, political sociology and the sociology of culture.

Dietrich Rueschemeyer teaches sociology at Brown University and is Director of Brown's Center for the Comparative Study of Development. He is the author of *Power and the Division of Labour* and co-editor of *Bringing the State Back In*. He is currently working on problems social knowledge and the origins of modern social policy.

Marilyn Rueschemeyer teaches sociology at the Rhode Island School of Design and at Brown University. She is the author of *Professional Work and Marriage: An East–West Comparison*, co-author of *Soviet Emigré Artists*, and co-editor of *The Quality of Life in the GDR*. She is interested in the impact of different political and economic systems on personal life.

Piotr Sztompka is Professor of Sociology and Chair of Theoretical Sociology at the Jagiellonian University, Krakow, Poland. His books in English include *System and Function, Sociological Dilemmas, Robert K. Merton: An Intellectual Profile*, and *Theory of Social Becoming*. His research focuses on sociological theory, history of social thought and the philosophy of the social sciences.

Kenneth Thompson is Professor of Sociology at the Open University, UK. His recent publications include *Emile Durkheim, Beliefs and Ideology*, and "How religious are the British?" in T. Thomas (ed.), *The British: Their Religious Beliefs and Practices 1800–1986*. He is current doing research on public controversies about religion in politics.

Preface

This book is the outcome of a conference organized by the editors at Jagiellonian University in Krakow, Poland, which took place between June 28 and July 1, 1988. The topic was "Social progress and sociological theory: movements, forces, and ideas at the end of the twentieth century." The meeting was the first material result of our ongoing efforts to organize an "invisible college" of sociological theorists on an international scale, an effort that has now come to fruition as a "working group" of the International Sociological Association, to be established as a Research Committee on Theory. The conference brought together twenty-six scholars from twelve countries. While only a selection of these papers eventually found their way into print, the success of the proceedings was as much due to the contributors whose work is not included here. To all of those who participated in the conference we wish to extend our warm thanks. We look forward to equally stimulating theoretical discussions in the future. We would also like to record our gratitude to Pat Johnson, without whose organizing skills the creation and continuing co-ordination of this international project would not have been possible.

Jeffrey C. Alexander, Los Angeles
Piotr Sztompka, Krakow

To the memory of Stefan Nowak,
who lived science as a vocation

Introduction

JEFFREY C. ALEXANDER and PIOTR SZTOMPKA

This volume is premised on the belief that it is neither too early nor too late to begin taking stock of our century.

When we do so, we cannot fail to be struck by a deep historical irony. Just as the nineteenth century ended with a *fin de siècle* period of brooding introspection and pessimism about the possibility for progress, so has our own. Certainly this does not mean that there has been no progress between these two end-of-the-century periods; nor does it suggest that the world views and social theory of the two epochs are the same. There has been much social progress in the meantime and even, we are so bold as to believe, significant progress in social theory itself. Still, the foreboding that presaged the beginning of the twentieth century has been vindicated in often tragic ways. If the present period is different, it is less because progress has been made than because, after another century of hope and despair, we are forced to reflect once again on why it has not been enough. If our reflections are just as urgent as our predecessors', they are also more cautious. This time, one hopes, the concept of progress may not be so easily given up.

Progress, of course, was initially a religious idea. Within the Judeo-Christian tradition the notion of linear development toward a utopian endpoint became a dominant preoccupation. If the Reformation brought this heavenly idea down to earth, the Enlightenment gave it for the first time a fully secular form. Despite romantic reactions against particular versions of secular progress, nineteenth-century culture and social thought were dominated by confident peans to the inherently positive nature of social development, even when these took on radical or communist forms. It was in the nineteenth century that there emerged the clear outlines of what might be called "progressivist" thought.

By the 1890s, however, there emerged a significant reaction against this progressive vision. The rigors of early industrial capitalism, the existential dangers of secularization, the continuing repression exercised in anti-democratic governments – these and other accumulating grievances against "modernity" created a growing sense of crisis and even decline.

1

The theorists who formed the basis for contemporary social science – people like Freud, Weber, Durkheim, and Lukàcs – were deeply affected by this first crisis of modernity, which exhibited most of the characteristics that we associate with the crisis of modernity today.

From the perspective of this first generation of social theorists, the events that transpired in the first half of the twentieth century would certainly have validated their concern about the endemic pathologies of modern life. Two world wars decimated Europe, killing off the best and the brightest of several generations and completely transforming the continent's institutional life. Depression and mass genocide reinforced the sense of a fundamental crisis in modern culture and society.

Yet, ironically, the Second World War seemed to have a purifying effect. From its ashes there arose the sense that a new "post-war world" had been created. After the Chinese revolution, millennial expectations for world communism developed to a heightened pitch. The welfare state brought new morale and equanimity to western capitalist nations. Decolonization and national liberation movements created intense expectations for modernization and rapid development in the Third World.

The 1960s brought these expectations to their highest point, marking the apotheosis of post-war optimism. By the end of the decade, however, these hopes seemed doomed to disappointment. Apocalyptic fears replaced millennial hopes. Western capitalist economies entered a long phase of stagnation. The prospects for social development in Third World countries looked increasingly bleak. World communism underwent a prolonged crisis and in the 1980s entered a period of long-term, ultimately fatal, decline.

Over the last decade progressivism has receded from its once commanding intellectual position. Its place has been taken by a vague congeries of artistic and intellectual movements that emphasize the irrationality of social development and the fragmentation of culture. The emergence of this perspective, which has been called postmodernism, casts doubt on linear conceptions of historical development. It marks the second crisis of modernity.

The essays in this volume explore in a myriad of ways – some in sharp detail, others in broad brush – the social reasons for this second crisis. Contributors discuss the increasing frequency of ecological calamities, the rebirth of religious cults, the emergence of nuclear war, the loss of traditional moral cohesion. In the end, however, most of the theorists who have participated in this volume sense a need to go beyond this all too familiar interpretive mode. They argue, instead, that there is not so much an objective decline of social and cultural progress as declining credibility in progress as a viable belief. Reciting the litany of contemporary woes may not be to the point. Was there ever an extended historical period in which societies were not threatened by serious objective dangers? Still, if the new crisis of modernity is real in a subjective sense, it can and will have objective results, not least in the field of social theory itself.

For social theorists, the growing disparagement of progress as a belief system has very specific consequences. It means that sociological theories based on the premise of automatic development, in either the social, cultural, or psychological spheres, are no longer considered true. It means that the social forces and causal sequences posited by such theories – for example, that industrialization, secularization, and differentiation will lead to emancipation through increased education and democracy – have been thrown into doubt. It means that the agents that such theories posit as the carriers of progressive change – groups like intellectuals, scientists, and the workers – are increasingly viewed as either much less significant than in earlier years or as having failed to act in traditionally expected ways.

The crisis of confidence in progress, in other words, has become a crisis in the explanatory power and emancipating potential of western socio-logical theory. Our contributors address themselves to this theoretical challenge within the framework of the postmodern movement. They demonstrate the inadequacy of our traditional thinking about the forces and carriers of social development, and they suggest that the very concept of progress itself must be reformulated.

The aim of these contributions is not to deny either the possibility of progress, or the vision of an emancipatory social theory. On the contrary, they demonstrate that there are still forces and carriers of progress. To find them, however, we must understand the notion of progress, and the whole notion of modernity, in a different, much less narrowly defined way. The theorizing in this volume aims to overcome the confinement of progressivist theory but not to dispense with the idea of progress more broadly defined. Armed with a different kind of social theory, it is possible to theorize, to evaluate, and even to measure progress in a postprogressive way.

The four papers opening the volume identify various aspects of the historical and intellectual context in which the issue of progress finds itself at the end of the twentieth century. The diagnosis is pessimistic but not fatalistic. In his chapter, "Between progress and apocalypse: social theory and the dream of reason in the twentieth century," Jeffrey Alexander defines some crucial presuppositions of the idea of progress and traces their reflection in social consciousness and social theory from the period of triumphant modernity in the nineteenth century up to the present postmodernist debate. The core assumption is human perfectibility: the possibility and likelihood of transforming the world for the better. The means to that end is the application of reason. The twentieth century embraces this "dream of reason" and all the hopes it entails. Almost immediately, however, it turned into the "nightmare of reason," and violence and force began their reign instead. Alexander suggests that apocalypse displaces perfection, and he outlines the strange, ambivalent experience of the twentieth century, that "wondrous and tragic time." On the one hand, there has been uncontestable progress in many areas of life, such as in technology, science, social emancipation, and human rights; on the other, there has been dramatic regress – two total wars, genocidal murder, state terrorism, totalitarian regimes, ecological devastation, meaningless consumerism. The author believes that theoretical discourse by its very nature is a form of self-reflection, a mental reconstruction of its time. The ambiguity of our century finds its expression at the level of social theory, in a taught dialogue between pessimism and optimism, reason and unreason. The author singles out four broad intellectual currents that have embodied the faith in reason, and the antirationalist standpoints that have developed in opposition to this faith. He identifies clear discontinuities in the work of leading masters of twentieth-century thought – Weber, Durkheim, Wittgenstein, Freud, Keynes, Lévi-Strauss, Sartre, Marcuse – and suggests that they result from the theorists' intellectual ambivalence about their social experience. But there is a sign of hope. Alexander ends on a mildly optimistic note. Reason is preserved, he argues, not only as the substantive social goal of twentieth-century theory but at the level of meta-theoretical reflection, as a tool for understanding unreason. Rational explanations of irrationality may be a way of curbing irrationality. Science, including social science, remains as the ultimate depository of reason, carrying it forward to the next and hopefully better century.

This line of argument is followed by Robert Holton in a chapter, "Problems of crisis and normalcy in the contemporary world." Holton finds that it is no longer the idea of progress, but rather the idea of crisis that has become the guide, not only in common sense but also in social theory. Crisis is perhaps the most symptomatic root metaphor of the late twentieth century. What is striking is not only its pervasive presence but also its radical change of meaning, from some extraordinary turning point in a line of development (for example, in the course of illness), to a chronic state of affairs without any clear prospect of resolution. Holton calls this the "normalization" of crisis. Two presuppositions of the old, traditional notion of crisis seem to have disappeared: (1) that it can be comprehended and overcome by rational means; (2) that there are vital social forces, agents of social change, that are able to carry human society forward towards a more healthy and sane future. As a result, people feel trapped in the present by contingency, randomness, and disbelief in the meaning or logic of history. They feel afraid to begin the future. In the strange symbiosis of technocratic crisis-managers and consumption-oriented households, the transcendent critique of contemporary society in the name of progress loses any footing. At the level of theory, the author finds important repercussions of this social climate in the notion of decentredness. In the work of Habermas, Luhmann, and Lyotard he finds the case of the decline of core principles of the progressivist creed, e.g., of notions like normative order, nation-state, and socialist movement. In conclusion, Holton calls for "postdevelopmental" modes of social analysis, and the recognition of post-*gemeinschaftlich* modes of moral integration, as befitting the new world of postmodernity.

For Carlo Mongardini some other aspects of postmodernity appear as crucial, and despicable. In his chapter, "The decadence of modernity: the delusions of progress and the search for historical consciousness," he focuses on the image of culture and history. In his reading, the concept of progress was always linked with the evolution of coherent, integral cultural wholes. Presently, however, we witness growing fragmentation and segmentation, in his view the dissolution of culture. Similarly, while the idea of progress was always rooted in historical consciousness – on recognizing the continuity of social processes stretching from the past toward the future – we currently witness the glorification of change for change's sake, as a value in itself. Without integration and continuity, the notion of progress is empty: in a period of "post-culture" and "post-history" there is no place for progress. The author gives his own account of the malaise and crisis inherent in the postmodern condition. He points to the destructuring of time, the instability of money, and the uncertainty of law as three symptoms of the new situation brought about by the fetishization of change. From the perspective of an individual, these processes lead to a feeling of intellectual and practical powerlessness, to cultural primitivism, and to the cult of fleeting aesthetic experience. There is, then, not only a social but also a psychological urgency to recover the visions of culture and history that can provide some new image of progress. What are the agents for such a cultural renaissance and a return to historical consciousness? Mongardini does not believe in traditional agents like political bodies (parties) or economically organized groups (classes). Instead he puts his faith in what might seem a peculiar triad: youth, a group that may revitalize culture; the churches, as depositaries of morals and traditional values; and intellectuals, as embodiments of reason. At the close of his chapter, Mongardini follows Simmel's hint that culture may be the core area of research for the sociology to come, and he exhorts sociologists to turn away from economic or political phenomena towards cultural and historical processes.

Klaus Eder attempts to search deeper under the surface of actual tendencies, explaining them by the dynamics of the hidden cultural themes, or codes, which underline the western heritage. His chapter, "The cultural code of modernity and the problem of nature: a critique of the naturalistic notion of progress," starts from the assumption that it is the redefinition of humanity's relation to nature, brought about by the ecological crisis, that is responsible for the demise of the traditional conception of progress. In these terms, Eder suggests that there is a fundamental ambivalence in western culture at the level of cultural codes, between the Greek tradition with its emphasis on blood rites and its consequent utilitarian treatment of nature, and the Jewish tradition with its restricted use of bloody rituals, its rigid rules of purity, and its prescription of a harmonious relation to nature. The first tradition became dominant: nature was treated as material to be shaped and conquered by society. The second tradition remained at the level of the collective unconscious; it has been triggered into prominence only by the recent ecological crisis, which has brought the sudden realization that nature cannot be taken for granted. This countercultural current, latent for centuries, became manifest and has assumed a new form in the ecological movement. Eder then moves to the level of theoretical discourse, which he sees as a reflection of these hidden cultural codes. He identifies a cultural conflict in recent sociological theory between the theoretical antinomies of rationality and romanticism, evolution and equilibrium, and, most importantly, utilitarian versus communicative reason. This ambivalence has produced two opposing ideas of progress, the technological and the moral. Eder claims that such opposition is no longer tenable and that a new notion of progress must be developed that treats technological and moral progress as indissolubly linked. These issues, he suggests, are exactly what is being contested in the new cultural and social movements.

The chapters we grouped in the second part of the volume address the question of agency. What kind of human groups, collectivities, and organizations are about progress at the end of the twentieth century? Who can be said to carry the torch of progress in our epoch? Obviously, new kinds of agents appear on the historical stage and traditional agents leave the spotlight. Some potential bearers of progress were already spotted by Mongardini. The theorists in this section extend the spectrum, discussing the role of such agents as intellectuals, social movements, and trade unions.

In his chapter on "Intellectuals and progress: the origins, decline, and revival of a critical group," Ron Eyerman traces the changing fates of the social category that was the offspring of modernity, the embodiment of its faith in reason, and the midwife of progress. He gives a historical account of the evolving self-identity and social role of intellectuals. Starting with the classical notion of an intellectual as an articulator of ideas and leader of action, the author shows that, while it had ancient roots, this idea was first fully articulated in the Enlightenment. Later, in the nineteenth century, intellectuals were viewed as the means by which various class interests – aristocratic, bourgeois, labor – could be transformed from an aggregate of individual needs into a collective identity. But, intellectuals also came to be perceived as ideologues, as producers of ideas and manipulators of consciousness devoid of any class roots. In the liberal

6

view, intellectuals were seen as self-conscious servants of a wide public interest, responsible for the education and moral advancement of the whole society. Later, with the full-blown development of modernity, intellectuals became professionals. They were incorporated into economic and bureaucratic systems and lost their critical spirit, a development epitomized by the role of "detached expert." Nonetheless, Eyerman believes that predictions about the demise of intellectuals are premature. Their degradation is being reversed by the wave of new social movements that are reactions to the disenchantment with modernity. Indeed, in environmentalism, civil rights, peace, and feminism, the author argues that a new role for intellectuals is emerging. They are "movement intellectuals." While similar in certain respects to what Gramsci called organic intellectuals, they articulate public issues that are related to the quality of life and human dignity rather than class interests, and they participate in group actions to defend such humanistic values. In this new way intellectuals may recover their old role as the critical agents of progress.

Dietrich and Marilyn Rueschemeyer take up the role of feminist movements. Their chapter, "Progress in the distribution of power: gender relations and women's movements as a source of change," puts forward a claim that the growing emancipation of women may become a crucial factor for substantial advances toward participatory democracy. They begin with a discussion of various models of democracy, evaluating them in terms of their feasibility and desirability. The Rueschemeyers argue that the core dimension of democratic order is the extension of participation. Greater participation makes democracy more real because it increases self-respect and the opportunity to pursue interests by political means. It is unlikely, however, that participation will be extended by authorities; nor will it be brought about as a by-product of other social processes, for example, by the enlargement of leisure time. Increased participation must be won, rather, by social movements, by struggles for ecology, peace, and women's liberation. The Rueschemeyers go on to trace the long and protracted process of women's emancipation over more than a century. They see this process as still far from ultimate success and show that in the political and economic domain there continues to be a striking under-representation of women. The key to further emancipation can be found in eliminating the gender division of labor, which depends on the emergence of a different kind of social structure. Whilst acknowledging that this project will encounter various obstacles and engender numerous dilemmas, they argue that it is a realistic historical possibility. Here, then, is the traditional vision of progress-through-emancipation, in a revised and more realistically compelling form.

David Kettler and Volker Meja focus on a more traditional kind of progressive agent, the trade unions. Their chapter, "The end of western trade unionism?: social progress after the age of progressivism," reassesses the role that unions play in postmodern society, arguing that they now primarily contribute to socially conscious political democratization. Kettler and Meja start with an overview of progressivist accounts of trade unions. Marx, Weber, and Durkheim provided three distinct versions of the relation between trade unions and social progress. By contrast to these earlier versions, the authors characterize the contemporary tendency as one of prevailing trade-union decline, punctuated by islands of eruption, notably in South Africa, South Korea, and Poland. As the context for their analysis of unions, Kettler and Meja adopt the concept of labor regimes, i.e., the rules, practices, and expectations that organize the labor market. This concept proves to possess considerable explanatory value for a comparative analysis of trade union rise and decline. In conclusion, Kettler and Meja evaluate the contribution of trade unions to democracy. In the past, unions served two vital functions: the institutionalizing of the "social question" (power sharing and economic distribution) within the political agenda, and the introduction of negotiating frameworks and arbitration mechanisms ("reflexive law") into the legal system. Kettler and Meja call these achievements the creation of an ethic of collective agreement, and they describe this as the project of the working class in a democratic society. With the institutionalization of the capitalist welfare state and the emergence of new economic exigencies in post-industrial societies, trade unions will probably lose this vital role. The authors argue, however, that unions will remain second-line defenders of the political rights they helped to establish, even as in non-democratic countries, they continue to play a central role in the struggle for democracy itself.

The chapters in the third section of our volume call attention to new social, economic, and political processes in the postmodern world, suggesting that these processes require basic re-evaluation of the theories and predictions of the progressivist discourse on modernity. The visible ascent of the sacred and the community contradicts the idea of progressive secularization. The globalization of economic management supplants immanent, evolutionary growth within the confines of isolated nation-states. The incorporation and cooptation of social movements into political elites requires the rejection of the mechanism of revolutionary struggle.

In his chapter on "Secularization and sacralization," Kenneth Thompson takes issue with one of the core claims of progressivism, namely that there will be an inevitable decline of religion and community concomitant with growing rationalization and differentiation. In a Durkheimian spirit, he believes that one should not think in terms of exclusive dichotomies or clear-cut directional processes. Concepts like sacred and secular, or *Gemeinschaft* and *Gesellschaft*, should be treated as co-existing in some dialectic interplay in all human societies. Each of them may be seen as generating countervailing tendencies: secularization provokes sacralization;

domination by *Gesellschaft* (societalization) encourages reaffirmation of *Gemeinschaft* (communalization). Thompson claims that in the late modern or postmodern world we observe not the decline of the sacred and community but only profound changes in their cultural manifestations. He calls attention to such salient phenomena as the revival of ideological and religious fundamentalisms; the proliferation of myth, magic, and folklore; the renewed assertion of ethnic and national bonds; and the growing importance of what he calls imagined communities and cultural totemisms. The common core of these developments is the shift of meaning from literally understood religion to generalized "sacrum," and from face-to-face communities to symbolic communities. Thompson demonstrates that sacralization and symbolic community are produced by a combination of discourses – religious, ethnic, national, political, economic, familial – each of which is undergoing profound re-articulation. Sects and cults, for example, are proliferating in response to the "mundanization" and "profanization" of established religious movements and faiths. In conclusion, Thompson links the perennial and universal presence of the sacred and the community with fundamental features of the human condition in the world, arguing that sacralization and communalization are typical processes in all human societies.

Hans Joas offers yet another challenge to the progressivist description of social change. Writing against the concept of automatic social development, he begins his discussion by pointing out that this idea was the object of widespread criticism among the classical generation of sociological theorists. Their resistance to such falsely optimistic conceptions of historical inevitability found expression, Joas suggests, in their exploratory efforts to develop theories of creative and open-ended social action, as demonstrated by Weber's discussion of charisma, Simmel's theory of aesthetic creation, and Durkheim's writing on unconscious religious creativity. However, it was only in American pragmatic theory, in Joas's view, that this search structured the fundamental understanding of action itself, producing the concept of expressive activity as a means of overcoming and resolving problems not only in individual experience but in society at large. Drawing on the more recent approach of the social psychologist Abraham Maslow, Joas suggests that these early pragmatic writers were developing a theory of "integrated creativity," in which expressive motivation is held to be balanced by moral commitments and rational insight. These considerations, Joas argues, point to the necessity for contemporary social theory to develop a much more forceful understanding of creative collective action, which he identifies as the independent contribution that social movements make to historical development. He brings this perspective to bear on what he regards as the limitations of social differentiation theory – the broadly progressive understanding of social change as functional specialization, rationalization, and pluralization which has been embraced, in one form or another, by most of the central figures in macrosociology. Joas argues that if creativity were really inserted into the center of social change theory, social differentiation could not be accepted as either a necessary or inevitable process. He shows how recent thinkers like Touraine and Castoriadis have broken away from such a perspective by emphasizing the fundamental role of historical imagination and the self-constituting qualities of social movements. In their terms, differentiation is not an objective tendency but an imagined and hence constitutive idea at the basis of western development. Only from this perspective, Joas suggests, can social theory understand that the very notion of differentiation has become a topic of contemporary social movements. In the postmodern world, arguments about the degree and character of social differentiation have become an arena for political and cultural contestation. This development has opened up the prospect of the "democratization of differentiation."

In her chapter, "The relative autonomy of élites: the absorption of protest and social progress in western democracies," Eva Etzioni-Halevy focuses on some basic political mechanisms of change. She suggests that the idea of revolution, which is fundamental to all progressive discourse in advanced capitalist countries, is outdated. She argues that it needs to be replaced by alternative principles and with her "demo-élite theory" she provides some. Her approach stems from the observation that there are various bases of power and that these depend on the kind of resources controlled, whether economic, political, or symbolic. As a result, in western democracies there is relative autonomy of the non-political from the ruling élites. The author traces the evolution of western democracies in this direction, finding the ultimate guarantees of the relative autonomy of élites in the electoral principle, freedom of association, and separation of powers. In contemporary societies, moreover, there is a proliferation of counterélites, representing new social movements, which can amass considerable countervailing power. In the democratic context, the strategy of suppression or coercion against the counterélites is not feasible because they can form alliances with other élites in non-state sectors. Hence, established élites have to use the alternative strategy of domestication, eliminating not the movement itself but its destabilizing potential. The result is the absorption of protest through the cooptation of movement leaders, and social movements become incorporated into existing power structures in exchange for moderation. Etzioni-Halevy argues that such incorporation (sharing of power) is, even from the point of view of the movements, a reasonable strategy, and not necessarily betrayal. Facing the unfeasibility of violent revolution, it is a way to gain momentum for incremental reforms, redistributing resources in the direction of greater freedom and lesser inequality. This is precisely how Etzioni-Halevy defines progress. She concludes that cooptation of non-established élites is a major process through which social progress occurs in western democracies. Her observations are strikingly relevant not only for western democracies, but also for the recent political, economic, and social transformations of Eastern European countries like Poland and Hungary.

The concluding part of the book includes two metatheoretical papers that attempt the conceptual specification, clarification, and elaboration of the idea of progress. They share the other authors' dissatisfaction with the current, received meaning of progress and – albeit in various directions and in different ways – try to reformulate it in line with contemporary theoretical tendencies.

In his chapter, "Models of directional change and human values: the theory of progress as an applied social science," Stefan Nowak strives for a less restricted, more open-ended model of progress by reminding us of some fundamental conceptual distinctions. He defines progress as any sequential, directional change that receives a positive social evaluation. It is this reference to social values that sets progress apart from sheer development and places it squarely within the domain of applied social science. The notion of progress always demands axiological relativization; we have to ask progress for whom and by which standards? But this does not make the notion itself unscientific or metaphysical. Nowak makes a crucial observation: because social change is often multidimensional, or syndromatic, various dimensions may not develop in a parallel direction. Dimensions may interact, amplifying or mutually blocking changes; they may be supportive or mutually incompatible. Such interactions may operate in an unintended and unrecognized fashion by means of latent effects. Hence, another relativization of the notion of progress is always necessary: we must specify the dimension (level, subsystem) of society which is undergoing change. This requires complex evaluational standards. If we move from identifying progress by empirical and valuational means to explaining progress, we need theories dealing with the dynamics of social transformations. Reviewing the present state of such theories Nowak arrives at pessimistic conclusions. While he finds most of them unspecified and in principle untestable, each does provide some insight for building a multitheoretical model of change, which is the only approach that will be able to grasp multidimensional, syndromatic processes. This is the long-range challenge for any social science account of progress.

Piotr Sztompka, in the closing chapter on "Agency and Progress," seems to make a step in this direction. His model of "social becoming" fits into the recent wave of postdevelopmentalist theories, emphasizing the active, constructive side of social processes, or the "creation of society by society." Within the framework of this model, the idea of progress can be fundamentally reformulated. The traditional concept refers progress to some future end-state of the process, or to some social utopia; the new concept relates it to originating, present conditions and defines progress

11

as the potential capacity for self-transformation. Not the quality of what actually becomes, but the potentiality for becoming is seen as the core meaning of progress. In other words, the progressiveness of society is measured by viability of human agency. Sztompka argues that such agency depends on five sets of factors: the traits of the actors, the properties of social structures, the features of the natural environment, the character- istics of historical tradition, and the image of the expected future. On this basis, he draws a contrast between an active progressive society, one with a high capacity for self-transformation, and a stagnant and passive society, devoid of self-transforming potential. Against the tide of contemporary pessimism, Sztompka believes that in the long run human society exhibits a progressive tendency toward growing activism and enlarged self- transforming capacities. The rationale for such a tendency he locates in human nature, in the inherent creativeness and educability that allow for the accumulation of experiences and innovations through time. This still does not mean that there is any necessity or inevitability of progress. The self-transcending, progressive tendency may be blocked, for its release ultimately depends solely on human actions. The specific type of progressive action befitting the intellectual is to articulate the theory of progress in such terms, which may in turn motivate others to such activism. By not only explaining progress but promoting it, such a theory may in fact become a self-fulfilling prophecy.

This argument seems like an appropriate place to bring our introduction to a close. The criticism of progressivism and the new explanations of progress that are offered in the following pages can be seen as intellectual efforts with a decidedly progressive aim. The transition from modernity to postmodernity means the rejection of some cherished beliefs, images, and creeds. But there is a way out of the present disenchantment with the idea of progress, and it comes down, paradoxically, to invigorating some aspects of the progress idea itself, which is one of the oldest and most challenging notions in the heritage of humankind. As we enter the last decade of the twentieth century, we hope the present discussion will stimulate others. Perhaps the theories and the societies of the next century will be better than our own.

PART I

Beyond progress
and
modernity

1

Between progress and apocalypse: social theory and the dream of reason in the twentieth century

JEFFREY C. ALEXANDER

Social theory is a mental reconstruction of its time, not a reflection but a self-reflection. Art is self-reflection in an iconic and expressive form. Theoretical self-reflection is intellectual and abstract. It leads not to experience and epiphany but to analysis and thought. Social theory cannot induce catharsis, but it can transform understanding. We need social theory if we are going to understand our world. As this great and terrible century draws to a close, this need has never been more important.

The thesis of this essay is that the twentieth century is a unique construction, an historically demarcated world, and that twentieth-century theory is differentiated from earlier theorizing in much the same way. This may be an illusion for future historians to correct. Certainly, neither theory nor history can hope to break out of the self-conceptions of its own time. At this point, however, the historical uniqueness of our century seems to be an empirical fact. It is certainly a social one, for in this uniqueness most of the participants in this century have fervently believed.

To comprehend the underlying motifs of our century, and eventually its social theory, we must clarify what initially marked the west off from other civilizations, the modern west from earlier periods in its history, and the twentieth century from earlier western modern societies. This distinguishing notion is "progress" and the possibility of perfection it implies.

All complex societies, of course, have had myths about the Golden Age. Only in the west, however, did people seriously begin to think that such a new age might occur in this rather than some extraterrestrial or fantastical world. This-worldly conceptions were formulated in Judaism three or four thousand years ago. If the Jews kept their covenant with God, the Bible promised, God would establish his reign of perfection on earth – what

15

came to be called the millennium. Because Jews were the chosen people, God promised to eventually redeem them. Christianity believed that Christ had been sent to renew this redemptive promise. We have lived in what might be called a millennial civilization ever since.

Yet Christianity still placed the millennium far off in the distant future. It would certainly not happen in our lifetimes. The lot of human beings on earth, at any given point in time, could hardly be changed. This dualism began to shift with the Reformation, which was much more emphatically this-worldly. Protestants, and especially Calvinists and Puritans, worked hard in this world, with the hope of bringing about the kingdom of God on earth. This initial belief in the possibility of worldly perfection was reinforced and greatly extended by Renaissance humanism, with its earthiness and optimism about improving nature and society. The Enlightenment translated this growing perfectionism into the vocabulary of secular progress. As Becker (1932) suggested in *The Heavenly City of the eighteenth-century Philosophers*, the philosophers believed in the imminent possibility of a secular golden age.

Perfectionism is the belief that the human world can become the mirror of the divine. This possibility has defined the essence of modernity. To be modern is to believe that the masterful transformation of the world is possible, indeed that it is likely.[1] In the course of modernity, this pledge to worldly transformation has been renewed time and time again. No matter what the disaster, the hope and belief in imminent perfection never disappears. The faith in perfection has informed all the great experiments of the modern world, big and small, good and bad, the incessant reformism and the revolutions launched from the left and from the right.[2]

With the Enlightenment and the growth of secular, scientific thought, the ethos of perfectionism became inseparable from the claims of reason.[3] Reason is the self-conscious application of the mind to social and natural phenomena. Through reason, people came to believe, we can master the world. Through this mastery, we can become free and happy. The world can be made a reasonable place. It can be reconstructed. Marx and Hegel produced their own versions of such perfectionism; neither believed in it less fervently than the other.[4]

In the twentieth century this fundamental tenet of modernity has been challenged and ultimately changed. The faith in progress has often been severely disappointed and the sense that there is the real possibility for perfection has diminished. This domination has not occurred in every place and at every moment, of course; in the end, however, it has so permeated modern life that it has deeply affected its core. Modern became postmodern long before the contemporary period. The experience of this century has been a tragic one. The originality of its social theory lies in coming to grips with this experience. This, at least, is the thesis I will seek to advance here.

The rational line: progress

I do not want to advance this thesis in a polemical or one-sided way. If one does so, the argument becomes myth and caricature, and loses its force. Our understanding of the twentieth century must be more subtle and more complex. To recognize its tragic proportions does not mean to ignore the hopes that it has inspired and the real progress it has achieved.

From the point of view of the present day, it is possible to look back on this century as a time of wondrous achievement. It is especially possible, and likely, for Americans to do so, but it is by no means impossible for Europeans.[5] Doing so reflects the particular historical vantage point of the present day; it also reflects the continuing intensity of the progressivist faith. History can, after all, certainly be reconstructed in different ways.

If we look back at the beginning of this century, we can see great hopes. In Germany and in the Austro-Hungarian Empire, large social-democratic parties existed, and their progress appeared to many as inexorable. By pledging themselves to control the market and by demanding full voting rights, these parties promised to incorporate the working classes into industrial economies and to democratize the state.[6]

Similar progressive forces seemed to be expanding in other industrialized nations. In England, radical Utilitarians and Fabian socialists had increasing access to power, and Marxian socialism itself was becoming a stronger and more militant force. In environments less hospitable to socialism, liberalism was developing a social program of its own. French "solidarism" and American "progressivism" were seen as prime examples of the successful mitigation of capitalism's harshest face.

The progressive view of our century can be sustained by drawing a straight line from these promising developments to the condition of industrial societies today. One can argue that Marxism, liberalism, social democracy, and even democratic conservatism have succeeded in transforming and, indeed, in perfecting modern life.

This rational line can be justified by pointing, for example, to the extraordinary increase in material wealth. Through the rationality of capitalism and industrial production, this affluence has ameliorated the conditions of everyday life throughout the class structure of advanced societies. These conditions are not limited, moreover, to consumption in a narrow sense. It is primarily as a result of this material transformation (Hart 1984, 1985: 29–49) that deaths in childbirth (for both infants and mothers) have been virtually eliminated and that such deadly diseases as tuberculosis have passed from the scene. One may point to the achievements of modern science, both pure and applied, which have contributed to such life-giving disciplines as modern medicine. The series of technological revolutions that has increased material productivity hundreds of times over make Marx's predictions about the exhaustion of capitalism

17

seem not just antique but almost reactionary. We are in the midst of what has been called the fourth industrial revolution, the transformation of information capacity that began with the transistor and miniaturization and, with the computer chip and super-computerization, has continued on an unprecedented scale.

The rational line can be further sustained by pointing to the expansion of human rights. T. H. Marshall (1964) drew an evolutionary model of the progress from civil to political to social rights. Over the last forty years, civil and political rights have been extended to religious and racial groups that had been excluded from western societies for hundreds and sometimes even thousands of years. Social rights have been expanded to groups who were considered to be deserving of their unfortunate fates only a century ago – like the physically and mentally handicapped. For the first time since the neolithic revolution ten thousand years ago, women are beginning to have substantial access to the institutional and cultural centers of society.

These advances may rightly be considered to be evidence of the advance of reason, and they are being applied to civilizations which did not initially share in the benefits of this-worldly millennial religion. Decolonization has extended "European" progress while allowing national aspirations to be freely expressed. Revolution, which has often been the vehicle for this decolonization, has been the primary trigger that has allowed modernization in the backward, unrationalized areas of the world. It, too, can be considered a successful example of the extension of world mastery which has helped to perfect life in the modern world.

On these grounds it may be argued that the twentieth century has been a time of progress, that this is not only a plausible view but also a valid one. Not only Americans and Europeans argue this view today, but articulate leaders in India, China, Brazil, and Japan as well. The twentieth century is a good and sensible world. Yes, evil and irrationality still exist, but their origins are outside of us. They stem from traditionalism and antimodernity, with religious fanatics in Iran, with tribal hostilities in Africa, with nationalist antagonism in Israel. Closer to home, they arise in impoverished groups who have not had the access to modernity that education and material comfort can provide. When we walk through our modern lives, organizing our lifeworlds with good sense and a modicum of comfort, it seems only reasonable to think that reason has prevailed.

The dream of reason

The reality of this vision of the twentieth century is underscored by the fact that it has produced a line of intellectual reasoning, a line of social theory, that goes along with it. I will call this the dream of reason. It is the image of this rationally perfected life in thought, but not of course a reflection of "real," material life alone. Because life is itself filled with ideas, the perfected life is filled with ideas about perfection. The reasonable life of today can be traced back to the dream of a this-worldly millennium that began thousands of years ago. Of course, while the millennial dream is religious, the dream of reason is postreligious. Still, the dream of reason operates with the metaphysical props of faith that were exemplified in Hegel's work a century ago.

We can see the dream of reason most distinctly by pointing to four spheres of modern thought: philosophy, psychology, art, and social engineering.

The most characteristic school of twentieth-century philosophy must surely be logical positivism, which believed that any thought worth thinking could be reduced to rational and eventually mathematical propositions. Philosophy from this perspective would be little more than a truth language, a code that would state the conditions for knowing. In this form, philosophy would allow language and thought to transparently reflect the external world. Words are induced from things that actually exist (Wittgenstein 1922). Thought is a rational induction from this reality. Philosophy must hone the relationship between words and things. Metaphysics will be abolished forthwith.

We should not be so blinded by the surreal dimension of modern art that we fail to see that much of aesthetic modernism is consistent with this rationalizing view. There is a clear movement in modernity which argues that art should be sparse, minimal, flat, rational, and "true." It should not be fictive but direct, not personal but objective. The great exemplifications of this are architecture and prose. The origins of modern architecture are the aesthetic dictum that form is to follow function. Those who created this style (Pevsner 1977) actually believed that their buildings represented no fictive design but only followed inevitably from the shape of engineering and efficient rational design. While this self-understanding may be false – engineering and efficiency do not have an implicit design – the International Style that resulted was of a decidedly rationalist bent – straight lines, angles, and flat surfaces.

A similar demand for directness, simplicity, objectivity, and efficiency characterizes twentieth-century prose. In the model of science, modern prose language aims to be translucent vis-à-vis its subject matter and denuded of "style" as such, as that notion was exemplified, for example, in Renaissance speech and writing (Lanham 1976). Connotation and ambiguity are pruned from articles and books. In the English language it was Hemingway who blazed this trail, with his short, flat, journalistic sentences. It was *Time* magazine that made this style the mass language of the day.

In psychology two contradictory movements reflect this sense of the ultimate reasonableness of the world. In Piaget's (1972) developmental

19

psychology, adult persons have developed the capacity for universalistic cognition and rule-oriented morality. These capacities develop from processes that are inherent in the life process. Individuals become rational because of realistic experiences. Faced with the growing complexity of reality, they act pragmatically and develop new modes of reasoning through trial and error. Behaviorism also sees individuals as acting in straightforward rational ways. Pavlov, Watson, and Skinner argued that people are formed not by subjective fantasy but by their environments, that they are molded into whatever they are pushed into being. Like pigeons and well-trained dogs, human beings are rational in a narrow and efficient sense. If we know their past conditioning, we can make predictions about how they will act in the future.

Theories about the possibility of rational planning have been reinforced by developmental and behavioristic psychology, but they also constitute an intellectual movement in their own right. This thought originates in the nineteenth century as a species of secular perfectionism, with people like Saint-Simon, Bentham, and Marx. It has become dominant in the twentieth century, elaborated by democratic socialist theorists of the welfare state like Marshall and Mannheim (1940) and by technocratic communist thought as well. The belief is that the world can be subjected to rational control, that the whole ball of wax can be shaped by reason into a desirable shape. Rawls (1971) is the greatest English-speaking proponent of this faith in perfection through reason. Habermas (1984) elaborates rationalism in a Continental, anti-Utilitarian romantic idiom.

The alternative vision of decline: the prophecy of Georges Sorel

With a very few exceptions, these rationalist streams of thought, no matter how brilliant and enlightening, have not represented the greatest and most original achievements of twentieth-century social theory. One reason is that they do not represent something that is really new; they are extensions of the perfectionist thinking of earlier days. But there is another, much more important reason as well. In its rationalist form, twentieth-century social theory cannot fulfill its self-reflective task. It does not tell us the absolutely essential things we must know about the new kind of society in which we have lived.

A straight line between the hopes of the turn-of-the-century period and the achievements of the present day cannot be drawn. There is, rather, a tortuous path.[7] If the newly dawning century embodied fulsome hopes for social reform, it was also known as the *fin de siècle* and the "age of anxiety." The dream of reason has continued to inspire the thought of our time, but it is the nightmare of reason that has captured the most profound theoretical imaginations of the age.

As an entree into this darker side of modernity, we might look briefly at the thought of Georges Sorel, the French revolutionary syndicalist who published his original and disturbing *Reflections on Violence* in 1908. Earlier I referred to the large socialist workers parties that were carriers for the ideas, forces, and often the reality of progress in that turn-of-the-century period. Sorel conceived of himself as speaking for a very different segment of the community of dispossessed. He insists (1950 [1908]: 66) that there remained large groups of workers, small employers of labor, and farmers – as well, one might add, as working-class leaders and intellectuals like himself – who bitterly opposed modernity and saw little hope for social progress within its rationalizing frame. These groups provided a constituency for a much more extreme left, one cut-off from the progressive and ameliorating groups of the socialist center. As Sorel explains, "Parliamentary Socialism does not mingle with the main body of the parties of the extreme left" (ibid: 67).

These parties are the revolutionaries. In one sense, of course, their ideal is not all that dissimilar from the reformers'. They, too, want a perfect society ordered by reason. They are certain, however, that such a society cannot be institutionalized in the "present phase" of social life. Reason has become an other-worldly ideal that can be realized only through violent world transformation. What has happened until now has not been progressive. Sorel denigrates "the trash of Parliamentary literature." He despises progressives and has no patience for democratic politics. Such appeals to reason, he writes, are "confused"; they serve only "to hide the terrible fear" that marks the inevitable tension between social classes. If socialism is to succeed it must become revolutionary. Rather than appealing to the rationality of the middle and upper classes, socialists must try to make them afraid: "The workers have no money but they have at their disposal a much more efficacious means of action: they can inspire fear." If the bourgeoisie are afraid, Sorel argues, they will engage in selfish behavior and eventually, repression. In his view this is all to the good. It unmasks the real, anti-progressive face of society, and it will inspire the proletariat to be revolutionary in turn.

Sorel believes that socialism must turn away from social and political reform toward the program of the general strike. As a collective act of deliberate violence, the general strike will inspire fear and usher in a cataclysmic revolution. This violence is associated by Sorel with the very group that according to the rational line embodies reason, the proletariat. Sorel has posed the fateful dichotomy of twentieth-century life. He has opposed violence and reason, rational progress with violence and force. Fifty years later Sartre (1976 [1968]) takes up violence in much the same way, promulgating it as a means of liberating debourgeoisification; from Sartre, Fanon (1965) took violence as the model for anticolonial revolt.[8] In important respects, however, Sorel's opposition of violence

21

to reason was more sophisticated; it was certainly more disturbing and more revealing.

Sorel's opposition is unusually revealing because he relativized this threat of revolutionary violence by calling it a myth. Whether there could or, in strategic terms, should be a violent strike was not Sorel's concern. Violent revolutionary was a myth in which workers had to believe in order to maintain their esprit de corps and to inspire repressive reactions in the ruling classes. Myth is necessary because people are irrational. They are moved by impulses, not by "observation of contemporary facts [or by] a rational interpretation of the present" (ibid., p. 99). "Infinitely simpler mental processes" are involved. Only by promoting the myth of violence can the socialists reawaken the spirit of alienation and hatred that creates the desire to destroy bourgeois society.

Sorel's theory is an apologia for left-wing terrorism.[9] It is also a prophecy of the irrationality to come.[10] Finally, it is a brilliant and representative invention of social theory in the twentieth century. Faced with the disappointment of his socialist hopes for progress, Sorel theorizes that individuals are not as rational as progressive theory had thought. Moving against the rational line, he establishes a commonality between modern actors and the myth worshipers of traditional societies. It is not surprising that Sorel himself wavers between revolutionary left and right. For, he has abandoned rationality not just as an explanation of human action but as a normative stance. He advocates irrationality in its most violent form. This, in fact, is where Sorel's thought differs from the more important twentieth-century social theory we will examine below. For while Sorel understood the pathologies of modernity, he could think of no way to overcome them.

The degenerate line: irrationality

Before we can get to this theory, we need to examine the life upon which they reflect. It can be argued that in twentieth-century life there has been a real declension, a decline that for many has made progress seem like a dream, or even a myth.

Since we have been thinking about Sorel, let us begin with socialism. Marxists and utopians alike have considered socialism (via revolution or reform) to be the very embodiment of reason. For Marx, communalization would overcome the alienation of reason and subjectivity upon which capitalism is based. As the twentieth century has unfolded, however, it has become increasingly clear that revolutionary movements of the left often intensify the "alienation of reason" in drastic ways.[11] This counter-intuitive fact should not be understood in essentialist terms. It has nothing to do with some inherent perversity of revolutionary action but with the sociological conditions under which revolutions typically emerge.

22

Revolutionaries represent groups who have been subject to quite terrible oppression and strains. Typically, they have been excluded from the legitimate centers of their societies and often from their very societies themselves; they have been denied access to universities, subjected to despicable prejudices, often jailed, sometimes tortured and murdered.

None of this mitigates what Marx would surely have regarded as the savage degradation of the revolutionary tradition in the twentieth century. In their alienation, revolutionaries, in and out of power, have not only advocated distorted and caricatured thought and speech but often acted barbarously, engaging in systematic force and fraud. For several decades after the outbreak of the Russian Revolution, not only socialists but also a wide range of thoughtful people regarded communism as a legitimate carrier of reason. The true nature of Russian communism was masked by its claims to reason and scientific "last resorts" (Emerson 1981). Wealth, technology, literacy, high culture, hygiene, and class inclusion have been the perfectionist references for official communist rhetoric.

It eventually became clear to many, however, that almost right from the beginning this revolutionary society has made of the hopes for perfection a bitter joke. Lenin initiated, and Stalin established (Johnson 1983: 49–103) a system that suppressed the very exercise of reason. Mao, Castro, and Eastern European puppet rulers followed in their wake. Twentieth-century communism has been more like the medieval church than a model for rationality and progress (Aron 1957). Ruled by an ideological pope and directed by a clerisy of party faithful, official communism spreads the dogma of the proletarian messiah, whose message and needs remain to be interpreted in approprate ways. Reason is monopolized by this communist church; it is impossible for private individuals to possess it. For the masses, coercion and violence are the only recourse. Russian communism subjected first counter-revolutionaries, then conservatives, kulaks, Jews, Christians, and "other" nationalities to unprecedented repression. Once in power, communist parties – these purported vanguards of reason and progress – have institutionalized vocabularies of double-think and systems of thought control that have come to symbolize the nightmares of reason in our time.[12]

Murder and massive political repression in China. Genocidal barbarity in revolutionary Cambodia and dreary failure in its occupiers, Vietnam. The overwhelming inadequacies of centrally planned state economies. Intellectuals who hope for human progress might well ask, what is left of the revolutionary dream of reason today? It may be that the communist version of this dream has become exhausted only two centuries after it began. Certainly intellectual disillusionment with the progressive promises of socialism and communism is one of the most distinctive developments of the late twentieth century (Alexander 1988).[13]

I have not begun with communism because it is the unique embodiment of bad faith and irrationality. This is the line of the conservative right in America and elsewhere, and it is a cop out intellectually and morally. One must acknowledge that anti-progress and anti-reason occurred throughout western societies, in capitalist and democratic countries as well.

The rational line describes the twentieth century as involving gradual democratization, the extension of rights and privileges to the lower classes, the opening up of ghettos, and the persistent spreading of secular rationality throughout society. In point of fact, even before the twentieth century truly began, much darker forces were beginning to brew. By the 1880s one could observe on the Continent, in France and Southern and Central Europe, a growing reaction against these very progressive forces. In the middle and upper classes powerful advocates of dictatorship and violence emerged. In Germany, a mystical and backward looking *Volk* ideology fermented (Mosse 1964), spreading even to intellectual classes (Ringer 1969). In France there was a sickening turn towards nationalist antisemitism. In the United States, the rigidly segregationist policies of "Jim Crow" began to spread through the Southern states, and "nativism" – cultural prejudice and social mobilization against foreign-born Americans – became an imperious collective psychology in the North.

These irrationalist forces fed directly into the First World War, the cataclysm that separated what afterward looked like an age of innocence from the wasteland that followed (Fussell 1975).[14] Sometime between 1919 and 1921, when he was the British Secretary of State, Winston Churchill jotted down on a piece of War Office stationary a retrospective whose embittered and apocalyptic tones capture the profound disturbance this war gave to the vision of progress.

> All the horrors of all the ages were brought together, and not only armies but whole populations were thrust in the midst of them . . . Every outrage against humanity or international law was repaid by reprisals . . . No truce or parley mitigated the strife of the armies. The wounded died between the lines: the dead mouldered into the soil. Merchant ships and neutral ships and hospital ships were sunk on the seas and all on board left to their fate, or killed as they swam. Every effort was made to starve whole nations into submission without regard to age or sex. Cities and monuments were smashed by artillery. Bombs from the air were cast down indiscriminately. Poison gas in many forms stifled or seared the soldiers. Liquid fire was projected upon their bodies . . . When all was over, Torture and Cannibalism were the only two expedients that the civilized, scientific, Christian States had been able to deny themselves: and they were of doubtful utility. (Quoted in Johnson 1983: 14–15)

Seventy years after the war's end, such activities could not possibly arouse such astonished indignation. They have become everyday occurrences in the political relations of the twentieth century.

In the chaos and devastation that followed in the wake of the First World War, there emerged at the end of the first third of the century what to earlier progressives would have been a totally unexpected event. This was the outbreak in Europe not of revolutions of the left but counter-revolutions of the right. In Germany, Austria, Italy, and Spain, radical right-wing movements came to power and began to dismantle what remained of the rational and progressive apparatuses of their respective societies. This reactionary movement reached its zenith in Germany, and the results are well known. Rather than the promotion of civility and inclusion, there was the genocidal murder of large segments of the carriers of progress, not only Jews but also intellectuals, communists, socialists, scientists, free-thinkers, and Christian idealists alike.

Alongside the spread of rational understanding, then, there has emerged in the course of this century an outbreak of brutality and violence on an unprecedented scale. This century invented total war, war to the death, war against not only professional armies but the masses of civilian populations. Americans are usually less sensitive to these developments than others, since none of this century's wars has been fought on its continental soil. It is a critically significant fact, however, that liberal democratic countries have become full participants in the ideology and practice of total war (see Gibson 1986 and Johnson 1983). Faced with Hitler's attack on Britain in the summer of 1940, Churchill wrote that "when I look around to see how we can win the war I see that there is only one sure path . . . and that is an absolutely devastating, exterminating attack by very heavy bombers from this country upon the Nazi homeland" (quoted in Rhodes 1988: 469). The leader who once had been repelled by total war had now come to embrace it. Even before the dropping of atomic bombs on Japan, allied bombing killed 260,000 Japanese and injured more than 400,000 more (Johnson 1983: 423). In their battle against the ruthless FLN in the first Indo-Chinese war, the French engaged in terror and systematic torture. In their own Indo-Chinese war, the Americans engaged in blanket bombing, with the intention, in President Johnson's words, of "bombing Vietnam back to the stone age." In contemporary America, one of the most democratic nations in the history of the world, the massively funded Central Intelligence Agency organizes secret classes on torture techniques for the military cadres of dictatorial nations; then it gives them the facilities to carry out this torture.

In part because of the strain of continuous warfare, this century has seen the spread of charismatic executive authority on an unprecedented scale. In Germany, China, and Russia, leaders have become living icons for their sometimes adoring, sometimes terrified, but almost always mesmerized and surprisingly compliant populations. In democratic countries charismatic executive authority has never disappeared. On the contrary, the cult of the personality seems increasingly essential for national integration and effective rational government (Harden 1974).

Finally, even when the darkest shadows of antimodernity have been avoided, the twentieth century has been haunted by a sense of disappointment with modern life. In the most successful countries, boredom and ennui often overshadow a sense of individual and collective purpose (see for example, Keniston 1964). This has resulted in one of the most revealing phenomenon of our time – the continuing attempts by those who have been spared the most awful modern brutality to escape from the progressive forces, ideas, and institutions that have achieved this. People flee from the demands of this-worldly perfection to the romantic alternatives of various addictions – to drugs and alcohol, to escapist religion, to visions of nirvana of a mystical and other-worldly kind.

The nightmare of reason

This historical declension of real life in the twentieth century – albeit a "real world" permeated by ideas – has had a pronounced effect on the world of intellectual thought. Reason has been experienced as a hollow shell, progress as inconceivable, and often actually undesirable. The very possibility that there is a higher point, an "end" towards which society should strive, has come to be thrown into doubt.

When social theory is caught up in the dream of reason it is post-religious but relies on a metaphysical prop. When it articulates the nightmare of reason, it is post-religious without a metaphysic. Paul Tillich, a great twentieth-century theologian who lived without the dream, described modern individuals as adrift and alone, without the traditional support from God. Yet Tillich maintained that this condition could spur them on to great strength and, indeed, even to greater faith, and he (1952) drew from Sartre the notion that what we need in the present, postmodern situation is "the courage to be." Nietzche drew the opposite conclusion, one more characteristic of the dark line itself. God is dead. Reason is a lie and abstract reasoning is lifeless and corrupt. From this Nietzche drew a kind of pre-fascist conclusion: we must escape from our present condition by transcending it. One of the ways we can do so is by identifying with an irrational superman.

But let us turn from this prophecy of alternative societies to efforts at creating alternative worlds of thought. Earlier I identified four intellectual currents of embodied reason. Here I will outline the antirationalist postures that have developed as alternatives. These alternative orientations crystallize the sharp departures from rationality and progress that have characterized our time.

Twentieth-century philosophy began with logical positivism and the confidence that analytic thought could know the truth. It is ending with hermeneutics, a philosophy which maintains that knowing reality in a manner that separates it from us is epistemologically impossible. Logical positivism was bold, ambitious, predictive. Hermeneutics is modest, exploratory, tentative, regarding the mere description of the object as a herculean task. In the earlier (1922) Wittgensteinean philosophy, words can reflect things; they are based on reality. In the later Wittgensteinean philosophy – *Philosophical Investigations* being the most representative single work of postpositivist thought – words refer not to reality but to themselves. We do not touch reality; we think within a self-referential cocoon of other thoughts and words. Saussure (1959 [1911]), the founder of structural linguistics and semiotics, made much the same point. There is no way to go from objects, from reality, to the word thoughts that characterize them. Between words and objects there is only an arbitrary relation. Influenced by logical positivism, earlier philosophy of science was concerned with the conditions for truth, verification, and the evolutionary progress of knowledge. Much of postpositivist philosophy of science glories in irrationality, asserts incommensurability, and theorizes apocalyptic revolutions.

Earlier I suggested that there does exist in contemporary aesthetics an emphasis on minimalism, realism, directness, and linearity. Much more widely recognized, of course, is the aesthetic movement in the opposite direction, toward surrealism. Particularly in the visual arts and in avant-garde literature there has been the destruction of the notion of a transparent reality. Artists neither refer to nor rely upon the rationality of human beings. Over the long duree, the discontinuities are striking: from Ingre to Abstrast Impression by way of Cubism; from Beethoven to Webern by way of Strindberg; from George Eliot and Tolstoy to Becket and Pynchon by way of James and Wolf. Interpretation theory reflects a similar trajectory. Earlier critics examined authors' intentions, historical contexts, and thematic development within actual texts. Beginning with New Criticism, these standards and practices became less applicable. The complexity and irrationality of motive, it is now believed, makes authorial intention impossible to discover. Similar difficulties accrue to the study of historical context. With Derrida, our lack of confidence in our own rationality has increased to the point that we are not certain there is a text.

Freud created the psychological alternative to the rationalistic images of developmental and behavioral approaches. Since assumptions about motives are the bedrock of social theory, this depth psychology has had a particularly powerful impact, whether orthodox, Jungian, or "humanistic."

Instead of rational motive, psychoanalysis begins with the passionate, moralistic, and irrational actor. In contrast to the self-confident and reactive individual, it suggests that the self is fragmented, contradictory, and difficult to find. Against the notion that reality is either obviously visible or increasingly becoming so, depth psychology emphasizes the difficulty of reality-testing and the omnipresence of distortion. Rather than an innate quality, rationality is something that may take years of treatment for an actor to achieve.

The intellectual alternatives to social engineering are at first sight less obvious. Theorists do not argue that society is impossible to change. They do, however, suggest that the standards for promoting and evaluating change are neither rational nor capable of providing accurate evaluations. Oakeshott (1962) has developed this approach in its conservative form, arguing that social change is encrusted by custom and inherently incremental and that efforts to plan change rationally only blind actors to these facts. Walzer (1983) and other "internalist" critics of Rawls and Habermas have developed this alternative more critically. They argue that justice cannot be understood in terms of abstract criteria and transcendental principles. It must be theorized from within the cultural practices of particular spheres of life. Social movements that ignore these structures encourage the domination and violence that has characterized the degenerate line of twentieth-century life.

Social theory as a bridge between two worlds

Many of the great thinkers who initiated twentieth-century social thought participated in two worlds. They experienced both the dream of reason and the nightmare that followed in its wake. They came to early maturity as believers in science, evolution, and progress. One thinks here of Freud's first career in psychophysiology, Weber's pre-breakdown Darwinian writings in political economy and comparative history, Durkheim's early scientism, and Wittgenstein's logical positivism. At a certain point in their development, however, these thinkers came face to face with the darkness and irrationality of their times. When Weber wrote, just after the turn of the new century, that "the rosy blush of . . . the Enlightenment [is] irretrievably fading" (1958 [1904–05]: 182), he gave expression to the darker perception that characterized an entire generation.

For many of these thinkers the First World War symbolized their disillusionment. In his lecture to German students immediately in the wake of war, for example, Weber rejected out of hand the evolutionary hope for reason.

I may leave aside altogether the naive optimism in which science – that is, the technique of mastering life which rests upon science – has been celebrated as the way to happiness. Who believes in this? – aside from a few big children in university chairs or editorial offices. (1946 [1917]: 143)

Three years before that war began, Durkheim wrote that "we are going through a stage of transition and moral mediocrity."

The great things of the past which filled our father with enthusiasm do not excite the same ardor in us . . . The old gods are growing old or already dead, and others are not yet born. (1965 [1911]: 475)

Just after the war began, Freud conceived of it as representing the disillusionment that all thinking people felt with the rationalist promises of the past.

We are constrained to believe that never has any event been destructive of so much that is valuable in the common wealth of humanity, nor so misleading to many of the clearest intelligences, nor so debasing to the highest that we know. Science herself has lost her passionless impartiality; in their deep embitterment her servants seek for weapons from her . . .

When I speak of disillusionment, everyone at once knows what I mean . . . We were prepared to find that wars between the primitive and the civilized peoples [and] wars with and among the undeveloped nationalities of Europe or those whose culture has perished – that for a considerable period such wars would occupy mankind. But we permitted ourselves to have other hopes.

We had expected the great ruling powers . . . who were known to have cultivated world-wide interests, to whose creative powers were due our technical advances in the direction of dominating nature, as well as the artistic and scientific acquisitions of the mind – peoples such as these we had expected to succeed in discovering another way of settling misunderstandings and conflicts of interests. (1963 [1915]: 107–8)

Just as Wittgenstein had been "a happy sunny child" in Vienna, so "his English acquaintances from before 1914 knew him as capable of great gaiety" (Janik and Toulmin 1973: 177). During the war Wittgenstein fought for Austria on the front lines.

From 1919 on, he became a lonely and introverted figure. He admitted to having been impressed by Oswald Spengler's *Decline of the West*, and he retreated more and more into ethical attitudes of extreme individualism and austerity. (ibid.)

After the war's end, even as the *Tracatus* made Wittgenstein famous, the author disappeared from the intellectual world. He taught school in a small peasant village and later became a gardener. When he returned to Cambridge and academic life in 1929, he did so with an entirely different outlook on life from that of his early, logical positivist phase. He had given up on progress in the conventional sense. "When we think of the world's future," he wrote in 1929 (1980: 3e), "we always mean the destination it will reach if it keeps going in the direction we can see it going in now; it does not occur to us that its path is not a straight line but a curve, constantly changing direction." These changes, Wittgenstein was certain, would bring ruin. He had a premonition of disaster: "The earlier culture will become a heap of rubble and finally a heap of ashes" (ibid.).

Cleansed of their earlier innocence, these thinkers devoted themselves to explaining how this darkness could have come about. Yet if they abandoned the dream of reason, they did not reject rationality as a normative goal. To explain irrationality constituted the principal intellectual challenge of their lives. They would do so in order to preserve the values of modernity in a less naive, more mature form.

Freud spent his later life outlining the pathways of unconscious irrationality. He allowed that the result of psychoanalysis would not be utopia but simply common unhappiness. He insisted, however, that this was far preferable to the fantasies of psychosis. Psychoanalysis could not eliminate the influence of the unconscious, but it could reduce its ability to distort reality. "Where id was," Freud suggested hopefully, "there ego shall be."

Weber demonstrated how modern rationality had historically arisen from religious commitments, and he believed that "world flight" would be the most common reaction of modern people once these commitments were withdrawn. He condemned these flights and any attempt to restore the metaphysical world. The secular rationality that was the heir to religious rationalization, he insisted, represented the only possible hope for humankind (Alexander 1989).

In his later work, Durkheim described how the mythical and symbolic underpinnings of modern thought made any conception of narrowly rational behaviour obsolete. At the same time, he hoped that his exposure of the social foundation of religion would allow this symbolic dimension of human life to be expressed in a non-deistic form, freeing the cognitive dimension of thought to be disciplined by the scientific method.

The case for a continuing commitment to reason is more complex with Wittgenstein. Alone among this first generation of great theorists, he experienced another world war. Is it surprising that in 1947, after this second shattering experience, he would ask whether it is so "absurd . . . to believe that the age of science and technology is the beginning of the end for humanity," or that he would entertain what he called a "truly apocalyptic view of the world" in which "the idea of great progress is a delusion" (1980: 56e)? When he announces his hopes for *Philosophical Investigations*, that great rational reconstruction of ordinary language, he does so in a subdued and pessimistic way.

> I make them public with doubtful feelings. It is not impossible that it should fall to the lot of this work, in its poverty and in the darkness of this time, to bring light into one brain or another – but, of course, it is not likely. (1968 [1945]: vi)

Still, this later theory of the conventionalized nature of ordinary language explained the impossibility of denatured objectivity in an extraordinarily lucid and rational way. Even while he expressed skepticism about "the idea that truth will ultimately be known" (1980 [1947]: 56e), it is clear that Wittgenstein continued to see "clarity [and] perspicuity as valuable in themselves" (1980 [1930]: 7e).

The great social theorists of the middle and latter twentieth century matured within the framework created not by progressive rationalism but by Freud, Durkheim, Weber, Wittgenstein, and other thinkers of a similarly postmodern cast. Keynes was weaned on the anti-Utilitarian platonism of Moore, and he developed a radically new theory of the irrationality of capitalist investment that could only have been drawn from Freud. Levi-Strauss grew up on Durkheimian anthropology and structural linguistics. Sartre cut his intellectual eye teeth on Husserl. Marcuse grew up on Heidegger, Freud, and Lukàcs. Parsons' intellectual fathers were Weber, Pareto, and Durkheim.

Yet, while these more contemporary thinkers differed from their illustrious predecessors in the fact that they never experienced an epistemological break, their commitment to postmodern thought was nourished by a similar confrontation with the darkness of modern life. Keynes rejected his earlier aestheticism after he was horrified by the barbarism of the Great War and politicized by the stupidity of the peace treaty that followed. In the middle of the 1930s, Lévi-Strauss fled to the Brazilian jungle and immersed himself in savage thought because of the repulsion he felt for the mechanization of modern society and the cold, abstract reasoning it employed.[15] Sartre lived at such a distance from French society that he experienced the Second World War almost as a relief (Hayman 1987: 149–78). He wrote *Being and Nothingness* in a German prisoner-of-war camp, and he took man's confinement in "non-being" as characterizing modern society as such. The true condition of being, Sartre wrote, is anguish; to talk about ideal values is only bad faith. Parsons conceived of his first great book as a response to the double shadow of fascism and Stalinism – "various kinds of individualism have been under increasingly heavy fire [and] the role of reason, and the status of scientific knowledge . . . have been attacked again and again" (1937: 5). Marcuse regarded even democratic industrial societies as totalitarian. "The fact that the vast majority of the population accepts, and is made to accept, this society," he wrote (1964: xiii), "does not render it less irrational and less reprehensible."

Neither did these later thinkers accept the nightmare of reason as humankind's necessary fate. Keynes intended to revive the hope for a humane economy in a post-perfectionist form. Lévi-Strauss, despite his fatalistic ruminations, regarded his life's work as a scientific contribution and urged other rational thinkers to resist the temptations of historicist thought. Sartre insisted that human beings do have the capacity for freedom, and he strenuously argued in his literature as well as his philosophy that this responsibility be taken up. Parsons tried to develop a voluntaristic theory that, through the internalization of values, would provide the basis for a more mediated and secure freedom. Marcuse insisted that transcendence was possible, if only his contemporaries would draw upon their innately human capacity for critical thought.

Conclusion

H. Stuart Hughes (1966) entitled his influential historical study of French social thought in the interwar years, *The Obstructed Path*. His thesis was that French society, and French social theory, had strayed off the normal and expected path of rationality and democracy into mysticism, radicalism, alienation, and antimodernity. My argument in this essay has been directed against this kind of "exceptionalist" view of antimodernity. Rather than as an accurate description of twentieth-century thought, it should actually be viewed as an expression of the dream of reason itself. The line of twentieth-century development has been a tortuous one, and the path of the theory that has reflected on this development has been obstructed. It is not just French theory between the wars that reflected alienation, radicalism, and irrationalism, therefore, but the major thrust of twentieth-century theory itself.

Indeed, it is American thought in the twentieth century that has been exceptional, precisely because it has been so untortured and perfectionist, so confident in the unobstructed access to rationality in modern life. In the postwar period, Parsons and Rawls provide perhaps the two best illustrations of this rationalist optimism. Hughes' first important book, *Consciousness and Society* (1958), provides an historical formulation of this American bias in a still influential form. In this classical work, which brought the whiggish thesis of *The Structure of Social Action* (Parsons 1937) into the domain of intellectual history, Hughes described the growing recognition of the irrational and surrealism in European thought and art merely as a deepening of progressive self-reflection. The bitter, often tragic, and enormously destabilizing social and intellectual origins of this turn away from rationality are simply unrecognized.

A taught dialogue between pessimism and optimism, reason and unreason, defines social theory in the twentieth century. Suspended between perfection and apocalypse, what marks off the greatest of this century's theorists is their attempt to mediate these dichotomies. While they have abandoned positivism and no longer see their times as embodying the dream of reason, most have not given up on science as a hope and none have given up on reason as a possibility. They recognize the omnipresence of irrationality with regret. Their theories are devoted to showing how the irrational works, in different spheres, in different modes, with different results. They show this by exercising their reason, and they hope to use their hard won understandings to find a way to a better life. This life will recognize the ineradicable need for irrational experience and for the concrete, expressive articulation of meaning. By augmenting our rational understanding, however, it may be possible for a form of social life to emerge that meets these needs in a less restrictive way.

This form of life has not yet emerged. As the second millennium of western history draws to a close, it remains a possibility devoutly to be wished. By reflecting on the unique character of this century, social theory may perhaps contribute to this task.

Notes

1. For the notion of "transformative capacity" as the rationalizing contribution of the Protestant Reformation, see Eisenstadt (1968). By emphasizing perfectionism and reason, I am adding to this evolutionary approach a more culturally-specific element of intellectual history.

2. For the centrality of millennialist ideas in modern revolutions and reform movements, see Walzer (1965) on the English Revolution; Tuveson (1968) and Bloch (1985) on the American Revolution; Miller (1965) on early national reform in America, "Christianity in Chartist Struggle 1838–1842" on Chartism and primitive Christianity; and Hyams, *The Millennium Postponed*, on the communist revolutions more generally.

3. At several points in his work, Weber suggested that, via the Enlightenment, the "charisma of reason" inherited Puritanism's this-worldly asceticism and became the embodiment of the world-mastering heritage of religious rationalization. For the connection of Puritanism to the first great manifestation of "reason," the scientific revolution, see Merton (1970 [1939]) and Tenbruk (1974). The connection between religious rationalization and the contemporary ethos of modernity has been almost totally obscured by Weber's instrumental and materialistic theorizing about the industrial society. The Parsonian tradition provides the antidote to this, but its generally optimistic, even pollyanna-ish thinking about modernity has made its contributions to theoretical reflection much less important.

4. For the religious and eschatological underpinnings of Marx's work, see Lowith (1949), of Hegel's, see Taylor (1975).
5. I doubt, however, that it is possible for Poles to take this progressivist line. For Germans who describe history in this progressive way, see the evolutionary change theories of Habermas and Munch. I will address the extremely interesting issue of national variation in the latter part of this essay.
6. Indeed, participation in these mass socialist parties seemed to have provided tens of thousands of low and middle status people not only with a firm conviction of the imminence of the new society but with an experience of actual salvation in this world. See, for example, the autobiography of Julius Braunthal, the Austro-Hungarian socialist leader, which presents Braunthal's participation and expectations in unmistakably millennial terms.

    It was a great day in my life when I went . . . to the Working-Class Youth Club to register . . . It meant for me the firm resolve to help bring about nothing less than the New Jerusalem on earth in my own lifetime . . . For me the fact that the world was constantly changing was beyond any question. My problem was whether or not the time for the "final change" in human society had come . . . From Marx's *Manifesto* and Friederich Engels' *Anti-Duhring*, which were among the first Socialist classics I had read, I believed that humanity had now entered the final stage of its history. (Braunthal 1945: 39–40).
7. Hughes (1958) used the phrase, "the obstructed path," in his influential intellectual history of French thought and ideology in the interwar years. His focus was the manner in which French social theory strayed off the path of normal and expected Enlightenment thinking, into irrationality, alienation, and antimodernity. My argument here is against this kind of "exceptionalist" point of view on antimodernity. Rather than describing twentieth-century thought, it should actually be viewed as an expression of the dream of reason itself. It was the twentieth century that ran into an "obstructed path" and a major thrust of European social theory (not just French thought between the wars) reflected upon it. It is American thought in the twentieth century that has been exceptional, precisely because it has been so untortured and perfectionist and has continued to express such confidence in rationality and modernity. Parsons and Rawls provide two of the best illustrations. Hughes' *Consciousness and Society* (1958) provides a formulation of this American bias in a still influential form. In this classic work, which was strongly affected by Parsons' *The Structure of Social Action* (1937), Hughes traces the growing emphasis on the irrational and the growing surrealism of European thought and art. This discussion, like Parsons' earlier one, is presented, however, as a story of intellectual progress. The bitter, often tragic, and enormously destabilizing social and intellectual origins of this turn away from rationality are simply unrecognized.
8. At first glance, it seems quite extraordinary that, in a century that has been humbled by the most horrid violence, this turn toward violence in radical philosophy has been so little remarked upon and so infrequently criticized. Thus, Sartre's *Critique of Dialectical Reason* has typically been taken by left thinkers (e.g., Poster 1979) as an argument for community – for the movement from serial to fused groups – rather than as an apologia for violence, which it also is. Aron's *History and the Dialectic of Violence* (1975) is the only serious critique of this theme in Sartre's work of which I am aware, and it has been virtually ignored. Aron argues that Sartre's work became so politicized that theoretical and ideological confusions are fused – "the taste for Revolution and a lack of it for reform have become a philosophical truth" (Aron 1975:

185). He attacks the degeneration of reason and the ultimate dehumanization that this position involves

> The strange alliance between Reason and violence, whereby the other – the conservative, the reformist, anyone who says 'no' to the revolutionary apocalypse – takes on the grim traits of the anti-man" (ibid.) . . . . It is by means of the class struggle, by the antagonism of groups where everyone wishes the death of the other, that the dialectical movement, whose completion is marked by the advent of totalizing Truth, progresses (187–88)

In regard to the link between Fanon and Sartre, Aron is critical not of anti-colonial violence as a strategic necessity but of its theoretical justification in anti-rational terms. "What I hate," he writes (p. 192), "is not the choice, *hic et nun*, at a particular conjunction of circumstances, in favour of violence and against negotiation, but a philosophy of violence in and for itself, not as means that is sometimes necessary for a rational politics, but a philosophy that lays claim to an ontological foundation and psychological function or effectiveness."

The intellectual promotion of violence, of course, is hardly limited to the left. Highly respected geopolitical thinkers, like Kissinger, advocate the strategic use of massive deadly force (see Gibson 1986).

That most commentators have been uninterested in the philosophical promotion of violence may, on further reflection, not be so surprising. It may in fact be the very result of the omnipresence of violence in this century's life.

9.   This is not an anachronistic usage, as Lenin's famous pamphlet, *Left-Wing Communism: An Infantile Disorder*, demonstrates.

10. "The notion that social change can be best achieved through revolutionary violence is very much an offshoot of the French Revolution and of its socialist heirs. Sorel's *Reflections sur la violence* took up an uncomfortable and hushed-up subject and made it the centre of a strategy destined to overthrow the bourgeois order. At a time when the Marxists of the Second International were pussy-footing about the desirability of a revolution, Sorel took the uncompromising step of affirming its necessity" (Llobera 1988).

11. For a discussion of the historical dialectic between absent and present reason, see Alexander (forthcoming).

12. Until recently, it was only "anticommunists" who made such critical claims. Ironically, the most recent documentation of the communist distortion of reason has come from newspapers within Soviet Russia itself. In spring 1988, in the wake of Peristroika, the final history examinations of more than 50 million Soviet schoolchildren were cancelled. In an extraordinary commentary on its front page, laced with expressions of bitterness, tortured guilt, and hopes for purification, *Izvestia* attacked the entire historiography of Soviet Communism as the inversion of the Revolution's rational hopes.

> The guilt of those who deluded one generation after another, poisoning their minds and souls with lies, is immeasurable . . . today we are reaping the bitter fruits of our own moral laxity. We are paying for succumbing to conformity and thus to giving silent approval of everything that now brings the blush of shame to our faces and about which we do not know how to answer our children honestly. [This process is] a purifying torture of revelation, or, to be precise, a second birth. (*Los Angeles Times*, June 11, 1988)

13.   "It is now the world of psychologically and morally exhausted societies (largely on a Marxist and post-Marxist pattern) that have lost their energy and appeal. They are seen, along with their philosophy, as antique fortresses jutting out of a wasteland of the past. In fact, their own chances of breaking out of this closure now depend largely on their success in following the new model set by America and its rivals and competitors in the Western imperium . . . At the time of Nikita Krushchev's reform regime in the early 1960s, and again under Mikhail Gorbachiev's drive in the mid-1980s to modernize the Soviet economy and partially open the society, there was discussion of a possible 'convergence' of the two adversary systems. But the pull of convergence was mostly one-sided, not toward the blocked societies of the East but toward the openness of the West."

This polemical statement is remarkable not so much for what it says as for who has said it – not a conservative cold warrior but the venerable New Deal liberal, Max Lerner (1987: 11–12), in the left-of-center American magazine, *The New Republic*.

14.   "In the weeks before the Armageddon, Bethmann Hollweg's secretary and confident Kurt Riezler made notes of the gloomy relish with which his master steered Germany and Europe into the abyss. July 7, 1914: 'The Chancellor expects that a war, whatever its outcome, will result in the uprooting of everything that exists. The existing world very antiquated, without ideas.' July 27: 'Doom greater than human power hanging over Europe and our people.' " (Johnson 1983: 12).

15.   Lévi-Strauss begins *Tristes Tropiques* with an account of his encounter with "one of those outbreaks of stupidity, hatred, and credulousness which social groups secrete like pus when they begin to be short of space" (1973: 18). He argues that "experiences such as these [are] starting to ooze out like some insidious leakage from contemporary mankind, which [has] become saturated with its own numbers and with the ever-increasing complexity of its problems" (ibid.). He concludes the book with this melancholic prophecy, not much different from the spirit of Wittgenstein's:

The world began without man and will end without him. The institutions, morals and customs that I shall have spent my life noting down and trying to understand are the transient efflorescence of a creation in relation to which they have no meaning . . . From the time when he first began to breathe and eat, up to the invention of atomic and thermonuclear devices, by way of the discovery of fire . . . what else has man done except blithely break down billions of structures and reduce them to a state in which they are no longer capable of integration? (ibid.: 472)

Bibliography

Alexander, Jeffrey C. (1988) "Back to Lippman," *The New Republic*, 198 (5), February 1: 15–16.

Alexander, Jeffrey C. (1989) "The dialectic of individuation and domination: Max Weber's rationalization theory and beyond," in Alexander, *Structure and Meaning: Relinking Classical Sociology* (New York: Columbia University Press: 68–100).

Alexander, Jeffrey C. (forthcoming) "General theory in the postpositivist mode: the epistemological dilemma and the search for present reason," in Steven Seidman and David Wagner (eds), *Postmodernism and Social Theory* (New York: Basil Blackwell).

Aron, Raymond (1957) *The Opium of the Intellectuals* (New York: W. W. Norton & Company).

Aron, Raymond (1975) *History and the Dialectic of Violence: An Analysis of Sartre's "Critique de la Raison Dialectique"* (New York: Harper & Row).

Becker, Carl (1932) *The Heavenly City of the Eighteenth-century Philosophers* (New Haven: Yale University Press).

Bloch, Ruth (1985) *Visionary Republic: Millennial Themes in American Thought, 1756–1800* (New York: Cambridge University Press).

Braunthal, Julius (1945) *In Search of the Millennium* (London: Gollancz).

Durkheim, Emile (1965 [1911]) *The Elementary Forms of Religious Life* (New York: Free Press).

Eisenstadt, S. N. (1968) "Introduction," in Eisenstadt (ed.), *The Protestant Ethic and Modernization: a Comparative View* (New York: Basic Books: 3–45).

Emerson, Robert (1981) "On last resorts," *American Journal of Sociology*, 87 (1): 1–22.

Fanon, Franz (1965) *The Wretched of the Earth* (London: MacGibbon & Kee).

Freud, Sigmund (1963 [1915]) "Reflections upon war and death," in *Freud, Character and Culture* (New York: Collier: 107–33).

Fussell, Paul (1975) *The Great War and Modern Memory* (New York: Oxford University Press).

Gibson, James William (1986) *The Perfect War* (New York: Atlantic).

Habermas, Jürgen (1984) *The Theory of Communicative Action*. Vol. 1 (Boston: Beacon Press).

Harden, Charles M. (1974) *Presidential Power and Accountability* (Chicago: University of Chicago Press).

Hart, Nicolette (1982) "Is capitalism bad for your health?" *The British Journal of Sociology*, 33 (3), September.

Hart, Nicolette (1985) *The Sociology of Health and Medicine* (Lancashire: Causeway Press).

Hayman, Ronald (1987) *Sartre: A Life* (New York: Simon & Schuster).

Hughes, H. Stuart (1958) *Consciousness and Society: The Reconstruction of European Social Thought, 1890–1930* (New York: Vintage).

Hughes, H. Stuart (1966) *The Obstructed Path: French Social thought in the Years of Desperation, 1930–1960* (New York: Harper & Row).

Hyams, Edward (1973) *The Millennium Postponed* (New York: Taplinger).

Janik, Allan and Toulmin, Stephen (1973) *Wittgenstein's Vienna* (New York: Simon & Schuster).

Johnson, Paul (1983) *Modern Times: The World from the Twenties to the Eighties* (New York: Harper & Row).

Keniston, Kenneth (1964) *The Uncommitted: Alienated Youth in American Society* (New York: Dell).

Lanham, Richard (1976) *The Motives of Eloquence: Literary Rhetoric in the Renaissance* (New Haven: Yale University Press).

Lévi-Strauss, Claude (1973) *Tristes tropiques* (New York: Washington Square Press).

Llobera, Joseph R. (1988) "The dark side of modernity." Paper presented at Madrid conference on the History of Sociology. Madrid, Spain, May 1988.

Lowith, Karl (1949) *Meaning in History* (Chicago and London: University of Chicago Press).

Mannheim, Karl (1940) *Man and Society in an Age of Reconstruction: Studies in Modern Social Structure* (London: Routledge & Kegan Paul).

Marcuse, Herbert (1964) *One-Dimensional Man* (Boston: Beacon Press).

Marshall, T. H. (1964) *Class, Citizenship, and Social Development* (Garden City, NY: Doubleday).

Merton, Robert K. (1970 [1939]) *Science, Technology and Society in Seventeenth-Century England* (New York: Harper & Row).

Miller, Perry (1965) *The Life of the Mind in America* (New York: Harcourt Brace).

Mosse, George (1964) *The Crisis of German Ideology* (New York: Grosset & Dunlap).

Oakeshott, Michael (1962) *Rationalism in Politics and Other Essays* (New York: Methuen).

Parsons, Talcott (1937) *The Structure of Social Action* (New York: Free Press).

Pevsner, Nickolaus (1977) *Pioneers of Modern Design from William Morris to Walter Gropius* (Harmondsworth: Penguin).

Piaget, Jean (1972) *Principles of Genetic Epistemology* (London: Routledge & Kegan Paul).

Poster, Mark (1979) *Sartre's Marxism* (London: Pluto Press).

Rawls, John (1971) *A Theory of Justice* (Cambridge, MA: Harvard University Press).

Rhodes, Richard (1988) *The Making of the Atomic Bomb* (New York: Simon & Schuster).

Ringer, Fritz K. (1969) *The Decline of the German Mandarins: The German Academic Community, 1890–1933* (Cambridge, MA: Harvard University Press).

Roth, Guenther (1976) "Religion and revolutionary beliefs: sociological and historical dimensions in Max Weber's work – in memory of Ivan Vallier (1927–1974)," *Social Forces*, 55 (2): 257–72.

Sartre, Jean Paul (1976 [1968]) *Critique of Dialectical Reason* (London: New Left Books).

Saussure, Ferdinand de (1959 [1911]) *Course in General Linguistics* (New York: McGraw-Hill).

Sorel, George (1950 [1908]) *Reflections on Violence* (New York: Collier).

Taylor, Charles (1975) *Hegel* (Cambridge: Cambridge University Press).

Tenbruck, F. (1974) "Max Weber and the sociology of science: a case reopened," *Zeitschrift fur Soziologie*, 3.

Tillich, Paul (1952) *The Courage to Be* (New Haven: Yale University Press).

Tuveson, Ernest Lee (1968) *Redeemer Nation* (Chicago: University of Chicago Press).

Walzer, Michael (1965) *Revolution of the Saints* (Cambridge, MA: Harvard University Press).

Walzer, Michael (1983) *Spheres of Justice* (New York: Basic Books).

Weber, Max (1958 [1904–05]) *The Protestant Ethic and the Spirit of Capitalism* (New York: Scribners).

Weber, Max (1946 [1917]) "Science as a vocation," in Hans Gerth and C. Wright Mills (eds), *From Max Weber* (New York: Oxford University Press: 129–56).

Wittgenstein, Ludwig (1922) *Tractatus Logico-Philosophicus* (New York: Harcourt, Brace).

Wittgenstein, Ludwig (1968 [1945]) *Philosophical Investigations* (New York: Macmillan).

Wittgenstein, Ludwig (1980) *Culture and Value* (Chicago: University of Chicago Press).

Yeo, Eileen (1981) "Christianity in Chartist struggle, 1838–1842," *Past and Present*, 91: 109–39.

2

Problems of crisis and normalcy in the contemporary world

ROBERT HOLTON

Contemporary social thought has become dominated, if not obsessed by the idea of crisis (Holton 1987). Crisis-talk is expanding on an epidemic scale. No-one needs convincing of the pervasiveness of crisis-perception. The problem is to determine what this situation signifies. Is the ubiquitous sense of crisis indicative of a deterioration in human welfare? Or is it more a symptom of exaggerated expectations about human capacities to improve the human condition? Should we expect current crises to be resolved, and crisis-talk to recede, or is crisis rapidly becoming a permanent fixture, part of the normal order of things?

One way of responding to these questions is to argue that the epidemic of crisis-talk does indeed reflect a deterioration in the human condition. It is not difficult to list many relevant indicators of this, such as the African famine, intractable warfare in the Middle East and Central America, mass unemployment, the AIDS epidemic, and increasing crime rates. The existence of such massive problems does not however explain how it has come about that crisis-talk has become normalized. Nor does it explain what Piotr Sztompka has called the crisis of crisis-awareness. By this he means the apparent moral indifference and insensitivity of contemporary society to the gravity of social problems. Sztompka asks do we really care about ecological crisis, famine, alienated labour, broken families, and alcoholism, if we are not ourselves unemployed, starving, and so forth (Sztompka 1984). Evidently crisis-awareness depends on issues of interpretation and judgement as to the presence of pathology according to particular evaluative criteria, and cannot be reduced to some simple calculus of human suffering.

The rationalist discourse of crisis has been designed as a means of identifying decisive phases in the development of social pathologies, and as a stimulus to crisis-intervention and resolution through social action. The model underlying this discourse derives, as is well known, from drama and medicine.

In the structure of a drama, crisis is manifest through a key moment or moments in a narrative wherein the dilemmas of human life and the fate of human actors are dramatized. This structure assumes that crisis is an abnormal and discontinuous feature of narrative. Similarly, in medical discourse crisis refers to a particular phase in the development of an illness which is decisive for the future. The resolution of the "crisis" will determine whether the patient will recover or will die. In both cases crisis is not a permanent state, but is a phase in a discernible process of development through time. In other words a rationally grounded narrative. Crisis, given the correct mode of intervention, can in principle be resolved, so as to recreate normality, and a sense of historical progress and continuity.

My argument in this essay is that this conventional framework of crisis-theory is currently being undermined by challenges to Enlightenment rationalism and a loss of faith in the possibility of social progress. The growing realization that there are limits to human and social perfectibility has eroded the distinction between crisis and normalcy. This process of erosion is to be seen in the increasingly nostalgic presentation of utopian expectations that crisis-ridden social pathologies can be progressively resolved.

Within this context it becomes increasingly difficult to justify "end-state" solutions to crisis problems – such as the utopia of *gemeinschaftlich* consensus or the utopia of free producers – by means of reason. A number of Marxists have picked up Romain Rolland's slogan, "Pessimism of the intelligence, optimism of the will," to depict this pathos of reason. There are, in addition, similar grounds for skepticism concerning Habermas' ideal of a discursively established consensus based on the procedural utopia of communicative action. Habermas' reconstruction of the notion of rationality from purposive-monologic to intersubjective-dialogic action, has been challenged by French postmodernists precisely because of its inflated evolutionary faith in the application of this new version of reason to social life. This challenge to Habermas is picked up in the latter part of this paper in terms of the debate with Lyotard.

Theories of social crisis have generally been responses to the rapidly extending processes of social differentiation associated with the advent of urban-industrial capitalism, and with the rationalization of social life into separate spheres. This differentiation master-process has posed massive challenges to the coherence and integration of society. Within this context, crisis theory has generally taken the form of an extended commentary on social pathologies deriving from social differentiation, together with modes of crisis-resolution aiming at improved co-ordination and integration of society.

This applies especially to crisis-theories in the Marxist tradition. These draw on the notion of emancipatory social change as the means of restoring unity, community, and wholeness in the face of pathological crisis-symptoms such as alienated labour, and the contradiction between social labour and private appropriation. The repertoire of crisis theory has been further extended and elaborated by the critical theorists of the Frankfurt School to embrace social structure, culture, and personality. Critical theory, however, is founded on a critique of instrumental reason as a privileged epistemology within which crisis may be diagnosed. This extends crisis-perceptions from the realms of overt and manifest pathologies, to include a latent symptomology based on that which is repressed. The utopian basis of the critical yardsticks in use in this diagnosis are very clear. If our knowledge of that which is repressed cannot be grounded in the conventional cognitive procedures of scientific rationalism, it must in some sense be derived from a philosophical utopia of alternative possibilities.

Jurgen Habermas' diagnosis of legitimation crisis and prognosis for a reconstructed rationality of communicative action is perhaps the most sophisticated synthesis of crisis theory and emancipatory social action yet atempted within this tradition. Habermas attempts to redefine the dream of social progress through reason by transcending the limits of instrument reason and possessive-individualism. In this endeavour, he is less equivocal about the legacy of Enlightenment rationalism than earlier critical theorists such as Adorno. Indeed Habermas' project may be regarded as a last-ditch attempt to salve a reconstructed evolutionary account of social progress from critics of Enlightenment rationalism such as Nietzsche and Foucault. Communicative action amounts to a reassertion of the emancipatory and redemptive potential of reason, a potential not grounded in a philosophy of consciousness, but inherent within sociality itself.

The rapid extension of crisis theory, in its various forms, since the 1960s, not only addresses critics of Enlightenment rationalism, but also alternative accounts of social progress. One of the major targets, in this latter respect, has been the blander forms of modernization theory and systems-theory which have developed since the mid-1950s. Such theories have been criticized for assuming that liberal-democratic institutions, such as the rule of law, the market, and representative democracy would produce an orderly, progressive, and relatively crisis-free future. Crisis theory has treated this prognosis – and the underlying liberal-democratic system theories of Parsons and Niklas Luhmann – with skepticism, both in relation to problems of Third World development and in relation to the western world.

Much of the major thrust of crisis theory, as advanced by Habermas, Offe, and radical political economists has been designed to emphasize the inadequacy of various modes of crisis-management. Particular criticisms have been leveled at varieties of social democratic, corporatist, and welfare state public planning options. These are criticized for their supposed inability to remedy problems of market failure, shortcomings in political steering capacities, and, above all, the increasing gulf between system-processes and the life-world. Given the absence of a demonstrably viable socialist alternative, the evaluative yardsticks at work in these critiques depend in very large measure on utopian projections of an alternative social order based upon the immanence of rational perfectibility. This either assumes a conflict-free environment, or, alternatively an environment in which no conflict or problem is opaque to the emancipatory gaze of reason. If all can be transparent to communicative action and intersubjective reason, there remains little scope for intractable crisis or persistent social pathology.

Set against the dreams of reason that underlie so much crisis theory is the growing challenge of two key assumptions within crisis discourse. The first of these assumptions is the claim that rationalism in some shape or form is capable of reaching an epistemologically secure understanding of social pathology and the means to crisis-resolution. This assumption is challenged, first of all, by the failure of the philosophy of science to come up with a secure basis for determining the adequacy of validity claims. This challenge is particularly acute in the social sciences where epistemological uncertainty leads to a proliferation of largely incommensurable para-digms, both between social science disciplines, and within them. The consequence, as Lyotard points out, is a diacritical clash of viewpoints and a radical uncertainty about the future rather than anything approaching a rational consensus about the truth, or confidence about the direction of social change.

There is of course a long philosophical pedigree behind these problems, as there is a reaction against Enlightenment rationalism. Parallel with these epistemological problems is what might loosely be called the Romantic reaction to the Enlightenment. This emphasizes personal desire and expressivity in contrast with rationalism of any kind. Amongst other things this tends to undermine popular conceptions of the progressive even heroic claims of science and scientists, and to elevate alternative cultural heroism of an aesthetic kind in areas such as music and film.

The second assumption of crisis theory that has been fundamentally challenged, is the erosion of belief in the availability of transcendental agencies of social change and programs. This erosion has been reflected in an accelerating shift from public politics to private consumption and the personal politics of desire. This has also been linked by some with a revival of the romantic ethic which encourages a restless pursuit of dreams and desires within consumption (Campbell 1987).

The decline of public politics is reflected in the shift away from radical labour movements, and a popular indifference to socialism as a privileged form of moral discourse about inequality, exploitation, and the conditions for their removal. New social movements have of course arisen in areas such as feminism, ecology, and the peace movement. Typically, however these movements are less interested in capturing state power than in transforming civil society as a sphere of autonomous rights for individuals and groups (Feher and Heller 1984).

Such challenges to rationalism have implications not only for crisis theory, but also for the wider belief in social progress. One of the current difficulties with rationalist social theory, with its underlying evolutionary presuppositions is that we have lost our capacity to claim to understand what lies beyond the current crisis. Those who believe in crisis cannot give us a convincing account of whether new patterns of normalcy will be established. Without any clear sense of the possibility of new patterns, crisis becomes a more or less permanent condition – a chronic illness or a dream without end. In place of the epic narrative we now have the soap-opera. Whereas the narrative structure of epic allows the possibility of the heroic resolution of crisis to reach a definite end-point, the structure of the soap-opera is radically open-ended. The endless serial form of the soap opera in which a multiple plot-structure is generated from a plurality of different characters' viewpoints, suggests that life has no unambiguous or stable meaning, and no clear line of narrative development (Ang 1987). Social experience is less and less part of an epic, and increasingly part of a soap-opera.

How then to characterize the constituent features of the contemporary social structure in the aftermath of the erosion of evolutionism. Within social theory, there are two prevailing characterizations. The first clings to crisis-ridden notions like late capitalism or disorganized capitalism. These highlight pathology but don't have much confidence about the direction in which the crises will be resolved or if they will be resolved at all. The second option is to attempt a more definite characterization of the present as a process of becoming, founded on notions like post-industrial society or postmodernism. These alternative approaches focus on certain new trends in social structure and culture, but remain somewhat enigmatic about the future. Characteristically we move beyond a previous phase but the new world cannot be given a wholly confident and unambiguous identity.

The notion of postmodernism is especially enigmatic. Does postmodern mean anti-modern, and if so is it a form of neo-conservatism as Habermas suggests (1982). Or is postmodern one of several modalities of modernism, albeit a modality that is corrosive of certain of the earliest formulations of the nature of modernism?

Certainly the notion of postmodernity has focused on a range of cultural, and aesthetic developments in the postwar world. Foremost of these is the awareness of limits to, and problems with, the projects of unlimited self-realization and personal authenticity in art and in the wider culture. Postmodernism, in contrast with modernistic avant-guardism emphasizes

43

the ubiquity of simulated rather than authentic experience. It also emphasizes the fundamentally decentered and diacritical nature of social experience under postmodernity, developments which are fundamentally corrosive of the search for rational consensus or holistic community. All is not solipsistic fragmentation, since local forms of communication are possible. The complexity of secularized individuated "language games," however evades social control, and indeed pervades not merely the life-world, but also the institutions that comprise "the system."

Is postmodernism then the coherent pattern underlying this incoherence, a new understanding of sociality? One problem with this way of beginning to rescue a coherent set of organizing concepts in the postmodernist debate, is the perception that contemporary social change transcends any specific substantive content. In so doing it also outstrips the capacities of social theory to produce coherent characterizations of the nature of the present. This applies both to the concept of modernity, and to postmodernity, which maybe did not turn out to be the next clear stage beyond the classical liberal-democratic notion of modernity. Modernization, in other words, has come to be associated, as Alain Touraine points out, with the process of change itself.

One of the most striking symptoms of this epoch of crisis-talk, and crisis-normalization is the breakdown of optimistic narratives of social change and historical evolution. Lyotard emphasizes this post-evolutionary characteristic of postmodernity, and links it to the collapse of faith in progress.

One noteworthy consequence of this feature of the crisis is that we are reluctant to begin the future. We are, so to speak, trapped in the present, encouraging time horizons which are characteristically short-term.

Niklas Luhmann, who has done most to theorize the troubled state of temporality within contemporary thought (Luhmann 1982), argues that in place of evolutionary evolutionism we are left with only two alternatives. One is a utopian plurality of projections – creating a surplus of possible futures, none of which seems immediately accessible. The alternative is short-run modes of crisis-management oriented to performance. The attraction of technocracy within this short-run perspective is that it defuturizes the future. This is achieved by reducing complexities associated with uncertain expectations about that which is to come. Technocracy seeks therefore to control surprise, and multiply short-run possibilities by maximizing performance. This leaves space for a symbiotic relationship between technocratic crisis-managers and private consumption-oriented households. Neither party has much of a stake in the future beyond tomorrow, and neither has the slightest interest in transcendent critiques of contemporary social relations. Post modernism, in this sphere, appears to represent the final eclipse of high culture with its rationalist and aesthetic aspirations for the plebeian culture of consumerism.

44

One of the major characteristics of postmodernism is therefore a recognition of the increasingly *gesellschaftlich* social relations of contemporary life. Postmodernism acknowledges that the contemporary life-world has moved increasingly beyond *gemeinschaftlich* and nostalgic presentations of social life, based on the search for a lost community and a personal quest for interpersonal authenticity.

Such *gesellschaftlich* relations proceed through the largely impersonal networks of communication and exchange, namely the market, and representative democracy. These impersonal networks rely on a formal universalism of procedural norms. This impersonal framework is the guarantor of a minimum sense of normative order, within which the largely incommensurable projects of private social actors are acted out. Within this pattern a public politically-centered culture of communicative rationality is undermined by a symbiotic relationship between technocratic crisis-management and private consumers. Crisis-managers seek to deliver and legitimize particular levels of formal economic performance, while private consumption-oriented households seek to appropriate shares of the social product for substantively incommensurable projects.

Habermas and most other crisis theorists regard this pattern as inherently pathological, and crisis-ridden. The social relations involved distort the possibility of communicative action, and constrain the potential of human actors to reach a rationally-grounded consensus based on mutual understanding. Instead the life-world is left at the mercy of colonization by "experts" who manage the impersonal process of system-reproduction. This reproduction process is legitimized wherever possible in his view by recourse to nature-like regularities beyond human intervention. The scope for social criticism is rolled back.

Against this vision it has to be said that the institutional matrix of liberal-democracy has proved remarkably resilient in the west, in spite of the diagnosis of multi-dimensional crisis. The shift away from liberal-democratic solutions to fascism or communism that occurred in the 1930s has not been repeated. To be sure, the character of liberalism has developed and expanded to take into account the expansion of support for social citizenship rights. None the less the crisis diagnosis has seemingly been undercut not only by crisis-management, but also by an apparent cultural shift away from the public politics of Enlightenment rationalism and the project of evolutionary social progress through the application of reason to social affairs.

Within this context, Habermas' vision has been criticized most notably by Luhmann and Lyotard, and the debates are well known. What follows is a selective summary of those features of the debates that relate to the argument of the present essay.

Luhmann has criticized the utopia of communicative action, seeing it as effectively a retreat from society. It may perpetuate "the illusion of a small and beautiful world," but it cannot "provide social security against change," and can no longer legitimize opinion. The implication of this argument against Habermas is that there is a functional advantage to the differentiation between the social system and the private life-world, in terms of the capacity to deliver the maximum amount of social utilities to those who wish to privately appropriate them for incommensurable purposes. Organic notions of community based on interpersonal interaction are dysfunctional to the management of large-scale secularized societies, with which a secure space for individual autonomy has been established.

Lyotard's critique of Habermas' notion of communicative action is ever more forthright (Lyotard 1984). In his view, the search for consensus among substantively incommensurable projects can only be enforced through greater or lesser amounts of terror. In the postmodern world, where God is dead, and rationality discredited, there is no hope for models of crisis-resolution, based upon a communicatively established consensus of substantive rationality. We are left instead with a set of temporary contracts between heterogenous actors, fractured by endemic episodes of dissent and conflict. Such interactions take place within a minimal and precarious normative order. Judgments are not based on a secure sense of pre-existing criteria, but on emergent rules which are discovered during the process of interaction, as a type of innovation. This whole approach owes a good deal to the later Wittgensteinean approach to language.

Lyotard's approach to normative order is therefore more minimal and enigmatic than that of Luhmann. As such it has received more critical attention.

We may agree with Lyotard that many social judgments do appear to anticipate the rules underlying them, but this does not in itself exhaust the analysis of judgment. One major objection is that Lyotard omits any account of participants' insights into structures of power and exploitation associated with the emergence of rules. It is therefore extremely doubtful whether the principle of domination has been effectively replaced by the principles of difference and diacritical discourse. What is at stake here is not the increasing scale of centralized state domination *per se*, since this apparatus, as Lyotard points out, is made up of individuals who themselves conduct language games with other incumbents of official roles. Language games can therefore be operated within bureaucratic constraints through networks of communication such as orders within the army, prayer in church, denotation in schools, narration in families, questions in philosophy, performance in business . . . and so forth.

The more telling objection is that Lyotard underestimates the importance of pre-existing power networks in constraining the substantive content of language games. In other words, his valuable critique of the idea of individual powerlessness, led him to overestimate the scope for individual autonomy within the atomized plurality of language games.

46

One way of pursuing the elusive character of the contemporary normative order is through a review of the notion of sociality itself. How far do conventional notions of sociality survive the current crisis?

One of the leading symptoms of crisis in notions of sociality is the idea of postmodern society as decentered. There are several components of this conception. One is the erosion of notions of sociality based on strong bonds of normative consensus. This process of erosion, foreshadowed in many respects by Durkheim, is reflected in part in the declining legitimacy of religious faith and the death of God. It is also evident in the convincing challenge mounted by Bryan Turner and his associates to the "dominant ideology thesis," whereby dominant classes were thought to require strong normative controls over subordinate classes (Abercrombie, Hill, and Turner 1980). Having said this, it is important to emphasize that there are two options currently facing debates about normative order. The first is that no normative consensus is required to hold society together. This implies that system integration can occur without social integration. The second option is that only loose or minimal normative bonds are necessary within contemporary society.

This former option is usually taken to involve a Hobbesian war of all against all, in which conflicting interests utilize power to enforce their will on others. This model seems applicable to the impact of Nietzsche on contemporary theories of postmodernism. In Habermas' view Nietzsche's influence has been to reinstate a conception of judgment based on "a capacity for distinction, which is beyond true and false, beyond good and evil" (Habermas 1982). In this approach value-judgments become reduced to issues of power rather than issues of validity. For Habermas this is no solution to the problem of normative order, because actors must still differentiate between power which deserves to be respected and that which does not. In other words norms are still required as the basis for evaluating competing power claims.

At the same time, since Habermas accepts that norms tend to be contaminated by the effect of power on pre-existing standards of evaluation, he is put in a predicament. Put crudely, communicative rationality depends for its own validity on power-contaminated notions of consensus and the legitimation of sanctions against those who defy consensus. The only way beyond this problem, as pointed out recently by Howard Caygill (1988), is to downgrade the status of communicative rationality to an impure pragmatism. Even the practice of rationality amounts to a non-coercive coercion by rational consensus over dissent.

The implications of this discussion seem to be that power and normative judgement are features of sociality that are simultaneously present. This suggests that the Hobbesian account of sociality remains inadequate. The alternative, however is not a return to ideas of strong normative consensus, dispensing with power. It is rather to see power as a necessary feature of normative structures. At the same time, there is no guarantee that such normative structures will be able to achieve coherence at the societal level. It therefore remains an empirical question as to how widely local instances of normative consensus can be diffused.

The net effect of this first set of debates is that norms and power structures are decentered to the extent that they are constantly subjected to criticism and change, within a plurality of multi-centered episodes of social interaction – or in Lyotard's terms "language games." These exist both in the marketplace and in bureaucracies. But it remains unclear whether they are really so diffuse and short-term as to undermine a centered model of social life.

A second set of arguments about the decentered character of contemporary society, concerns the collapse of the idea of a politically-centered society, built around the nation-state.

The idea of a politically-centered society is not a recent one, but derives from the classical world, and key concepts such as polis. Within the modern process of nation-state building, society and sociality became closely associated with the central political apparatus, which served to integrate the population within a given territory in conditions of relative stability and security. Nationalism, at this time, functioned as a mode of social integration.

The paradox of the contemporary western world is that while the state apparatus has grown in scale and widened its social and economic functions, the binding force of nation-states has become less internally powerful. This is reflected in the waning influence of nationalism within popular culture in most nation-states. It is also reflected in a growing differentiation between politics and culture, between the state and civil society. As Alain Touraine has said, "The State is no longer a principle of unity of social life; it is perceived as a super businessman or as a bureaucrat or a totalitarian power" (Touraine 1984). The only contemporary supporters of the state as an organic unifying force, are the new class of state-employed professionals engaged in social planning and human service delivery. Their influence within the political structure is however insufficient in most western societies to offset the more powerful political formations represented by Thatcherite new rightism or pragmatic corporatist crisis-management. The new class within the public sector is also sometimes outflanked by certain of the new social movements who do not aim to capture state power.

One area in which the decline of political centeredness is most noticeable is in the secular halt, and in some cases, decline in the importance of labor and socialist movements. Their strategic concern to capture the centers of public power in typically nineteenth-century fashion has been overtaken by the decenteredness of private consumerism, and by the transformation of relations between politics and society from issues of political principle to issues of pragmatic crisis-management. State economic planning and regulation mechanisms in the west are characteristically dominated by short- to medium-term manipulation of economic relationships, oriented to achieving a relatively predictable environment. Crisis may be a chronic feature of such activities, given heightened levels of expectation about material well-being. The task of crisis-managers is to see that crisis never moves into an acute phase. This pragmatic framework of short-run adjustment cannot alleviate that chronic restlessness in postmodern discourse, which Agnes Heller has termed "the dissatisfied society." Without the benefit of evolutionary optimism, and a confident future-oriented perspective on life, dissatisfaction represents the chronic condition faced by contemporary individuals. This condition is not however the same thing as crisis, but rather a leading quality of normalcy in postmodern society. In short, dissatisfaction is not crisis, except from the outdated nostalgic viewpoint of a non-coercive *gemeinschaftlich* social theory in which consensus is somehow possible.

This brings us to the problem of how postmodern dissatisfaction is connected with the new social movements – and in particular the symbolic shift from red to green (Feher and Heller 1984). This issue is a very complex one. In the first place it is not at all clear how influential social movements will be in a world dominated by pragmatic crisis-management and private consumption. We should not assume that new social movements will occupy a similar strategic position in contemporary society to that occupied by labor movements in the late-nineteenth and early twentieth centuries.

Secondly, it is something of an over-simplification to suggest that the new social movements do not aim to capture state power, but rather to transform civil society. There are elements within both feminist and ecology movements which have become increasingly oriented to political conflict within the central political apparatus. It is therefore premature to suggest that the new social movements will remain politically unincorporated.

Thirdly, and having made these qualifications, it is clearly the case that there *is* something new about the new social movements. This principle of novelty is to do with the transformation of civil society, and what Touraine calls "the use of the capacity of society upon itself." These social capacities are now decentered, to the extent that they are not managed through the central political apparatus. Touraine makes the further point that the new social movements are reshaping notions of sociality. Society . . . "is no longer defined by common values or permanent rules of social organisation" . . . It is rather "a field of debates and conflicts whose stake is the social use of the symbolic goods which are massively produced by our post-industrial society."

In the discussion of political decenteredness there is a major weakness in most arguments, namely the relevance of the theory of interstate relations within the international context. In an epoch of superpower domination, supported by military resources designed to protect the territories of superpowers, it seems superficial to emphasize the problem of decenteredness outside the sphere of domestic politics. Military power, as Michael Mann reminds us, is characteristically more tightly centered than ideological or economic power (Mann 1986). In other words, the means of coercion continue to give a coherent structure to the international activities of certain more privileged nation-states. This problem follows through to the role of new social movements. In a recent interesting exchange within the British journal *Economy and Society*, Paul Hirst (1987) argued that peace movements cannot make peace, only nation-states are in a position to do this. The pressure of peace movements on nation-states is important, but it does not automatically produce fundamental results. Nor can peace movements spontaneously deploy the resources of civil society to achieve international peace. There is a sense in which Hirst's argument is supported in a more general way by historical evidence of the failure of labor movements in 1914 to prevent the outbreak of world war. This was a prime political example of civil society being unable to spontaneously prevent war. The conclusion one may draw from this is that certain core nation-states remain tightly centered in specific territories protected by military might. Any definition of contemporary sociality must recognize this.

Conclusion

My concluding comments return to the problem of the status of crisis-talk in social theory. If we are to retain the idea of crisis, I believe we should restrict its use to the acute rather than chronic features of social pathology. Once crisis is extended promiscuously to all instances of conflict, anxiety, or dislocation we will lose the capacity to discriminate between acute pathology and normalcy. The widespread tendency of theorists to operate in this promiscuous manner is however a reflection of an extreme reluctance to accept the new *gesellschaftlich* and pragmatic features of postmodern sociality as normal. This reluctance is, I believe, rather fruitless. The test for sociology is whether it can maintain a capacity for social analysis in an epoch of disenchantment with ideas of progress, reason, and political utopia. The test can be overcome I believe, but we will need to abandon the search for a lost paradise of community and consensus, and forget the dreams of a world made free through the progressive application of reason.

This also means that the problem of what a moral imagination looks like in the postmodern world requires reappraisal. Instead of the association of morality with public politics and the achievement of strong collective moral bonds, the status of morality within a pragmatic *gesellschaftlich* order needs reconsideration. The question we must now ask is not "Will *gemeinschaftlich* morality ever revive?," but rather is a moral orientation possible within the symbiotic structure of pragmatic accommodation between crisis-managers and private households mediated through representative democracy. Has morality been overtaken by the twin forces of managerial domination and personal desire? Or are there modes of moral conduct present within this postmodern culture. And are these limited to monologic ethics of individual virtuosity permitted to a mere handful of autonomous intellectuals? Or are there more widely diffused moral codes built perhaps around more mundane networks of inter-personal responsibility.

Acknowledgments

This paper is an amended version of a paper first delivered to the international conference on Social Progress and Social Theory, at the Jagiellonian University, Krakow, Poland in June 1988. I am grateful for the comments made during the conference by Jeffrey Alexander, Ken Thompson, S. N. Eisenstadt, and David Kettler, all of whom helped me to think through the paper's argument more thoroughly, and I hope rigorously.

Bibliography

Abercrombie, Nicholas, Hill, Stephen, and Turner, Bryan S. (1980) *The Dominant Ideology Thesis* (London: Allen & Unwin).

Ang, Iain (1987) "Popular fiction and feminist cultural politics," *Theory, Culture and Society*, 4 (4): 651–8.

Campbell, Colin (1987) *The Romantic Ethic and the Spirit of Modern Consumerism* (Oxford: Blackwell).

Caygill, Howard (1988) "Postmodernism and judgement," *Economy and Society*, 17 (1) February: 1–20.

Feher, Ferenc, and Heller Agnes (1984) "From red to green," *Telos*, 59: 35–44.

Habermas, Jürgen (1982) "The entwinement of myth and Enlightenment: re-reading *Dialectic of Enlightenment*," *New German Critique*, 26: 13–30.

Hirst, Paul (1987) "Peace and political theory," *Economy and Society*, 16 (2): 205–19.

Holton, Robert J. (1987) "The idea of crisis in modern society," *British Journal of Sociology*, 38 (4): 502–20.

Luhmann, Niklas (1982) *The Differentiation of Society* (New York: Columbia University Press).

Luhmann, Niklas (1984) "The self-description of society: crisis fashion and sociological theory," *International Journal of Comparative Sociology*, 25 (1–2): 59–72.

Lyotard, Jean-François (1984) *The Post-Modern Condition* (Manchester: Manchester University Press).

Mann, Michael (1986) *The Sources of Social Power, Vol. 1, A History of Power from the Beginning to 1760AD* (Cambridge: Cambridge University Press).

Sztompka, Piotr (1984) "The global crisis and the reflexiveness of the social system," *International Journal of Comparative Sociology*, 35 (1–2): 45–58.

Touraine, Alaine (1984) "The waning sociological image of social life," *International Journal of Comparative Sociology*, 25 (1–2): 33–44.

3

The decadence of modernity: the delusions of progress and the search for historical consciousness

CARLO MONGARDINI

Culture and progress

The idea of progress is closely linked with the idea of culture and tradition. It is impossible even to conceive of progress if there is no consolidated and robust cultural system. Both the image of the past and that of the possible future, as well as the conception of the developmental routes leading from the present to the future, can emerge only in the condition of stability and relative internalization of the cultural system. On the other hand, if the condition is one of the precariousness of culture, it is the present which is emphasized, while the past is only fairy tales and fantasies, and the future only an extended, extrapolated present. The crisis of the idea of progress is merely an indicator of the crisis of a culture. And this is doubly true with respect to modern culture which developed from the myth of progress.

The observation, therefore, that nowadays the idea of progress has largely disappeared takes us back to the structural weakness and fragility of contemporary culture. I think the central theme of sociology at the end of the century will be that of culture and its destiny. And this is because the entire structure of culture, which is founded on tradition and seeks to define and establish the roles of the social actors, has been thrown into crisis in recent times by a process of change, which cannot any longer be considered as progress, but rather indicates the limits to progress.

What will be the destiny of this vast, symbolic, formal structure to which human individuals have always attached the certainties of collective life and which today can no longer define values and norms and is witnessing the fragmentation of institutions which manage to survive by dint of a rigid defence of the status quo? On the one hand, the development of modernity has made it necessary to extend the definition of the formal rules of behavior to the very minutiae of social relationships. On the other hand, almost to counterbalance this, the premise of modernity that change is a value in itself has cancelled, or at least left only the appearance of rigidity in modern culture. The monolith of culture has shattered into a thousand splinters which can be experienced only in a pseudo-aesthetic way.

The preconceptions of every cultural form have been called into question. Nowadays, no religion, no moral values or knowledge can be founded on undisputed premises and certainties. Old issues, such as economic development and class conflict, the Welfare State, and post-industrial society, which were the focus of sociology in the 1960s are fading out, confronted by today's dramatic question: what is happening to modern culture? And more generally: what is the fate of human culture as such? Isn't it the case that talking of the so-called "postmodern," we are already in a "postculture" that makes it more and more difficult to establish social relationships in a stable, orderly, rational, and clearly defined way?

The theme of progress is thus inseparably linked to that of culture. Progress is synonymous with evolution, development, and not fragmentation, segmentation, dissolution. Progress means generating a new culture in which values are transformed, reshaped, but not cancelled or rendered meaningless. To put it otherwise, progress is a process of society's structuring its new social forms; change that produces culture and not change that destroys it. It is the emergence of indisputable, firm reference points for collective action. In proposing an alternative, utopian ideal of society, Marxism countered bourgeois world with a form of culture that upset the order of values, but did not annihilate those values. In assuming change as the only value, and the aesthetic experience as the only common bond, postmodern culture destroys itself as a culture. Now, this presupposes either a radical modification of the anthropological premises on which society is built, or a phase of transition out of which the forces able to re-establish the form of a new and different culture have to emerge.

The components of such a new culture must allow the social actor to move at will from the certainties of the norms which organize and define collective life to the impulses of emerging needs which lead him to seek out what is useful and new. It is not possible to escape this configuration and eliminate one or other of these poles within which social processes take place. Different epochs put emphasis on one or the other of these points of reference for behavior, but collective life is unthinkable if we suppress one or the other of these necessary requirements which social behavior manifests.

But the major aim of our epoch seems to be the extension of quantitative forms of society, ignoring or eliminating other aspects of human social participation. In this way, the idea of progress has identified itself more and more with economic progress, and culture, particularly in the last few decades, has become ever more dominated by economic rationality. The whole complexity of a social bond, as understood by classical sociological thought like that of Simmel or Pareto, has been reduced to a simple submission of an individual to the rules of the group in order to satisfy egoistic strivings. The social actor has come to be considered in a simplified manner, solely as a bearer of utilitarian tendencies, and all that is important in a society became identified with economic calculus. The idea of "rational choice" precludes the possibility of considering the real complexity of factors impinging upon the social actor.

The predominance of the economistic ideology in the last decades permitted, in a way, a certain measure of control of reality, as eruptions of passions were avoided by orienting the public mentality toward rational, calculating attitude. But this created the conditions for a distortion of the idea of culture and the idea of progress. The economistic mentality contributed towards stabilizing society, but at the same time created a great potential of instability by excluding from the consideration of daily life such crucial components of the social link as moral passions, religion, or solidarity. The underemphasis on culture and progress led to a simplified view of social activity, with its predominant stress on the immediate present of mundane life and on economic components of the social fabric.

By such a "retreat" into the present and into the code of rational calculus, humanity is perhaps easier to grasp intellectually, and to manage and control politically, but such a logic inevitably loses contact with reality, and creates the vehicle for the decadence of culture. That is why contemporary culture possesses on the face of it a stabilized and consistent structure, but in fact exhibits a substantial weakness in the solidity and depth of a social bond. That is why the idea of progress has been progressively eroded, and replaced by an economic mentality.

The distorted view of culture created the vehicle of radical changes in values, which are evident these days in the increasing influence of non-economic forms of social life: religious communities, ethnic loyalties, solidaristic, and voluntaristic movements, revival of local traditions, and so forth. This tendency will reintroduce on the sociological agenda the issue of complexity of the social order, and the significance of the idea of progress in a postmodern society.

If, therefore, our concern as sociologists in the years to come will be directed towards the sociology of culture, the reason is the necessity to identify the directions and trajectories of change through which seemingly destructive tendencies will be capable of engendering transformations of one cultural form into another. What appears as the "concept and tragedy in a culture" (Simmel 1976: 106), as the dilemma of culture, is how the idea of progress, born of modernity, can be reproduced in postmodern culture, even though its core value (change for change's sake) seems to deny the very possibility of progress.

Modernity and the myth of progress

The emergence of modernity as the organization of material life and as the ideal of a break with tradition,[1] is a parallel development to the rise of the bourgeoisie. It finds in progress the myth needed to represent its vested interests. But progress is not an empty idea; it is received, encountered, shaped earlier as a complex and unified framework of meanings and objectives,[2] and in turn it can generate meanings that legitimize collective action. Thus, through the concept of progress all history can find its interpretation, but it is by means of a particular image of progress arising from the modern period of bourgeois experience that modern history is interpreted. From the myth of progress, however defined (as scientific, social, or technological progress), history derives both meaning and an immediate this-worldly, earthly purpose, replacing the other-worldly, divine purpose of history as construed by pre-modern societies.

There is, then, a close connection between the bourgeois world, modernity, progress, and historical consciousness. The various ideologies of the nineteenth century were in fact interpretations of this interdependence, that is to say interpretations of the myth of progress as bound up with bourgeois history. Their interpretation of progress gave social and political significance to the objectives of collective action and helped promote change, in the belief that human beings could achieve happiness through attaining these objectives.

However, the modification in the framework of values and meanings in modern culture was enough to strip the idea of progress of all of its earlier sense. The urge for change became the glorification of change. Change was seen as a value in itself; a change without purpose is consequently a change only in appearance, a change in order to preserve the status quo, not a change in order to transform and generate new and more adequate forms of society. The "cunning of modern reason" lies in the fact that in its fight against the tyranny of totality, finality, unity, coherence, it has devised a tricky way of preserving by innovating.

The history of modernity is drawing to an end in the present period of "postmodern" and "post-history." Postmodernism becomes the last ideology adopted by modernity to save itself. In all cultural forms change no longer serves modernity as a tool for achieving the goals stipulated by the idea of progress, but has become an end in itself. Therefore, the ideologies and the myth of progress lose meaning. There begins a period of no progress and no history, a period of "postculture," where the individual – with his personality attacked on all fronts by the fetishism of objects – is surrounded by the present, has lost the "truth" and a sense of history, and abandoned all means for the control of reality. The growing discomfort of contemporary people comes mainly from the fact that along with their identity, historical consciousness, and the ideal of progress, they are also abandoning all the elements of culture that used to permit them to interpret and control reality. And it is precisely these elements of culture which permit them to escape the certainties of the stable present and produce the future as an alternative, as something different, as a project more suited to emerging needs which collective life endlessly generates. Change *per se* does not produce anything new. The extreme form of change for change's sake is the most refined and totalitarian form of preservation and conservation, it is in fact the total negation of progress. In change for change's sake, that is change which destroys without constructing, there is no longer progress, because the passage from one stage to the other, from one frame of reference to another, is eliminated, and hence there is the elimination of the points of reference by means of which historical continuity can be recognized.

But change for change's sake also calls into question the anthropological premise of certainties and guarantees on which social action can be developed and expanded. Uncertainty creates unease and limits the possibility of developing social relations in contexts in which modernity requires their more formal development. An ever-widening gulf is formed between materialistic culture, developing according to patterns of modern rationalism, and spiritual culture, life-giving tendencies, symbolic structures, which tend to withdraw into small and intimate circles of limited and fragmentary experience. Nor does the pseudo-aesthetic approach serve to bridge the gulf, tied as it is to the contemplation of the present and immediate experience. The aesthetic solution is the most refined representation of change for its own sake. In fact, unity is constructed out of the intuition of the moment, an intuition with no duration or continuity. Besides, in the aesthetic approach there is no progress or regression; there is rather a flight from reality through fleeting impressions and the power of the imagination. From the symmetry of the universal idea of progress constructed by modernity, we pass to the extreme fragmentation, to a universalized individuality, to the tiny experience of the moment, a neo-romantic vision which destroys the illusions of rationalism that has become excessively abstract, but in itself does not produce anything more than primitive forms of fantasy, magic, regression, and negation of history.

The framework of reference of a culture within which progress, the process of emancipation of humanity, is located, cannot be replaced by pseudo-aesthetic fantasy. Even if we can comprehend and rationalize the motives for this leap from traditional forms of previous culture – which are seen as empty and lacking in meaning for contemporary culture – to the opposite extreme, nevertheless, we cannot replace the impact of reality by fantasy and we cannot satisfy with magic the need to control reality meaningfully. Nor can the complex world of values, meanings, and ideals be replaced by superficial stimuli, appropriating the center of the world for oneself, living with sensationalism and kitsch (Mongardini 1985). The extension of materialistic culture is counterbalanced by a reduction of individuality, and thus the further development of modern economic rationality clashes with new needs which do not fit in with the economic model. The devaluation of life clashes with the ideological tension towards primary human values. The limitation of experience to the immediate present, to daily life, clashes with the need for historical consciousness. The consideration of life as a "show on a large scale," conflicts with the need to become a leading actor, but only in small, intimate areas of communities and groups.

If the result of the postmodern condition is – to paraphrase Simmel – that everything is interesting but nothing is really significant (Simmel 1976: 106), then underlying postmodern ideology with its neo-romantic solutions there is another reality, the reality of the individual permeated with tensions towards the search for meaning and the foundations of a new culture. In other words, there is the search for a way out of the postmodern condition.

The postmodern condition

The crucial problem in contemporary culture is the conflict between the ideal of progress which is unilinear and too abstract by comparison with the complexity and the emerging needs of the contemporary individual, and an attitude which is not a deliberate rejection of progress or modernity, but simply an almost primitive desire to re-evaluate the individual as a fragment of experience, denying relevance to the historical continuity, the certainties of the culture, and the validity of progress. Against the emptiness of the form which characterizes the end of modernity, we discover not an alternative future, but a present which spreads out and gains strength through dreams and fantasies. It is as if elements of humanity for long repressed by the layout of modernity were trying to have another chance in an explosion which has not yet the force of negation but has the superficiality of denying relevance to the totality of history, culture, and humanity. Here emerges the contrast between material life which continues to develop according to modern rationalistic patterns in economics, technology, and politics without, however, any vision of the goals and ideals it once had, and the vastly altered condition of non-material culture. A radical cultural revolution has begun, well hidden under the postmodernist surface. It is a long-developing, silent revolution, in comparison to which postmodernism is merely modernity's latest effort at defending itself. Like it or not, postmodernism marks the end of the old order. It makes it possible for us to see the radical change in relevance and in the priority of needs, choices, objects, and experiences in material life.

When we talk of postmodernism, then, we must distinguish postmodernist ideology from the postmodern condition. Postmodernist ideology represents a modernity on the defensive, a modernity which has given up its ideals and even its myth of progress. It reacts to modern culture's "limits of development" by radicalizing and secularizing the central concepts of modernity. It substitutes a myth for a disintegrating system and thus performs its function as the last ideology of modernity. The cleverness of the postmodern idea is in the fact that it constitutes, as a matter of ideology, precisely what it declares itself unwilling to be, namely a global representation and control of reality in the face of modern segmentation, a form of historical consciousness in the face of "post-history," a search for a single and collective identity in the face of psychological and social inconsistency in the contemporary individual, a semblance of intellectual and spiritual culture in the face of fetishism of objects and images.

Even more than the postmodernist ideology, therefore, it is the postmodern condition which should be our focus, because there we can see the ideal of progress wiped out and recreated. In the postmodern condition the idea of modernity becomes itself problematic. We witness precisely that unease that Simmel described as a result of the removal of life and individuality from the objectified forms of culture. But this has always produced an enormous potential for revolution. This potential is, however, largely absorbed, in the postmodern condition, by change. Thus, change, considered as a value, on the one hand negates modern culture because it destroys the certainties and specificity of cultural phenomena, on the other hand saves it, in so far as it attracts and rechannels the revolutionary potential which would otherwise turn against the forms of modernity. Once again, distinguished from the postmodern condition, postmodernist ideology is not a successor of modernity but its necessary line of defence. Any change that is not real since it is not founded on values and cultural processes, is only a hallucination. If it can be seen as saving modernity by defusing the revolutionary charge present in contemporary societies, it can also be seen as condemning it because it produces a culture which is a negation of culture, precisely because all cultural forms require certainty, identity, consistency, and weight. That is why postmodernist ideology does not solve, but on the contrary aggravates the problem of culture and will make it the central problem of collective life in the years to come.

A tiny example of this problem is the unease of contemporary man in establishing and administering his own time and in reconciling social time and individual time (Taboni 1984). The pressure on the individual of social times generated by group activities, and his inability to put them in order, to establish priorities and co-ordinate different needs, typically illustrates the decadence of the culture and the individual's loss of identity and historical consciousness. The unease in modern culture is clearly illustrated by the great and widening gap between formal organization of objective time and the experience of subjective time. Along with the destructuring of time, the increasing instability of money and uncertainty in the law, as a consequence of its hypertrophy, certain basic modern institutions have been thrown into crisis, namely those upon which the rational model of collective life has been built.

All this makes for an increasing sense of unease experienced by the contemporary individual. The cultural tools which enabled him to control his reality are less effective. The historical consciousness which permitted him to interpret events is lacking. The image of progress, that was associated in modernity with the idea of increasing security and greater control over reality, is transformed into its exact opposite. The disillusionment with progress is the product of loss of control over reality combined with a diminishing sense of identity and historical consciousness. Losing control over reality means for the individual insecurity and growing uncertainty; it means finding oneself in the condition of cultural backwardness, a far cry from the image of established rationality, the image that modern ideology has cultivated. It means finding oneself in the condition of a savage, maybe no longer face to face with nature, and yet face to face with society as it has been shaped by modern rationality (Maffesoli 1988). That is to say, the individual becomes estranged from his own world; he is a foreigner at home, alienated from that formal rationality that he has assisted in creating in the belief that thus would he finally have definite control over reality.

If we take away the ideal of progress, the postmodernist history is like a tree that cannot bear fruit. It has lost its earthly goal without acquiring superior objectives. The future as extended present (Luhmann 1976) is simply the enclosure, the "golden cage," defining the limits and delusions of modern man. As material culture develops, unconcerned with any definition or justification, so also the disillusionment with progress grows in the form of weakened historical consciousness and cultural decadence. Without the guiding principle of history, the idea of progress cannot hold up (Simmel 1976: 153).

The riddle of history

Postmodernism is thus also postculture, or culture without history. Let us not confuse the mass of historical images or references in contemporary culture with historical consciousness. This is history which is not used as awareness, reflection for the purpose of interpreting an event, but rather as a stimulus, a show, a form of regression. The overabundance of historical reference does not imply, then, historical consciousness. Historical consciousness is in the first place a sense of continuity, the psychological use of the past in order to understand the present in terms of the future. Historicity is not automatically history, but merely a form of regression in periods of decadence (Mongardini 1983).

Postmodernism offers us a culture without history (and therefore a negation of culture) and a history without culture (post-history). Both are anchored in the present, in the experience lived out here and now, which in fact is not the experience at all, as the term implies past accumulation to be compared with the present (Jedlowski 1986). Life cannot be reduced to the present: it needs a past and a future.[3] Reduction to the present is simply an attempt to petrify the status quo, and therefore, in our case, the last effort at self-preservation on the part of modernity. In fact, change and reduction to the present may seem logical contradictions, but "change" is meant here not as real, but simply as a means of rechanneling the revolutionary potential which has built up in modern culture.

Compared with modernity which attributed an exaggerated importance to the role of its own culture, one can observe in postmodernism an important historical shift. This is an effort to save that culture by ignoring the assumptions of culture in general. It amounts to an attempt to enforce the meaning of modern culture by adopting in postmodern culture the products of modern fetishism liberated from the necessity of coherence and conformity with the values that generated them.[4] Postmodernism has also desired to liberate them from the guiding principle of historical consciousness which gave everyday life a sense of stability, continuity, and tradition. In the absence of this guiding principle, there is a crisis of identity which passes from the level of the individual to the entire culture. Hence, the psychological urgency for the contemporary individual to recuperate historical consciousness which will grant him the ability to see life as a process and not as a simple event, to order the contents of his experience in a line of development which has sense and therefore can be interpreted.

By breaking down reality into processes without reference, unity, or purpose, postmodernism has substituted a modernity-fetishism for reality, multiplying individual expectations, seriously overheating social imagination through distorted visions of man, his possibilities, and his limits (Bonichot 1987). Far from being a solution to the modern crisis, this has merely caused the fundamental, historically recurring problem to be posed again – the problem of reconstructing a culture and a set of inseparable ideas of tradition and progress, establishing values from which an identity can be derived, the images of "me" and "us," which Elias speaks about (Elias 1987).

Emerging groups

Tradition and progress are ideas which have historical consciousness as their necessary foundation. The reconstruction of historical consciousness is the task of any line of thinking that wants to find a way out of postmodernity. Finding this way out is the task for new groups emerging on the social scene that are trying to overcome the destructuring phase of culture, which is at one and the same time a phase of ideological tension, of segmentation, and of psychological unease. Bourgeois history and its actors have no more strength or imagination. To give a new dimension to culture and to get away from contemporary tribalism (Maffesoli 1988), new groupings are needed. They have to revitalize the ideas of history, future, and progress. There is also a need for a new idea of truth and morality, since they are also essential for the consistency of any culture.[5]

How can we identify these groupings? It seems to me obvious that a cultural renaissance and especially a return to historical consciousness cannot spring from either economic groups or traditional political groups. The former marked out their boundaries by declaring the "limits to development" in the 1970s and by passively accepting the loss of meaning in the ideal of progress. Even technology is no longer a leading force, but has lost its sense of breakthrough into the future. Technological change is almost a banal ritual. Digital society, press-button society no longer excites us. Technological innovation is more of a means for regaining and controlling time, than a way of satisfying essential needs. Technology is generally seen as a set of signs rather than a set of tools necessary for transforming human existence (Bonichot 1987). The rationalization associated with economic and technological development is therefore a future with many anxieties and very few real gratifications. As Toennies has said: "Man can cause his own destruction by using reason" (Toennies 1979: 278).

It would seem that the contemporary individual has grasped all the terrifying doubts that result from this conviction. Does it mean that we are moving toward a society "without economy?" Are we going toward a society in which the idea of progress will not necessarily be associated with economic growth? The answer is yes; the problems of economic development are beginning to seem less crucial than the negative consequences they produce in various areas of life (e.g. ecological destruction, pollution, worsening quality of everyday life in urban agglomerations, etc.).

As for traditional political groups, the argument is much the same. These groups have been too often led to some form of totalitarianism. While modern rationality, according to Max Weber, led to "disenchantment," these groups have constructed a political universe that was a "system of enchantments," a "magic world" – to arrive at unity by means of the colonization of an increasingly varied and heterogenous social life (Burdeau 1983). From the time of the French revolution the growing hegemony of political ideas with their global function (Sorel 1963: 670) has served "to exclude reason in favour of magic" (Burdeau 1983), in the cause of creating and reinforcing the sources of power in the face of social segmentation. It can be seen even more clearly today that political groups have lost meaning, have undergone separations cutting right through the traditional groupings in the form of opposing opinions, sects, lobbies, factions, secret associations. They have lost the basis of consensus, and the legitimacy of representation. Faced with these processes, the post-modernist solutions adopted in the form of neo-conservatism and pseudo-aesthetic anarchy (Habermas 1985: 4–5) seem to have very little effect.

If we search for emerging groups able to re-establish historical consciousness, the vitality of tradition, the idea of progress, and other basic cultural premises, we must above all look to the young. It is only a new generation that can overcome the stagnation of the dominant groups and proclaim their indifference toward the superficial stimuli and materialistic paraphernalia that modernity can no longer revitalize, nor justify. Only the young will be able to counterpoise to this retreat into the present, a courageous search for new meanings and future values.

Next, since we are talking of refounding a culture, we must consider the churches and religious groups. Collective solidarity must be re-established to give strength to the norms which bind the activity of individuals to common rules, and so create the foundations for reactivating the image of progress. The norms and rules which potentially may have the strongest hold over "postmodern" individuals – uncertain, inattentive, and pre-occupied with mundane, practical, and material affairs – are undoutedly the moral and religious norms. The churches are by far the most prestigious depositaries of moral and traditional values. The religious groups represent the constant search for perfection in man. Surely, they can play an important role in refounding a culture and the idea of progress, provided that they can solve the present conflict between modern universalistic rationalism and postmodern segmentation and sectarian-ism. What is needed is for the church not only to offer all the riches of its experience and tradition but also, to find a way of using to best advantage the full heritage of modern culture.

Finally, a group which could play an important role in refounding a culture are the intellectuals. By intellectuals I do not mean the "stage-intellectuals" who are today's ideologues of modernism and postmodern-ism, but those for whom the goal is still the truth attained by reflection and research. If they can relearn to perform a critical function, and present a valid defence against the temptations of totalitarianism, the intellectuals will be able to play a decisive part in the solution to the problems of culture that face us as we come close to the twenty-first century.

63

Conclusion

The problem of culture and its revitalization seems to be the key problem in our epoch, and the one on which the fate of modernity depends.[6] The refounding of the idea of progress is strictly linked with the solution to that, more primary, issue. Beginning these days a new phase in the discussion and struggle for new culture, we are also starting a new discussion on what progress is, what social forces are its bearers, and under what conditions it can flourish.

Social movements have always represented collective needs, but have been unable to express a political synthesis; they have not known how to find their roots in tradition, or how to paint a credible image of the future. Thus, they have remained prisoners of the political crisis of modernity. Regressive, neo-romantic tendencies produced efforts to substitute political synthesis with aesthetic intuition. They were blind to the fact that the crucial chance of surmounting the contemporary crisis lies in getting out of this blind alley in which modern culture has found itself.

Refounding the idea of progress and thus restoring a historical and political vision to society requires in the first place coming out from that "retreat into the present" into which – as Norbert Elias indicates – intellectuals, politicians, and journalists have fallen, exploiting time and again all forms of regression, sensationalism, and pseudo-aesthetism, frequently bordering on kitsch. The emphasis on the present is like a drug which obliterates consciousness of the past, and sends us blindfolded into the future. To reconstruct an image of the future and rethink the idea of progress means overcoming this crippled quality of our culture which lives only in the present tense.

Out of critical awareness of this condition, so typical of postmodernity, a new phase in the struggle for culture is emerging; a struggle which sometimes covertly, sometimes openly has been an undercurrent of the whole epoch of modernity, often providing stimulus for various totalitarianisms, as politics has tried to solve by means of universal solutions, the conflicts, weaknesses, and fragmentations of modern culture. In this phase, it is true, modernity is only able to defend itself by putting forward the idea of change, giving up the vision of the future and an idea of progress, and entrenching itself in the present, that can only be lived in regressive – anarchic and pseudo-aesthetic – forms. But in doing so, in the long run modernity condemns itself. It no longer manages to hold together the cardinal elements in its own culture. It slowly undermines and destroys the foundations of modern bourgeois culture: time, money, rights, morals.

The idea of progress was linked to these themes, and vacillates with them. Must we believe, then, that we have come to the end of all culture and that society is destined to fall back into primitivism and tribalism with no escape? Or should we think that we have arrived at a turning-point, after which the problem of culture will become the crucial challenge for the coming decades?

A new idea of progress will emerge by means of a slow and convoluted process of refounding the pillars of culture. Till then, it remains for sociology to be only the interpreter of decadence, and of the search for historical consciousness as critical consciousness. Its attention, then, will no longer be mainly directed – as was the case in the 1960s and 1970s – towards economics and politics. The coming years will witness instead the great ascent of the analysis of cultural phenomena and processes.

Notes

1. On the break of modernity with tradition and on the necessity for tradition as a source of identity and of spatial and temporal [cultural] allocation, see Shils (1981); Tabboni (1984).
2. "It is evident – observes Simmel in a chapter entitled 'The meaning of history' – that the concept of progress presupposes a final situation that has to be ideally present in its absoluteness, because the approach to it, that is a higher degree of its realization, may characterize the later condition as relatively advanced" (Simmel 1982: 147).
3. "Life – writes Simmel – incorporates its own future in a way that has no analogy with what is not alive . . . While everything which is not alive has only the present moment, what lives extends in an incomparable way into the past and the future" (Simmel 1976: 84).
4. Here once again we want to make reference to a general consideration of Simmel, who points out that there is "a general destiny of cultural elements according to which objects have a developing logic of their own, which is not a conceptual or natural logic, but only a logic of their development as cultural works of man. As a consequence, they split off from the direction in which they could perhaps have formed part of the personal development of the human spirit" (Simmel 1976: 104).
5. These ideas cannot be replaced by mere aesthetic contemplation of events. Postmodernity boasts the rediscovery of the aesthetic justification of life. This is supposedly the great news and the profound revolution it performs. From the point of view of postmodern culture, the aesthetic dimension of experience undoubtedly offers considerable advantages. In time and space, it can be relegated to the infinitely small; it can change, cross, multiply (as happens in Gehlen's idea of "posthistoire"). In addition, the aesthetic dimension – that is a continuous manipulation of one's attitude in relation to the present – can be created by means of a wide range of means, from profundity of feeling to superficiality, all the way to outright kitsch. Thus morality is replaced by the various games and means of a pseudo-aesthetic attitude. Even morality is turned into a show, an image, and is experienced aesthetically.
6. This was already intuitively grasped by Simmel (see Simmel 1918).

Bibliography

Bonichot, C. (1987) "Le mythe de la modernité," Bulletin of Microsociology, December.

Burdeau, Georges (1979) La politique au pays des merveilles (Paris: Presses Universitaire de France).

Burdeau, Georges (1983) "Politica e magia," in C. Mongardini (ed.) Il magico e il moderno (Milan: F. Angeli).

Elias, Norbert (1987) Die Gesellschaft der Individuen (Frankfurt: Suhrkamp).

Habermas, Jürgen (1985) Der philosophische Diskurs der Moderne. Zwolf Vorlesungen (Frankfurt: Suhrkamp).

Jedlowski, P (1986) Il tempo dell'esperienza. Studi sul concetto di vita quotidiana (Milan: F. Angeli).

Luhmann, Niklas (1976) "The future cannot begin," Social Research 43: 130–52.

Maffesoli, Michel (1988) Le temps des tribus (Paris: Meridiens).

Mongardini, Carlo (1983) "Razionalita e storicita: due modi di rappresentare il pensiero della decadenza," in P. Bisogno and R. Tonini (eds) Razionalita e storicita (Rome: La Goliardica).

Mongardini, Carlo (1985) "La socializzazione del Kitsch," in Epistemologia e sociologia (Milan: F. Angeli).

Shils, Edward (1981) Tradition (Boston: Faber and Faber).

Simmel, Georg (1918) Der Konflikt der moderner Kultur. Ein Vortrag (Munchen-Leipzig: Dunker & Humblot).

Simmel, Georg (1976) "Concetto e tragedia della cultura," in Arte e civilta (Milan: Isedi).

Simmel, Georg (1982) I problemi della filosofia della storia (Casale Monferrato: Marietti).

Sorel, Georges (1963) "Le illusioni del progresso," in Scritti politici (Torino: UTET).

Taboni, S. (1984a) Tradizione e coscienza storica (Genoa: ECIG).

Taboni, S. (1984b) La rappresentazione sociale del tempo (Milan: F. Angeli).

Toennies, Ferdinand (1979) Comunita e societa (Milan: Comunita).

4

The cultural code of modernity and the problem of nature: a critique of the naturalistic notion of progress

KLAUS EDER

The problem of nature

Our growing awareness of the worldwide ecological crisis has damaged, perhaps completely, our conviction in the rationality of modern society. Rationalization itself has come to sound increasingly negative as we disentangle it from the idea of progress. More and more, we are experiencing a deep ambivalence toward the model of rationalization that underlies, accompanies, and has directed European-type modernization processes.

The challenge of the "problem of nature" contributes to a new understanding of the culture of modern society. It could even contribute to a fundamental revision of the code of modern culture. For it challenges the basic element of this code: the boundary between nature and culture. In acknowledging the problem of nature we are putting the symbolic foundations of modern culture at stake. Nature, traditionally seen as sharply separated from the world of culture, can no longer be considered as external and opposed to society. The relation between nature and culture has to be redefined and the cultural code of modern society reorganized.[1] The problem of nature also sensitizes us to an ambiguity in the *rationality* ascribed to modern culture. It forces us to fully re-evaluate the normative assumptions of modernity, even to redefine the progress that is supposedly its fruit. Thus the ecological crisis provides an opening for ideas (and movements as carriers of these ideas) that define rationality differently from the prevailing definition.

Modern culture has so far been dominated by a conception of rationality that takes nature as a means to other ends. This rationality in fact excludes any moral considerations from the realm of nature. By defining nature as the locus of the emotional, of the non-rational, or even the irrational, the

67

subjugation of nature to ends defined by culture becomes the model of rationality. This is what disenchantment is about. Increasingly, there are reactions against this form of rationality. Radical new discourses on nature, both everyday and intellectual ones, plead for the repeal of "disenchantment," and call instead for "re-enchantment." Re-enchantment is played off against disenchantment, the core idea of rationalization.

These allegedly "non-rational" or "irrational" discourses and ideas, thematizing "the other side of modernity,"[2] rely on a conception of practical reason that does not exclude moral considerations from the realm of nature. It is a practical reason based on a sympathetic identification with nature, on a quasi-social relation with nature. It is a practical reason compatible with a re-enchanted nature. It is a practical reason that might even lead to an alternative form of rationality in modern society. Such a communicative conception of practical reason is opposed to the utilitarian conception of reason dominating the modern relationship with nature and shaping its modern culture.

This modern duality in practical reason can be traced back to its Greek and Semitic origins. These cultural traditions represent two cultural codes, the one based on the myth of a bloody origin of humanity, the other based on the myth of a paradisiac origin. They represent a "bloody" culture and an "unbloody" culture that define the cultural universe we still live in. The "bloody" side could explain some of the cruelties that were part of the rationalization process shaping modern society: cruelties against the human body, against animals, against nature as well as against culture.[3] This could explain the ambivalence of modern society toward rationalization, an ambivalence so deep seated that even Weber struggled with it, though inconclusively.[4]

Expanding thus the notion of the cultural traditions that shape the European experience of modernization to include the unbloody as well as the dominant bloody one, we deliberately take into account counter-processes that have inadequately been described as "antimodernization" or "traditionalistic regressions." The new definition of the cultural code of modern society that ultimately emerges is not based on the notion of a culture beyond modernity (e.g. postmodernity), but rests on a broader notion of the culture of modern societies that dominates social evolution today.

Disentangling rationality from progress

The Marxian heritage

Let us start with a critical approach for describing the rationality constitutive for the progress of modern society: the Marxian approach. In Marx the close relationship between progress and the rationality built into the development of the forces of production is beyond question. That development, freed from the bonds of feudal relations of production, is foreseen as the mechanism that will eventually break apart the irrationality of the social relations of production in capitalism and generate rational ones.[5]

In the meantime, our experience of the development of the forces of production has indeed been that they are no longer blocked but actually fostered by the social relations of production. But the emancipatory effect is contrary to what Marx thought it would be.[6] The development of the forces of production has contributed towards legitimating the relations of production, whether capitalist or socialist. And it has reduced the relation to nature in modern society to a mere instrumental one. It has led to "progress" in the subjugation of nature, which is tantamount to "regress" in the social relations with nature. This double effect points to the limits of one of the most important images modern society has produced of itself: that of being a progressive society. It is in Marx's idea of how the forces of production develop that we find the key to the ambivalence of rationalization characteristic of modern society. This can be attributed to the questionable logic that a society free from domination can be based upon a nature dominated and defeated by this society. To the extent that the rationalization of society is seen as being dependent upon developing forces (!) of production, the idea of a rational society is bound to a utilitarian type of practical reason. In order to go beyond this restricted notion of practical reason, we must start to redefine the relationship of society with nature beyond the idea of "forces" of production. Looking at it as a symbolically mediated relationship will enable us to elaborate the idea of a social relation with nature as a model for other types of practical reason constitutive for the social relations, be they of production, exchange or consumption.[7]

Going beyond the perspective inherited from Marx we can reconstruct the theoretical idea of forces of production as a cultural category, as a specifically defined cultural form of appropriating nature. Then we can extend our notion of a social relation to nature and see the basic forms of social life from production to consumption as being determined by specific cultural definitions of that relation to nature.

The way societies in history manifest this varies. But modern societies surpass most other societies in applying the crudest form of a social relation to nature: that of an instrumental use of nature. Nature is nothing but an object. Modern society belittles as primitive the opposite attitude, that of treating nature as a person, and claims as "progress" this version of relating to nature. Increasingly, however, it appears to be bound to a process of self-destruction which is in turn destructive to the notion of progress built into the cultural code of modern societies.

Correcting this perspective has become the more urgent as the development of modern society runs into the ecological crisis that threatens its further material reproduction. Progress must be disentangled from the idea of subjugating nature. Instead, the idea of progress must develop in a way that relinquishes that subjugation. We have to go beyond Marx.

The Weberian radicalization of Marx

The usual proposition is to look at Max Weber. Yet Weber's work is only a radicalization of Marx, generalizing it by assessing rationalization from the point of view of the universalization of formal rationality.[8] Weber's concept of rationalization refers above all to calculability. His analyses of bureaucracy and law, of economic life and religious ideas, are impressive pieces of historical work and interpretation. His scrutiny even includes those phenomena opposed to the incarnations of rationality in formal organization and formal law, in modern economy and modern culture. But they are treated as "aberrations" from the ideal path of formal rationalization seen as constitutive for modern society. He subsumes these aberrations under the heading of material rationality[9] which is then nothing but an illegitimate child of formal rationality.

Weber's religious studies do not hinder him from seeing modern culture as the apotheosis of formal rationality.[10] He is convinced that the logic of formal rationalization is inevitable in modern society. He is not unaware of its costs. His metaphor of the "iron cage" describing the outcome of formal rationalization and his metaphor of the "new polytheism" deriving from formal rationalization suggest that formal rationalization inevitably leads to irrationality. But these scarce hints are insufficient grounds for crediting Weber with exposing the ambivalence of modern culture.

We really need to start afresh. We have to construct anew the traditions modern culture is made of and determine their relative influence. This will not (and cannot) be done here. But we can point to the different traditions that merge within modern European culture and their consequences, both manifest and latent, for coexisting and sometimes competing strategies of conceptualizing nature. We can sketch the programmatic of a new look at the culture of modernity, a look forced upon us by the problem of nature.

A theoretical reorientation: two types of modernity

Reconstructing the code of European culture

Two cultural traditions

The roots of the ambivalence of modern culture can be found in the Greek and Jewish history that, through the Christianization of Europe, constitute our cultural heritage. A unique blend of two traditions whose internal contradictions are complementary, modern culture has developed the alternative options available within them according to the Greek model.

Ancient Greek society was characterized by a model of political domination legitimized by extensive bloody sacrificial rites. These sacrificial Delphic rites represented the real symbolic base of the society. The political system was held together primarily by this symbolic code and only secondarily by its democratic ideology (in fact this was an intellectual invention of later Greek history!).

Good evidence for the dominance of the bloody model underlying Greek culture comes from the cultural orientations of those social groups opposed to it. Most important were Pythagorean groups who defined themselves by their vegetarianism, a value orientation clearly opposed to the bloody rituals. Vegetarianism can be seen as a symbolic rejection of the dominant culture. Logically, persecuting these vegetarian groups became the way of reinstating the dominant culture.[11]

Jewish society on the other hand, was characterized by a cultural code that succeeded in institutionalizing cultural restrictions upon its forms of political domination. This was the decisive difference between the Jews and their neighbors. The non-sacrifice of Isaac is one of the myths marking the historical point when the Jews began abstaining from human sacrifice even while their neighbors continued to practice it. Increasingly the Jews restricted the shedding of blood. This restriction was rationalized by recourse to the ideal of a non-bloody paradise in society. Because in reality it was impossible to completely circumvent bloodshed, rules of ritual purity became enormously important. These rules put strong limits upon the practice of bloody sacrifice and other practices concerned with animals and other forms of nature. The rules became more and more complicated as social life increased in complexity. The unique canon of dietary prohibitions and rules characteristic of Jewish society thus represents a cultural tradition that tries to limit the opportunity for using an other (be it human, animal, or nature as such) as a mere object. It favors instead a culture that puts symbolic limits upon such uses.[12]

Jewish obsession with ritual purity explains why its political society never really developed the social dynamism characteristic of Greek or Roman society. Yet, the code had tremendous cultural validity. Intervention from outside could not change it. The Jews were never mobilized by political élites the way neighboring societies were. The Romans knew why they were trying to force the Jews to eat pork. It would have been the best way to destroy the symbolic basis of their culture. The early Christians also belong within this cultural code. The Romans saw them as a radical Jewish sect. The cultural basis of their persecution was – like the later persecution of the Jews in European culture – rooted in the cultural divide that distinguished them from, and even opposed them to, the bloody tradition of Greco-Roman culture.[13]

Thus the cultural code of Europe has a complex heritage. On the one hand we have the Greeks, a society that mobilized its social, economic,

71

and political dynamic by putting rather loosely structured controls upon the use of power. On the other hand, we have the Jews, a society that integrated its economic, political, and social dynamic into a cultural world that put rigid limits upon the use of power. The Greek model became the dominant model in the development of European society. The contradictory Jewish model has always been circumscribed and ghettoized, or has been persecuted.[14]

The analysis of this double tradition allows us to broaden our conception of the cultural code underlying European culture. Both the dominant and the latent traditions have contributed to the process of modernization. Christianity, as the symbolic system mediating between and blending these two traditions, has not only reproduced but even intensified this strange constellation of two codes in one culture. The cyclical outbreaks of protest and rebellion, of "heterodoxy," in Christian culture can be seen as attempts to reverse the relationship between the two cultural codes. The movements associated with, for example, St Francis and John Hus are carriers of a cultural orientation opposed to that institutionalized in Christian culture.[15]

This dynamic of European culture has had costly effects. Its history is one of suppressing the alternative tradition within modern culture. The persecutions of heretics, of witches, of the Jews are – added to the destructiveness of the religious wars – proof of it. The alternative tradition has therefore remained – due to bloody force – part of a "collective unconsciousness."[16] Now, however, the dominant cultural tradition has come increasingly under attack as incapable of grasping the problems it produces, and above all the problem of nature. This process forces modern society to confront the other cultural tradition that up to now has remained outside the discourse about modernity and modernization. The "collective unconsciousness" has begun to be publicly discussed and collectively shared. The effects of this process of discovering and uncovering a latent tradition upon the cultural evolution of modernity cannot be exaggerated. They will certainly change modern culture.

Two conceptions of nature in modern culture

The problems modern society has run into in its relation with nature have ended the latency of its "other" tradition, the one deriving from Jewish culture. This second tradition proposes solutions to the "problem of nature" incompatible with those of the first one. The problem of nature has made us aware of the basic and elementary opposition of Greek and Jew.

Looking into the two traditions we can find two conceptions of nature rationalizing two contradictory ways of relating to it. The Greek tradition utilized nature without restrictions. Nature (like a sacrificial animal) was not only an object of politics. It was treated as a means to other, namely human ends. The logic of this coding, permitting the shedding of blood without any cultural restriction, underlies the dominant relationship with nature in modern society. The Jewish tradition, on the other hand, restricted the use of bloody rituals by binding the sacrificial acts to the model of a paradisiac state of nature. The ritual rules of purity were attempts to reinstate at least partially the biblical paradise where men and nature were subject to a higher law and lived together in peace. This coding implied a harmonious or peaceful relation with nature, whereby nature is defined in such a way that limits its use as such by human beings.[17] Thus we can describe the basic code of European culture as one pulled between a bloody model, derived from the code of the Greek city state, and an unbloody countermodel, derived from the Jewish code of ritual purity. These two roots still operate on a basic structural level, each defining a different relation of man to his outer world, to nature. This duality shows us again the deep ambivalence built into our culture.

The key to modern rationality nevertheless remains the Greek code. The category "poiein" (the work of the artisan) that Greek culture differentiated from, and favored over, the category of "prattein" (the work of the peasant) indicates the direction of the Greek cultural outlook: the proper relation with nature was not praxis, but poiesis.[18] Nature was material to be shaped by man. The normative implication is far-reaching: by defining nature as a material we have been able to operate on it without limits, even to engage in a bloody relationship. The history of European civilization can be seen as an atempt to channel this bloody interaction by rationalizing and civilizing its "manners."[19] But it has not changed the code of this culture that favors the unlimited use of nature, non-living and living alike.

With this cultural code in mind, it becomes easier to understand some practices and movements in European history based on a different relation to nature that today manifest themselves on a much broader scale within the ecological mood and movements. We can decipher a cultural meaning in romantic love for animals, in modern vegetarian movements, and in animal rights movements.[20] As part of a countercultural movement, provoked and suppressed at the same time by the dominant culture, these have been the social carriers of the latent alternative tradition of relating to nature. Today they are becoming the key to a new, spreading type of rationality in modern society.

Until the twentieth century this counterculture existed only in discrete social niches, either persecuted or scorned. But as the problem of nature has become more insistent this old countercultural tradition, which in fact offers an alternative to the most pressing problems of modern societies, has assumed new life. This tradition lies at the base of what we call the ecological movement.[21] This new movement is a cultural as well as a social movement. As a social movement it continues the conception of "material" rationality of the old social movements, the working-class movements, and the bourgeois movements. As a cultural movement it goes beyond this rationality and pleads for a rationality that puts into question not only the social relations of production, domination, and consumption, but also the symbolic forms serving as the medium of these social relations. It pleads not for social relations that correspond to some criteria of justice, but for social relations that correspond to some criteria of purity (Eder 1989). Thus changing the symbols that allow for symbolically mediated communication, the ecological movement is transforming the cultural underpinnings of social life in modern society. It is here the possibilities for a type of communicative practical reason have to be sought.

Two cultures in modern culture

Contradictory discourses in modern culture

As we have seen, modern culture contains two competing conceptions of nature. Let us now focus on a theoretical description of the cultural code specific to modern society. To describe this double code three pairs of conceptual oppositions will be used: rationality and romanticism; evolution and equilibrium; and utilitarian and communicative reason.

A first opposition contrasts ways of perceiving and experiencing nature. Rationality comprises orientations toward nature that value efficiency in some form or other. Romanticism rejects these orientations, basing its understanding of nature upon norms taken not from logical insight, but from intuitive knowledge.[22] The two orientations are tied to two differentiated spheres of value: the cognitive and the aesthetic. The first has been embodied in modern science, the second in modern art. The rationalist-scientific conception reduces nature to what can be experienced by the senses and deduced from sensual experience through theoretical reasoning. The romanticist–aesthetic conception extends the range of experiences of nature beyond the scope of science. Its experiences are therefore found in aesthetic forms rather than in the form of scientific discourse.

A second opposition thematizes the time dimension underlying modern relationships of nature with culture.[23] This relationship can be seen as one of evolution or as one of an equilibrium, as one based on a linear time conception or as one based on a cyclical time conception. The idea of evolution has played an important ideological function in the self-description of modern society. Referring to a "scientific" conceptualization of social development, it has simultaneously fulfiled ideological functions while legitimating the superiority and expansion of modern western culture. From the evolutionary perspective, nature is an object upon which selective pressures exerted by human society act to shape and change its forms. The net result of such pressures is adaptive advances toward a greater control of nature. This process is seen as unavoidable.

The idea of an equilibrium between society and nature can be traced back to the image of a natural state. Its most simple version is a return to nature, widespread in romantic thinking. But there are other variations, based on as many equilibria as there have been paths of history. These equilibria are not identical with a natural state but represent different culturally defined states of the relation of society to nature. The equilibrium that allows for the reproduction of society in nature depends upon the cultural form society gives to its natural environment. This idea of an equilibrium presupposes an interactive relationship between society and nature, thus expanding the one-way relationship characteristic of the idea of an evolution based on the increasing mastery of nature by society. Uniting both aspects it arrives at a conception where nature and society evolve together; in a process mediated by culture.

A third opposition derives from differing a priori assumptions about practical reason. Utilitarian reason is strategic, calculating the effects of the use of nature upon nature. It dominates the economic ideology of modern society. Communicative reason, on the other hand, treats nature as a symbolic good and restricts the uses of nature to what can be justified on moral grounds. This type of relation with nature is encouraged by the new counterculture. As it acts upon nature, practical reason can vary between two extremes. One extreme applies a utilitarian ethic and the other an ethic of upholding universal a priori principles. Thus when speaking of practical reason we need to distinguish between two interpretations.

The utilitarian interpretation idealizes the "rational man," freed from social and cultural restraints and mobilizing his self-interests. This concept has become the point of reference for the "formal" rationality of this society. The communicative interpretation idealizes an interactive mankind composed of equals free to air their differences. This form of practical reason has partially succeeded in the political realm (where it has been incorporated into human rights advocacy, or in the moral idealism of cosmopolitanism) and, as Habermas claims, for example, in private bourgeois life, in the modern family. Both are seen as embodiments of communicative practical reason, whereas the economic and administrative systems are seen as bound to the dominant strategic or utilitarian type.[24] Both models of rationality can be identified in modern society. They are manifest when the two cultural models of relating to nature come into direct confrontation.

Logically speaking, the ecological movement can stimulate both models. Ecological thinking can be considered the most advanced version of the dominant utilitarian mind, a radicalization of modern economic ideology. But ecological thinking can also stimulate the countercultural tradition. This potential for ambivalence within the ecological movement is represented today for example in the split between the "realistic ecologists" and the "deep ecologists."

As ecological problems have increased and attitudes that were once latent gained respect, a dual relation to nature within the cultural code of modernity has come to light. The price has been an unequivocal notion of modernity. We are presently left with the phenomenon of two cultures in one culture, of two definitions of modernity within modernity. The theoretical puzzles thus produced still await resolution.

Two cultural models of modernity
It is the conflicting conceptions of nature that give us the key to the most basic differences between the "two modern cultures." They are basic in the sense that they thematize the competing rationalities underlying these two cultures. The cultural rationalities at issue can be conceptualized as "culture as profit" and "culture as communication" (Sahlins 1976, Leach 1976). Both rationalities can be seen as specific versions of practical reason. The one is the utilitarian version based upon the rationality of efficiency and maximization. The other is the communicative version based upon the rationality of equality and discursive argumentation. In terms of discourse theory the difference can be described as one between a monologue and a dialogic form of practical reason.[25]

Thus we can now identify two forms of practical reason that determine the rationality of modern culture. Both utilitarian and communicative reason have been operative in the history of modern culture in Europe. The bourgeois culture of the eighteenth and nineteenth centuries mixed these two rationalities and produced the illusion of one. The cultural changes brought about by the labor movement then separated them and left them without any systematic relationship. Now, the ecological crisis of present-day advanced industrial societies has made us aware that the cultures are dependent upon one another. This gives us a chance to escape both the illusory eighteenth-century fusion and the realistic nineteenth-century separation of these two rationalities. And it forces us to find a new way of relating the two.

The theoretical task before us then is to end the separation between the two cultures as it manifests itself in a dual social theory: one half concerned with the realm of strategic and utilitarian action and the other concerned with the realm of communicative action. We can no longer, as Habermas (1981) has proposed, separate two different social worlds by merely analytically distinguishing between system and life-world. Separating the two cedes the realm of nature to the systemic sphere dominated by a culture-as-profit orientation. Moreover, we have to acknowledge that morality pervades the realm of nature as much as technology pervades the realm of men. This being so, we can no longer separate two notions of progress in modern culture, the one defined as technological progress, the other as moral progress. They are indissolubly tied together. There is a problem, however, in how duplications of concepts key to the culture of modernity can be circumvented.

The practical task before us is to criticize the use modern society has made of the notion of progress to describe its development. Having lost faith in the progress we have made so far, we have turned this self-description into an illusion. We have to revise the notion of progress. It is the only way modern social science discourse can maintain its use in the self-description of modern society.

Revisions of the notion of progress

Bourgeois culture and progress

The bourgeois culture of the eighteenth and nineteenth centuries tried to fuse the utilitarian and communicative traditions of practical reason under the heading of progress. Technological progress and moral progress would be but two sides of the one coin. Progress, realized through science and technology, would be a means of freeing society from the limitations of nature and would thus contribute to the moral progress of mankind. This optimistic expectation of Enlightenment culture was based on the belief that everything that challenged traditional forms of belief, above all science and technology, contributed to the moral progress of mankind.

Then, as the social thinkers of the nineteenth and early twentieth centuries became aware of the negative social consequences of modernization they began to differentiate the conception of progress. Some challenged the inevitability of moral progress so self-evident to the Enlightenment. Marx was one of the most important of these critics. Moral progress was still not at hand; it was something society still needed to struggle for. This could be done in two ways: either by imposing morality "from above" or by claiming a morally better world "from below."[26] Marx himself was ambivalent with respect to these options. But whatever the solution proposed, the progress ascribed to the development of the forces of production remained unquestioned. The mastery of nature still could serve as a model of social progress. Only a few challenged this idea. These critics were labeled "romantic." The justice of the utilitarian relationship with nature was simply too self-evident to modern society. No critique of the technological model of progress had any real chance under these historical circumstances.

This situation has, however, changed. With the expansion of the ecological discourse the progressive character of our relation to nature is no longer self-evident and the rationality of that relation is now subject to challenge. The notion of progress, under increasing pressure since the coming of the ecological crisis, has become the central ideological and practical concern of advanced industrial societies. The new problem posed by the ecological crisis is not simply that of survival; it is the problem of a "reasonable" relation to nature.

Now that even the notion of technological progress, that aspect of modernization that once seemed to be its most clear-cut advantage, causes cultural irritation, we can no longer assume an empirical basis for the idea of progress. Since claiming moral evolution causes similar irritation, progress seems to be a fiction. It would be easy to give up progress as a meaningful theoretical category and to relinquish it as a mere ideological category.

But the idea of progress is more than an ideological force in modern society. It is a category that contains "counterfactual" postulates and is also used in this way. Progress is still considered to be something that has to be produced. We simply have to understand and analyze better. We need to understand its practical use beyond that classic situation where "natural progress" was a culturally shared idea. What we as sociologists can contribute to the analysis of the use of the notion of progress is to push the disturbing disillusion about "natural progress" into active "de-illusioning." We can:

- de-illusion the idea of a self-propelling progress in modern culture
- de-illusion a unilinear progress
- de-illusion European-type modernization as a model.

This de-illusioning process has already been accomplished with respect to the idea of moral progress. We have research criticizing modernization theory as either ethnocentric or as inadequate for grasping pathological paths of modern development. But only when we criticize technological progress, this last bastion of self-evident progress, will the idea of progress begin to be freed from naturalistic fallacies. Then there will be nothing but a concept ready to be filled with meaning. The theoretical problem before us then is to relocate the idea of progress within the present social and cultural struggles and to define the limits of possible choices in such struggles.

The range of possible choices

We are left with the thesis that after the loss of a substantive idea of progress we are open to cultural struggles to define and redefine its contents. As a corollary, the cultural traditions underlying modern European culture are in fact being used by competing and even antagonistic collective actors to give a new content to this idea. The analysis of such collective actors, of cultural movements, then becomes the key to explaining the fate of the notion of progress so central to the self-description of modern societies.

Thus we have come to view progress as the "definitional" result of "symbolic struggles" (Bourdieu 1984) in modern society. It turns out that the notion of progress is a means by which social actors try to influence social change. It is not inherent in modernization. It has no unequivocal validity. The notion of progress is a way of describing and validating an emerging cultural model. It refers to a field of social conflict between actors seeking to define the direction of social change. Within social science discourse, such a theoretical idea can be found in the concept of a "self-production of society" (Touraine 1977).[27]

But the range of possible notions of progress used to legitimize a cultural model of social development is not without limits. Combining two fields of human action (nature and culture) and two cultural orientations of human action (communicative action and utilitarian action) gives us four possibilities for the practical use of the notion of progress:

(1) To restrict the notion of progress to the field of strategic/instrumental action. The idea of dominating nature then defines the rationality of cultural practices. This is the model that permeates modern societies.

(2) To restrict the notion of progress to the field of moral action. Moral evolution is the privileged field of the idea of progress. This restriction excludes the relation of man to nature from the agenda of rational practice. This notion has become the model of the new humanist critique of the perversions encountered in modern societies.

(3) To reduce the notion of progress in both dimensions to its function in the reproduction of social systems. Actors are the environment of social systems that behave like strategic actors. Such an idea can be found in Luhmann's system-theoretical approach. The reification of social practice here is worth a hard look because the collective experiences of the dominance of systems in modern societies foster such a conclusion.

(4) To generalize moral action across nature and culture. This implies a form of practical reason in our relation to nature that allows us to recouple technological and moral progress. This would involve changing some basic cultural conceptions of nature in order to be able to treat it according to some standards of a morally grounded practical rationality.

The first two conceptualizations of progress are the classical ones claiming a "natural progress." They no longer work. The choice between technological progress in nature and moral progress in society is no longer operative. We can no longer equate technological and moral progress under the heading of formal rationality. But we can give both processes either a "strategic" or a "communicative" direction. The choice then can ultimately be reduced to the alternative between progress in the dimension of "culture-as-profit" or in the dimension of "culture-as-communication," the third and fourth possibilities above.

The third possibility is probably an escapist strategy. It simply denies the constructive aspects of collective communicative action and discourses.

The idea of progress appears as nothing but an element in the "auto-poiesis" of society (Luhmann 1984) and is thus an overtly ideological notion. The fourth possibility is the most promising as a starting point for disentangling the concept of rationality from the historical model of European-style progress based on the overpowering of nature. A way of discovering the historical possibility of such a concept is to analyze how present social struggles and discourses mobilize competing cultural traditions (the Greek and the Jewish) to produce competing definitions of progress. We do not need to give up the idea of progress. We simply need better theoretical tools for a sociological analysis of its use in modern society. The tools are there – we need only adapt and apply them.[28]

Conclusion

The idea of progress has in recent years increasingly been put into question. The key experience contributing to disengaging the idea of progress from the idea of rationality has been the ecological crisis. This crisis has made modern culture appear to foster a way of organizing social life that is self-destructive. The crisis has nourished cultural movements that counter modernization. There are groups and discourses that plead for re-enchantment as opposed to disenchantment. Modern culture has started to react to this experience by putting into question its key concepts: rationalization and rationality. Modernization based on rationality appears to be only one of many alternative ways of organizing modern social life. It appears to be nothing but the social form forced upon the majority of societies in the world by a dominant European culture and its American and Russian derivatives. Modernity is a cultural force that has imposed upon us a form of social evolution that cannot control its own consequences.

New, alternative ideas and movements are increasingly being directed against this type of modern rationality. These counterprocesses are not adequately described as antimodern or traditionalistic regressions. Instead, they represent another type of rationality and rationalization within the legacy of modern culture. The increasing concern with nature that we experience today is symptomatic of a fundamental cultural cleavage within the culture that underlies, accompanies, and regulates the development of highly complex societies in European-type modernization processes.

This cultural cleavage is traceable to the Semitic and Greek origins of modern culture. Two conflicting traditions, one of bloody sacrifice and one of unbloody (vegetarian) paradise, still define the cultural universe within which we live. Expanding the notion of cultural traditions constitutive for the European experience of modernization, and conceptualizing it as the manifestation of competing codes of modern culture, we are able to identify not one but two types of relationships with nature in modern society. Thus we arrive at two types of rationality encountered in modern culture: utilitarian rationality and communicative rationality, and at two types of culture within modern culture: culture as profit and culture as communication.

Ultimately, we have the outline of a new theoretical notion of progress. It is one that puts into question any social theory premised on its own progressiveness in terms of the European version of progress. The current ecological crisis has destroyed the last bastion of the belief in natural progress and the mastery of nature. Social theory should continue the task of disillusioning this self-ascription, of disengaging European-style progress from the notion of modernity.

Notes

1. I have treated this topic at length in a book entitled *The Socialization of Nature. Studies in the Social Evolution of Practical Reason* (Eder 1988). There I treat the "problem of nature" from a theoretical as well as an historical and cultural anthropological point of view. Nature is seen as the basic element of the cultural code of a society. The notion of a cultural code can be traced back principally to Claude Lévi-Strauss. For its sociological application within a Parsonian framework see Münch (1986).

2. This is the way, Schäfer (1985) puts it. He points to ideas, scientific knowledge, and social movements counter to the dominant modernity. Following this lead we do not plead for something beyond modernity, but for a notion of modernity that incorporates the protest against it as part of modernity. Eisenstadt (1986) argues similarly when criticizing modernization theory.

3. Here I refer to historical experiences that are intimately related to the rise of modern society, above all to witch-hunting in the seventeenth and eighteenth centuries and fascism in the twentieth century. It is difficult to exculpate modern society from these events without criticizing the very social and cultural conditions that have led to or made possible such events.

4. Here I refer to Weber's idea of the "battle of the gods" that goes along with the formal rationalization of modern society. This quotation comes from Weber's famous speech on "Science as a Vocation" (Weber 1922: 582–613). For a discussion see Schluchter (1988). See also below, note 10.

5. This "mechanism" can be seen as neutral with respect to its outcome. But such an interpretation of Marx is – as I see it – inadequate. There is in Marx a conception of man's relation to nature that offers ultimately a "productivist" notion of rationality. For this claim see Eder (1988), 30ff. See also Habermas' critique of Marx in Habermas (1979). Habermas' critique is insufficient because he substitutes the social relations of men among themselves for the basic relation of man to nature. This solution to the Marxian problem of nature separates two spheres of human action and thus overlooks the internal connections between both spheres of action. The problem of nature forces us to give up the idea that nature is subject to instrumental and culture to communicative action.

6. This self-negating character of rationalization has been treated by Hork-heimer and Adorno as the "Dialectic of Enlightenment" (Horkheimer and Adorno 1947). The domination of nature is seen as extending over society as a whole. The dialectic ends in the universal domination of instrumental reason. Reconciliation with nature ("Versöhnung mit der Natur") as mediated by aesthetic forms is the only chance to escape instrumental reason. This idea found a politically radical expression in Marcuse (1964). For a systematic discussion of, and a different solution to, the "Dialectic of Enlightenment" see Habermas (1981) 489ff.

7. Such a relationship with nature has normally been associated with some kind of romanticism or even irrationality and therefore been excluded from scientific discourse. This might explain why the problem of nature does not exist in the social sciences. It has been left – as something exotic – to cultural anthropology and recently to the history of mentalities. For an interesting cultural anthropological treatment see Douglas (1966, 1975). For a historical account see Thomas (1983).

8. For this notion of rationality in Weber see especially Schluchter (1981). The model from which Weber has taken the structure of formal rationality is modern positive law. Its rationality lies not in its ability to produce justice but in its ability to produce comparable and calculable results.

9. Habermas (1981) claims that there is no concept of formal rationality that does not imply some minimal material assumptions. Therefore the distinction between formal and material rationality is only a matter of relativity. This point was already made by Marx who showed that the formal rationality of modern law presupposes assumptions about subjective rights (e.g. property rights) and the modern fundamental rights of freedom.

10. Weber's central problem is to show how even religious traditions helped shape the form of rationality prevalent in modern European culture (Weber 1920). His theoretical strategy contributes to underestimating competing cultural traditions, and it explains the irritations Weber runs into when he examines the cultural developments of his times. For an interesting analysis of Weber's sociology of religion and its relation to the new "battle of the gods" see Schluchter (1988). For an extension of this Weberian program see Eisenstadt (1986).

11. This short analysis refers to recent research on Greek society that goes beyond classic euphemisms. Classical Greece consisted not only of some philoso-phers but also of a political system that has had a decisive influence upon the history of political domination in Europe. It was by isolating the Greek philosophical traditions from their social and political context that the idea of the Greek miracle became possible. But this obscured the understanding of the effects of this type of thinking. We can do better when we try to understand the social and political context within which this thinking arose, to which it reacted, and which it helped to rationalize. For the literature used, see especially Detienne (1972, 1979), Detienne and Vernant (1971, 1979).

12. The ritualistic character of Jewish culture has often been emphasized. But the meaning of this ritualism has normally been missed, to be "explained" by religion in what amounts to a tautological explanation. But religion does not "explain" the meaning; it arranges and rearranges the content that gives meaning to rituals. In this sense religion is a (mytho) logical system giving coherence to myths that rationalize ritual action. In Jewish society the main myth is that of the fall from paradise and the resultant longing for a world without blood. Judging the real world from the angle of the paradisiac ideal

structured norms and values that guide social action (cf. Eder 1988, 200ff.). It led to the preoccupation with blood and gave rise to rules of purity that allow for addressing the problem of blood. The "purity" of the unbloody state of nature then was extended into rules for the most elementary daily activities, especially eating. For an analysis of the ritual rules of eating from this point of view, especially the eating taboos, see Eder (1988), 27ff.

13. There were attempts in ancient Israel to oppose the ritual foundation of political domination by challenging the religious authorities upholding the code. Attempts by some political leaders to bring about polytheistic "regressions" (allowing for a return to bloody sacrifice), and to adapt Jewish political society to the model characteristic of their neighbors generally failed. For more details see Eder (1988), 200ff.

14. The social fate of Jewish culture within European culture is revealing. The aggressions against, and persecutions of, the Jews in European society through to modern times can be explained by the structural location of this cultural tradition within European culture: representing the model opposed to the dominant one.

15. The literature on messianic movements in medieval culture is abundant. An interesting case is that of the early heretics, especially the Cathars, who thought salvation consisted in escape from flesh. Mistrust of flesh is the most basic characteristic of this heretic tradition. The procreation of flesh and the consumption of its products (meat, milk, eggs) were bad, part of the kingdom of evil (Moore 1975). For later heretics continuing this tradition see Leff (1967). For a general macrosociological account of the role of such movements see Eisenstadt (1982). In order to reconstruct such symbolic systems we have to go behind the intellectual and theological disputes. These disputes were – beyond their manifest content – carriers of a latent content, representing and rationalizing the two opposed and antagonistic cultural traditions analyzed above.

16. Cultural codes of ritual purity have entered into and been fostered in the course of European history as conscious movements of protest against modernity and modernization. The history of cultural movements outside the main stream of political and economic development has only recently become the topic of scientific historical research. Concerning the research on protest movements and its implication for the theory of modernization see Eisenstadt (1981, 1986).

17. This takes up the argument made above with respect to these traditions. In the following, the consequences of the opposition of nature and culture for the conception of nature will be emphasized. See Soler (1979) and, building upon Soler, Eder (1988).

18. This difference taken from Greek philosophical thinking points to an ambivalence inherent in Greek culture. The "poietic" tradition was favored via its elementary cultural codings. But at the same time the cognitive means criticizing it was developed by elaborating the concept of "praxis." The latter concept has influenced different strands of modern social thought, from early Karl Marx to Hannah Arendt, Jürgen Habermas, and (in a different way) Pierre Bourdieu. For a discussion of this difference see Eder (1988), 306ff.

19. One example is the development of the knife and fork for eating meat. See Elias (1971). This rationalization can be seen as an attempt to generalize the dominant code of modern culture at the level of everyday life.

20. These phenomena have gained increasing attention in the last few years. For some German contributions see, e.g., Schimank (1983), Sprondel (1986), Weiß (1986), Hepp (1987) and Eder (1988), 225ff., 256ff. For important

earlier works see Honigsheim (1956) and Gusfield (1966). I would like to call the carriers of such discourses cultural movements, thus distinguishing them from social movements, constitutive for the rationalism (and rationalization) of modern culture. Here I adopt Touraine's idea of social movements as the "producers" of modern society (Touraine 1977, 1981). At the same time I try to extend it to include the cultural movements up to now at the margin of the historical process in such a theory of the "self-production of society."

21.   There is no consensus concerning the usage of the term "ecological movement." For the most common use of the term in Germany see Brandt (1982) and Brandt et al. (1983). I restrict my use of the term to those groups that are concerned about the destruction of the natural environment (e.g. by pollution) by political and economic institutions and organizations, but not by the people that consume nature. In this sense the ecological movement is primarily a "social" movement. The modern natural food movement (from vegetarian to healthy eating groups) is not a social movement but a "cultural" movement. Therefore I would like to distinguish between the ecological movement and the alternative nutrition movement pointing to differences in the way social and cultural movements thematize the relationship of man with nature (see Eder (1988), 256ff.). An example of such a cultural movement within the ecological movement is the "deep ecology movement." For a discussion of its ambiguities see Luke (1988).

22.   Romanticism thus appears as a tradition that continues – mediated and fostered by the "Greek" tradition of the Enlightenment – a relationship with nature that is to be found in the Jewish heritage. This interpretation allows us to see romanticism as being more than a mere reaction to the Enlightenment (e.g. Timm 1978). Rather, it can be seen as an attempt to create a more comprehensive Enlightenment. This is possible when we see romanticism as a movement resulting from a different strand of European culture trying to adapt to the exigencies of modern life. For a classic sociological discussion of romanticism as a cultural movement see Honigsheim (1956). For a more recent treatment see Weiß (1986). Campbell (1987) shows that romanticism contains an ethic that has decisively shaped the modern "spirit of consumerism." The emphasis on consumerism is another way of correcting the productivist conception of modern culture inherited from Marx. And a sociological analysis of the romantic tradition is one means of doing so. The consequence of such an approach is a closer look at the symbolic constructions underlying our forms of consuming nature – and here the Jewish tradition offers a way of criticizing the mere instrumentalist approach to our ethic of consumption.

23.   The opposition between nature and culture can be solved by "temporalization" in two ways. First there is the possibility of advancing from nature to culture. This can be called the "progressistic optimism" of modern culture. Then there is the possibility of returning from culture to nature. This has been a general topos of cultural critique in modern culture (and Rousseau is only the most famous representative of this type of thinking). Such temporalizations again point to the two competing traditions modern culture carries. For an interesting discussion of different conceptions of time within European culture see Wendorff (1980).

24.   Here I refer to Sahlins' work on "Culture and practical reason" (1976) which uses "practical reason" in the sense it has been used in modern society, i.e. in the utilitarian sense. Pointing this out Sahlins contributes to the de-illusioning of modern practical rationality. But he underrates the other meaning of practical rationality, one that is contained in modern society within the limits of the private and public realms. As long as decisions about

the direction of social change are made outside these limits Sahlins's point is well taken. The meaning carried by the claim of practical rationality is a means of criticizing its more restricted version. The perception of this problem will be stimulated – and here I follow Sahlins without hesitation – by the definition and redefinition of our relationship to nature, by the way we consume nature.

25. This interpretation of competing concepts of rationality and reason is taken from the theory of communicative action (Habermas 1981). In a reconstruction of political modernization in nineteenth-century German society I have tried to develop systematically the idea of an egalitarian and discursive relationship as the organizing principle of modern civil society (Eder 1985). I differ from Habermas when defining the competing notions of rationality. Habermas opposes functionalist reason to communicative reason, an opposition that detracts our attention from those rationalities that determine actual social conflicts. The problem centers on how we try to organize and orient collective action in a given situation (or given systems of social action). The problem is to construct an adequate theory of practice. And here I propose the theoretical alternative to be between utilitarian and communicative rationality (Eder 1988). Sahlins (1976) and Leach (1976) seem to me to argue in the same way. These alternatives are themselves a manifestation of the double tradition characterizing the cultural heritage of modern society.

26. This constitutes an interesting field of historicosociological analysis. It involves undertaking historical comparisons of such strategies, and analyzing the social conditions and consequences of such strategies. I have tried this approach with the case of late nineteenth-century German society when the dominant model of bringing about "moral progress" was one of imposing it from above (see Eder (1985)).

27. This discussion is the necessary follow-up to the type of cultural analysis I present. For after analyzing culture the interesting question becomes culture in action. We have treated progress as an expression of a dominating cultural tradition and now we arrive at a sociological treatment of progress as being the result of symbolic struggles, the carriers of which are competing social and cultural movements. The theoretical efforts and disputes from Luhmann to Habermas and from Bourdieu to Touraine can be given a new objective meaning from this perspective.

28. To combine such different strands of theorizing within European sociology seems to me a promising effort. Europe, being that part of the world where the problem of nature was invented and radicalized, offers a context of social thought that can objectively confront and possibly treat the pressing new problems of advanced industrial societies.

Acknowledgment

Thanks are due to Barbara Young who went through several versions of this paper trying to clarify the argument and to improve as much as it has been possible the "Germanic English" characteristic of the first versions of it.

Bibliography

Bourdieu, Pierre (1984) *Distinction. A Social Critique of the Judgment of Taste* (Cambridge, MA: Harvard University Press).

Brand, Karl-Werner (1982) *Neue soziale Bewegungen. Entstehung, Funktion und Perspektive neuer Protestpotentiale* (Opladen: Westdeutscher Verlag).

Brand, Karl-Werner, Büsser, D., and Rucht, Dieter (1983) *Aufbruch in eine andere Gesellschaft. Neue soziale Bewegungen in der Bundesrepublik* (Frankfurt/New York: Campus).

Campbell, Colin (1987) *The Romantic Ethic and the Spirit of Consumerism* (Oxford: Blackwell).

Detienne, Marcel (1972) *Les jardins d'Adonis. La mythologie des aromates en Grèce* (Paris: Gallimard).

Detienne, Marcel (1979) "Pratique culinaires et esprit de sacrifice", in M. Detienne and J.-P. Vernant (eds) *La cuisine du sacrifice en pays grec* (Paris: Gallimard: 7–35).

Detienne, Marcel, and Svenbro, J. (1979) "Les loups au festin ou la cité impossible", in M. Detienne and J.-P. Vernant (eds) *La cuisine du sacrifice en pays grec* (Paris: Gallimard: 215–37).

Douglas, Mary (1966) *Purity and Danger* (London: Routledge & Kegan Paul).

Douglas, Mary (1975) *Implicit Meanings* (London: Routledge & Kegan Paul).

Eder, Klaus (1985) *Geschichte als Lernprozeß? Zur Pathogenese politischer Modernität in Deutschland* (Frankfurt: Suhrkamp).

Eder, Klaus (1988) *Die Vergesellschaftung der Natur. Studien zur sozialen Evolution der praktischen Vernunft* (Frankfurt: Suhrkamp).

Eder, Klaus (1989) "Cultural movements against modernity," (Manuscript, München).

Eisenstadt, E. N. (1981) "Cultural traditions and political dynamics: the origins and modes of ideological politics," *British Journal of Sociology* 32: 155–81.

Eisenstadt, S. N. (1982) "Heterodoxies, sectarianism, and dynamics of civilizations," *Diogenes* 120.

Eisenstadt, S. N. (1986) *A Sociological Approach to Comparative Civilizations: The Development and Directions of a Research Program* (Hebrew University of Jerusalem: Harry S. Truman Research Institute).

Elias, Norbert (1971) *Über den Prozeß der Zivilisation. Soziogenetische und psychogenetische Untersuchungen* 2nd edn (Frankfurt: Suhrkamp).

Gusfield, Joseph R. (1966) *Symbolic Crusade. Status Politics and the American Temperance Movement* (Urbana, IL: University of Illinois Press).

Habermas, Jürgen (1979) *Communication and the Evolution of Society* (Boston: Beacon Press).

Habermas, Jürgen (1981) *Theorie des Kommunikativen Handelns. 2 Bände* (Frankfurt: Suhrkamp) English translation: *Theory of Communicative Action* (Boston: Beacon Press 1984).

Hepp, Corona (1987) *Advantgarde – Moderne Kunst, Kulturkritik und Reformbewegungen nach der Jahrhundertwende* (München: Deutscher Taschenbuch Verlag).

Honigsheim, Paul (1956) "Romantik und neuromantische Bewegungen," in *Handwörterbuch der Sozialwissenschaften* (Göttingen, Vol. 9: 26–41).

Horkheimer, Max (1967) *Zur Kritik der instrumentellen Vernunft* (Frankfurt: Suhrkamp).

Horkheimer, Max, and Adorno, Th. W. (1947) *Dialektik der Aufklärung* (Amsterdam).

Leach, Edmund (1976) *Culture and Communication. The Logic by which Symbols are Connected* (Cambridge: Cambridge University Press).

Leff, Gordon (1967) *Heresy in the Later Middle Ages. The Relation of Heterodoxy to Dissent* (2 volumes) (Manchester: Manchester University Press).

Luhmann, Niklas (1984) *Soziale Systeme. Grundriß einer allgemeinen Theorie* (Frankfurt: Suhrkamp).

Luke, Timothy (1988) "The dreams of deep ecology," *Telos*, 76: 65–92.

Marcuse, Herbert (1964) *One-Dimensional Man* (Boston: Beacon).

Moore, Robert I. (1975) *The Birth of Popular Heresy* (London: Edward Arnold).

Münch, Richard (1986) *Die Kultur der Moderne. 2 Bände* (Frankfurt: Suhrkamp).

Sahlins, Marshal (1976) *Culture and Practical Reason* (Chicago: University of Chicago Press).

Schäfer, W. (1985) *Die unvertraute Moderne. Historische Umrisse einer anderen Natur- und Sozialgeschichte* (Frankfurt: Fischer).

Schimank, Uwe (1983) *Neoromantischer Protest im Spätkapitalismus: Der Widerstand gegen die Stadt- und Landschaftsverödung* (Bielefeld: AJZ-Verlag).

Schluchter, Wolfgang (1981) *The Rise of Western Rationalism: Max Weber's Developmental History* (Berkeley, CA: University of California Press).

Schluchter, Wolfgang (1988) "The battle of the gods: from the critique to the sociology of religion," *National Taiwan University Journal of Sociology*, 19: 165–78.

Soler, J. (1979) "The dietary prohibitions of the Hebrews," *New York Review of Books*, June 14: 24–30.

Sprondel, W. L. (1986) "Kulturelle Modernisierung durch antimodernistischen Protest. Der lebensreformerische Vegetarismus," in F. Neidhardt, R. M. Lepsius and J. Weiß (eds) *Kultur und Gesellschaft. Sonderheft 27 der KZfSS* (Opladen: Westdeutscher Verlag: 314–30).

Thomas, Keith (1983) *Man and the Natural World. A History of the Modern Sensibility* (New York: Pantheon Books).

Timm, Hermann (1978) *Die heilige Revolution. Schleiermacher – Novalis – Friedrich Schlegel* (Frankfurt: Syndikat).

Touraine, Alain (1977) *The Self-Production of Society* (Chicago: University of Chicago Press).

Touraine, Alain (1981) *The Voice and the Eye* (New York: Cambridge University Press).

Vernant, Jean-Pierre (1971) *Mythe et pensée chez les Grecs. Etudes de psychologie historique* (2 vols.) (Paris: Maspero).

Vernant, Jean-Pierre (1973) "Der Begriff der Arbeit bei den Griechen," in K. Eder (ed.) *Seminar Die Entstehung von Klassengesellschaften* (Frankfurt: Suhrkamp).

Vernant, Jean-Pierre (1979) "A la table des hommes. Mythe de fondation du sacrifice chez Hésiode," in M. Detienne and J.-P. Vernant (eds) *La cuisine du sacrifice en pays grec* (Paris: Gallimard).

Weber, Max (1988 [1920]) *Gesammelte Aufsätze zur Religionssoziologie I–III* (Tübingen: Mohr).

Weber, Max (1988 [1922]) *Gesammelte Aufsätze zur Wissenschaftslehre* (Tübingen: Mohr).

Weiß, J. (1986) "Wiederverzauberung der Welt? Bemerkungen zur Wiederkehr der Romantik in der gegenwärtigen Kulturkritik," in F. Neidhardt, R. M. Lepsius, and J. Weiß (eds) *Kultur und Gesellschaft. Sonderheft 27 der KZfSS* (Opladen: Westdeutscher Verlag: 286–301).

Wendorff, Rudolph (1980) *Zeit und Kultur. Geschichte des Zeitbewußtseins in Europa* (2nd edn) (Opladen: Westdeutscher Verlag).

PART II

Rethinking the agents of progress

5

Intellectuals and progress: the origins, decline, and revival of a critical group

RON EYERMAN

Although defined in various ways, intellectuals have often been portrayed as the bearers of progressive ideas and leaders of progressive historical change. This is especially true in Marxist and liberal traditions of social thought. While the latter stress the benefits of education and its connection to democratic norms of inclusion and participation, the former look to intellectuals for insight into the causes of human misery and the course of human history. This essay will look at the ways social theorists have linked intellectuals to social progress and the ways intellectuals have actually participated in politics and political movements. In this context, I define intellectuals historically, as an emergent group with direct connections to the ideologies and movements of the nineteenth century and trace the evolution of this notion in twentieth-century sociology. Central to the ideologies and movements of the nineteenth century is the idea of social progress and the distinct role of intellectuals in its historical realization, and much of modern sociology, as we know, is rooted in just these traditions. In the process of this exposition I outline a new theory of intellectuals, one which builds upon the entirely disparate work of Antonio Gramsci and Alvin Gouldner. The basic idea here is that intellectuals, those who call into question the basic taken-for-granted assumptions of a social order and of their "progressive" transcendence, are an emergent category, not a distinct social strata, whose appearance depends upon historically contingent factors. Who are tomorrow's intellectuals and what the content of their message will be is something now only taking form.

As has been recounted by Carl Becker, the idea of progress has roots in Judeo-Christian notions of history and redemption. The idea of progress also has direct links to the concept of the intellectual, for the modern reformulators of these ancient traditions were the original *philosophes*, the participants in the Enlightenment who propagated for the march of reason on earth, providing the ideological groundwork for the French Revolution and a source of inspiration for influential German thinkers like Hegel and Marx, as well as liberal thinkers like Mill. This doctrine called for direct human intervention into the ways and processes of the world and was founded upon the belief that a rational social order could be constructed on earth. Historical change, the movement toward such an order, was, indeed, progress. Condorcet, student of D'Alembert and admirer of Voltaire and the last of the *philosophes*, wrote about moving the unleashed historical forces of revolution along paths of reason and virtue to the land of Enlightenment and progress. These ideas were shared by later "intellectuals," positivist as well as romantic and utopian, reformist as well as revolutionary. In fact, they were shared more or less by "intellectuals" generally, forming a sort of basis to the identity-formation of a social group and the basis for a self-proclaimed historical mission. It was this faith in progress based on human reason that led many disenchanted members of the bourgeoisie to join the new workers' movements, as these were viewed, along with the rising and aggressive bourgeoisie, as motors of social change. In the concepts later, Marxist formulation, intellectuals were identified as the articulators of these new class identities, which were thought basic ingredients for class struggle and, thus, progressive social change. Liberalism, on the other hand, focused on creating a new institutional framework in which these various new "interests" could be represented, respected, and contained. Intellectuals were here assigned the task of providing the ideals and the leadership, as well as that of helping to construct the framework within which these conflicting interests could be harmonized or at least maintained, and thereby progress achieved.[1]

This classical notion of the intellectual as articulator of needs and interests and progressive leader has roots in ancient thought, but more directly in the Enlightenment and, especially in connection with the struggle for national unification associated with the transition to modernity in German idealism. In the European revolutions of 1848, "intellectuals," poets, and philosophers as well as fledgling young publicists and writers, joined in the struggle to build new collective identities as well as institutions – classes, parties, and nations. Through their activism the idea began to take form that intellectuals were a social group with a distinct historical mission to perform. Part of that mission was to help realize "progress" by overcoming a "traditional" social order rooted in tired ways of living and thinking. New forms of thought, art, and science, new social relations and political groups were set in motion to shape the future as progress. It was the intellectuals who claimed to perceive the laws of this motion, taking for themselves the role of leading blind social forces in the right directions.

Intellectuals and progress: Marxism and liberalism

The very idea of "intellectuals" thus first emerged in the new political context created by the transition to modernity. In those confrontations surrounding the spread of the market economy and the power of private property and the struggle over their control, in the framework of newly forming classes and movements, intellectuals pursued a group awareness and sense of mission, either as active supporters or opponents of modernity. Through their role in budding movements, individual members of the bourgeoisie became "intellectuals," part of a group in conflict with their own class and also with the newly forming working class. On the other side, more conservative "intellectuals" formed a sense of their identity and common mission to resist and counteract the new working class. The conflicts from which the working-class movements arose produced and inspired intellectuals on both sides of the new left–right political divide.

The European workers' movements turned "worker" into a household word. Intellectuals were instrumental in the processes that made this possible. The most well-known are of course Marx and Engels, but there were many others. However, the Communist Manifesto (1848) not only helped to make famous the opposition between "bourgeoisie and proletariat," it also popularized the idea of the revolutionary intellectual. Although the term "intellectual" does not appear in the text, the very appearance of the text, its manner of production and distribution, helped to constitute the intellectuals as a distinct group with a mission to perform. In the early phases of the workers' movement, and later on, the term intellectual was often used in a derogatory manner to refer to those non-manual workers who would give themselves a special place in the movement; the model of course were members of the bourgeoisie. Alvin Gouldner records the clash between Marx, the bourgeois intellectual, and the former tailor's apprentice Wilhelm Weitling, over the issue of working-class self-emancipation, i.e., from "movement" intellectuals as well as from the bourgeoisie in general (Gouldner 1985: 95ff.). This "anti-intellectualism" was a theme that would reappear in many forms and contexts, but its political origins at least lie here in the early struggles of the European labor movement.

In such internal conflicts, déclassé writers, journalists, and professors formed a sense of their own collective identity, which later would be given theoretical standing as well as tactical significance in Lenin's classic "What is to be done?" (Lenin 1977 [1902]). Citing Karl Kautsky, the leader of German socialist orthodoxy, Lenin made the famous proposition that revolutionary class consciousness could not emerge spontaneously from within the working class itself, but would have to be "brought to it from the outside," carried, that is, by progressive bourgeois intellectuals. It is worth citing Lenin-Kautsky in full, not only for the role given to intellectuals in the workers' movement, but also for the connection between intellectuals and progress.

> . . . socialism and the class struggle arise side by side and not one out of the other; each arises out of different conditions. Modern socialist consciousness can arise only on the basis of profound scientific knowledge . . . The vehicle of science is not the proletariat but the bourgeois intelligentsia: it was in the minds of individual members of this stratum that modern socialism originated, and it was they who communicated it to the more intellectually developed proletarians who, in their turn, introduced it into the proletarian class struggle where conditions allow that to be done. Thus, socialist consciousness is something introduced into the proletariat class struggle from without and not something that arose within it spontaneously.[2]

Spontaneity, the great mass awakening that later Marxists would champion was anathema to cautious movement intellectuals like Lenin and Kautsky. For them, intellectuals were not so much producers of ideas which sparked insight, but rather carriers of a progressive way of thinking which articulated universal (class), rather than particularistic, interests and which thus provided guidance as well as grounding. Accordingly, intellectuals provided a necessary foundation for well-grounded, and organized, progressive social change. In order to be "progressive," action leading to change had to be intellectually well grounded and politically well organized. Intellectuals, according to Lenin and Kautsky, were important to the working-class movement in both these respects: providing it with insight and organization. Because Lenin-Kautsky identify science with a particular social stratum their ideas could later be used to legitimate giving "intellectuals" (defined by function and skill) a dominant position in working-class organizations and related political parties. Robert Michels' (1959 [1911]) study of the German SPD was an early sociological formulation of just this process.

The idea that progressive intellectual activity was class based was modified by a later movement intellectual, Antonio Gramsci. Gramsci (1971) separated the intellectual activity of methodical, reflexive critical thinking from the social stratum which may, historically, have first formulated it as "science." As intellectual activity, critical thinking is open to every human being, he wrote; only in a hierarchically ordered, class divided society is such activity limited to specific social strata. Since class society needed to be overcome, subordinate social classes and the social movements they created were still dependent on "traditional," bourgeois, intellectuals for the well-grounded insight provided by this way of thinking. But this was now made an historically contingent rather than

94

a transcendent condition. In Gramsci's formulation, it was at least theoretically possible that subordinate social classes could produce their own "organic" intellectuals.[3] His own life may have provided him with the basis for this idea. Although the son of a middle level provincial functionary, Gramsci struggled hard to overcome social as well as physical handicaps to become an urban "intellectual," but he was hardly traditional. Rather than choosing the worn paths available to a petty-bourgeois son of the provinces, following his father into the local bureaucracy, or totally escaping this background to become a fully fledged "bourgeois intellectual," as a scholarship student at the University of Turin Gramsci combined his academic studies with participation in socialist organizations and writing articles for socialist newspapers, where he stressed the links between cultural and political activities. Providing the working-class movement with the intellect for the "intense labor of social criticism, of cultural penetration and diffusion," was how Gramsci and his fellow socialist students saw their role as progressive intellectuals (Fiori 1973: 103). It was through providing this service that students became intellectuals and progressive at the same time. If they were not traditional, Gramsci and his fellow socialist students certainly played the classical role given to Marxist intellectuals.

It was not a long step from this political-cultural analysis to a concept of the intellectual, referring to a person rather than a process, based on social function, either in relation to social movements or to society in general. Thus, in later accounts, the intellectual was made identical with the ideologue, the producer of ideas and culture, the manipulator of symbols and mobilizer of opinions, even where this function was not directly linked to a social stratum or given a class basis.

This more general notion of the intellectual has historical roots in the Dreyfus Affair, as Daniel Bell (1980) has made clear. But it really came into force with the integration of the labor movement into the established political frameworks of European society, when progress was given over to faceless forces like technological development, such institutions as the state, or organizations like the party something which will be discussed later on. In the Dreyfus context, the term intellectual had a negative connotation but a positive effect, at least when judged from the point of view of the formation of group identity and sense of special moral mission for intellectuals. Through being labeled intellectuals in a newspaper article a group of French writers discovered they had more than one common interest: they were "intellectuals," who, perhaps, were also "progressive" in that they stood together for enlightened social relations against censorship and discrimination. This helped to feed the growing idea that intellectuals had a transcendent moral mission, something which could involve different issues in different contexts, but which was beginning to find a common theme: giving public voice to the silenced and the silent, defending the right to free expression and the force of enlightened argument (Bell 1980).[4]

This conception of the intellectual also has classical roots which were revived with the Enlightenment and the French revolution. Its more modern usage however is directly linked, as is its Marxist counterpart, to the confrontations surrounding the emergence of the workers' movements and the European transition to modernity. In terms of historical appearance, it was not a specific function that produced the group, as would be portrayed in later sociological discussions of intellectuals, but rather the two emerged simultaneously – the notion that intellectuals might have a special function (and mission) arose as part of the self-awareness of the group.

In sum, in its Marxist conceptualization, intellectuals were those non-Bohemian writers and publicists, a segment of the bourgeoisie, who deserted their class of origin to give intellectual guidance to working-class movements, forming in the process "a dynamic unity," as Max Horkheimer (1972) put it, for progressive historical change.[5] Their role was to transform particularistic, "trade union consciousness," i.e. the "natural consciousness" of the working class through articulating universalistic interests and orientations. It was this orientation that would set humanity free and lead history on the path to progress. Intellectuals, in other words, acted as mediators of historical progress: they helped translate needs into interests and bind forces into political movements with clear goals and the powerful organization to achieve them.

Intellectuals and progress in liberal thought

In the liberal thought which sometimes competed with Marxism for the attention of subordinated groups and social movements, the notion of the intellectual has a moral grounding and entails a distinct educative mission. Here the idea of social progress, and the moral mission of intellectuals as its carriers, has its origin in the emergence of what Jürgen Habermas (1962, 1974) has called the "bourgeois public sphere." In the salons and cafés which sprang up in Europe in the seventeenth and eighteenth centuries Habermas argues, a growing stratum of an increasingly self-conscious and confident social class, the bourgeois intelligentsia, could constitute itself in a moveable and continuous "public discourse." Through its dialogues and their more permanent public record in newspapers, journals, and books, the bourgeois intelligentsia could help constitute as well as influence wider public opinion and the "general public." Habermas and others have shown this influence to be both cultural and political (Hohendahl 1982). The new bourgeois intellectuals affected public taste in art and literature, as well as forming the basis for influencing opinion for and against established political powers. It is here that our notion of the "critical intellectual" and the "public intellectual" have their roots.

The practice of the critical intellectual, the two terms being intimately linked in the new bourgeois public sphere, involved publicly speaking out on issues of general moral and political importance. It involved taking a stand as well as attempting to mobilize and influence others. It involved, in other words, moral example and political persuasion. The role of the bourgeois intellectual was to educate the public through the display of intellectual ability and moral example. The notion of the general or the public interest is central for the self-consciousness of the intellectual in this conceptualization. The intellectual is he who rises above self-interest to speak for the general good, standing on universal moral principles in the process. In this sense, the education through reasoned example provided the public by the intellectual moves from the particular to the general, as in the Marxist view.

The idea of progress connected to this notion of the intellectual involves educating individuals about their own critical abilities and their moral responsibilities. Progress here meant uplifting individuals through widening participation in the reflexive thinking of the public sphere. The idea of progress as public education, if not as an educated public, has links with the working-class movements discussed above. In Europe, a central organizing activity of early working-class movements concerned culture and education, a theme later taken up in the United States by "progressive" intellectuals and parties. In Sweden and other European countries the origins of the working-class movement can be traced to the literary circles organized and led by "bourgeois intellectuals," which aimed at uplifting the laborer. Often with a religious basis, these groups gathered craftsmen and laborers in bourgeois homes to listen to university scholars lecture on topics that were thought to be of general cultural interest. Labor historians have recorded the conflicts which followed on from these two ideals of progress. Marxists and other revolutionary intellectuals were concerned that this "bourgeois moralism" would lead to the embourgeoisement of the working class and to dreams of individual social mobility, to individual revolutions, rather than to class struggle and collective social progress.

Organized progress: consolidation and modernization

The common classical Marxian and liberal link between intellectuals and progress came together with the consolidation of social forces for modernization in European social democracy. To speak in necessarily simplistic terms, the "success" of working-class movements, which meant both the defeat of the radical left and their integration (in subordinated form) into the routinized democratic processes of the new, more strongly cohesive (politically and culturally) European nation-states, meant, as Daniel Bell would later put it, "the end of ideology." It also meant the transformation of intellectuals into intellectual laborers and their redeployment as part of the new "state sector." Once the center field of intellectual praxis, the production of ideology became a routine part of the output of the new public sphere organized through the state. The alliance between the newly constituted intellectual labor and the tamed working-class movements accomplished through expanding the structure and function of the state is the basis of modern social democracy and a new "non-ideological" idea of progress.

With these changes as basis, the locus of "progress" was shifted from intellectuals and enlightened social forces to institutions constituted through, and brought under, the leadership of the state.[6] It was now the state that would provide enlightened leadership, guiding the production of knowledge as well as goods, the socialization of knowledgable individuals, controling the market and the new mass media. The idea of progressive change was thus institutionalized in the policy and planning functions of the state, competing in some contexts with the private corporation, and localized in an educated public. In the newly integrated European state, progress became a taken-for-granted system function rather than the self-proclaimed mission of any social group or class.

This great transformation was reflected in the self-perceptions of "intellectuals" and recorded in theories of social change. An aggressive and dominant structural-functional sociology, with its stress on equilibrium and on integrative modernization, identified progress with societal differentiation; scientific-technological change; an "education revolution" which combatted parochialism; the spread of representative democracy; and most significantly, with the rise of the professions and the professional, who, it was hoped, would hold it all together. In line with their integration into the system of modern societies, intellectuals were transformed into professionals, their identity circumscribed by occupational and social function. No distinct group identity and no moral mission was associated with the term.

The liberal functionalism associated with modernization theory retained, however, a tempered normative definition of intellectual labor in its expectations about the role of the professional and the professions in modernized society. As modernizing élites, the professionals organized through the legal/bureaucratic framework of the modern state were said to represent and express progressively evolved personality structures as well as forms of conflict resolution for social reintegration, as compared to either dynamic entrepreneurs or charismatic political or religious leaders, i.e., classical intellectuals. With their depersonalized personalities and the ability to separate reason from emotion in scientific objectivity, professionals could mediate conflicts in a more rational way than either force or money, as the alternatives were laid out. Thus progress here implied the rationalization of society through the legal/bureaucratic state and the incorporation of intellectuals in the process. As professionals they were the state's leading arm, the incarnation of progress. Of course, educating the public still had a role to play, but now as bureaucratized and steered public education it could be more concerned with role socialization than critical reflection and public discourse.

The inter and postwar periods marked by state expansion and intervention, rapid technological change, and the installation of a managerial political culture, consolidated modernity. This also solidified a new role for the integrated intellectual – the professional, a part of the intellectual labor organic to the new social system. As in the early stages of this process intellectuals were active participants in this historical transformation. Not only in the sense that they helped conceptualize the terms which defined the new situation, in the sense meant by Zygmunt Bauman (1987) when he rightly notes that all definitions of intellectuals are bound to be self-definitions, but also in the more profound sense that they helped mediate the historical process at work. As rationalizing intellectuals they helped consolidate the role of the "expert," and the managerial political culture grounded on a rational-scientific world view, which not only supported modernization but also provided professionals with their legitimate role. In another place (Eyerman 1985) I have described how Swedish intellectuals in the 1930s and 1940s supported the statebuilding policies of the Social Democratic Party through their rationalizing role, objectifying, isolating, and transforming into problems behaviors that previously had been taken for granted. These intellectuals used cognition in an instrumental way, thematizing issues such as social problems, for which they could provide solutions. Like their counterparts in the classical mode, rationalizing intellectuals, who would soon become rationalized professionals, claimed to do more than articulate vaguely felt interests: they also claimed to provide solutions and answers grounded in science, an instrumental cognitive process to which they, by definition, had privileged access. The difference between the classical role and this transitionary intellectual role as rationalizer, is that the interests being articulated and the solutions proposed were not those of dynamic social classes in the formative stage, but those of rather passive prospective clients for an expanding and consolidating state. As professionals, intellectuals would become part of the new progressive authority; as rationalizing intellectuals, they were helping to consolidate the new legitimating political culture and their own place in it. Linking the notion of progress to the state was part of this process.

In neo-Marxist accounts, often colored by the same functionalist assumptions, intellectual labor soon became a problematic category, in a "contradictory class location," somewhere between labor and capital on a structural map.[7] Marxism, even in its Leninist variants, had always been suspicious of intellectuals and very reluctant to assign them a special mission. More importantly, however, intellectual labor became a problem for neo-Marxists because of its largely unanticipated growth.

The classical liberal notion of the intellectual as social critic and mobilizer of rationally grounded public opinion is similarly threatened by the fundamental changes that accompanied modernization, in the conditions for the formation of public opinion, and the constitution of that public itself. The rise to dominance of the mass media and the ability to manipulate rather than merely influence public opinion, the rise of mass culture and the consequent decline of "serious" public interest and debate threatens the classical liberal ideal of both the role of the intellectual and the idea of progress.

This threat has most recently been elaborated from opposite poles of the American political spectrum by Russell Jacoby (1987) and Allan Bloom (1987). Jacoby laments the fall of the public intellectual, a composite of Marxist and liberal ideal, and the rise of the academic specialist in his place. This fall is traced by processes which undercut the possibility for critical intellectuals to survive in the creative atmosphere connected to what was earlier described as the "bourgeois public sphere": the rise of commercial mass media, including "information" conglomerates and the corresponding decline of serious journals and newspapers which could support as well as give space to intellectual discourse. Modernizing urban renewal projects destroyed the neighborhoods and the cafes in which intellectuals could live cheaply and congregate. Most importantly of all, the incorporation of the intellectual into the university, and its accompanying specialization, Jacoby claims has narrowed his or her focus as well as audience.

In addition to these historical processes, which, ironically, classical intellectuals helped to set in motion, Marxist and liberal ideals of progress are threatened by the rise of fundamentalist social movements with, from their points of view, anti-intellectual and thus regressive ideologies. Fundamentalism is anathema to the classic ideal of the intellectual because it encourages censorship and dogmatic interpretation rather than free intellectual exchange and often takes on antimodern, and thus from that point of view, retrogressive form.

Disorganized progress: the new social movements

The first real break with the intellectual as professional and the managerial political culture surrounding institutionalized social progress began with the American student revolts in the early 1960s.[8] These revolts can be interpreted as a rebellion against what was perceived as the degradation of intellectual activity and a rejection of the role of intellectual as producer of knowledge in the new knowledge industries. Those traditions that stressed the classical role of the intellectual as moral spokesman and carrier of progressive ideas, like Marxism and liberalism, as well as those more independent thinkers with the same message, C. Wright Mills in the US, Camus and Sartre in Europe, played a significant role in formulating the grounds for this rebellion. It is not by chance that the early formulations of the new student left concerned the role of the intellectual and that the focus of their revolt was first of all the new "multi-universities," perceived by themselves and their opponents as centerpieces in the modern, "knowledge industry."[9]

The idea of progress as a system function was also an integral part of this critique, something which would be further developed when environmentalism emerged as a social movement in the early 1970s.[10] Ironically, or perhaps necessarily, it was the beneficiaries of the dream of progress who were now among its most strident critics. Spurred by the American civil rights movement, which revealed that "progress," even as a blind system function, was discriminatory, and, later, by the growing insight that scientific and technological "development" did not automatically translate into economic or social progress, this essentially liberal critique turned radical and Marxist. It also built upon and revived alternative political traditions developing into a global social movement that inspired other "new" social movements which, among very many other things, opened new critical public spaces where the idea and the practice of "movement intellectualism" could re-emerge.

The basis for the re-emergence of the classical notion and practice of the movement intellectual with the new social movements is entirely different from the original setting of the transition to modern society. These new social movements express reactions against the idea of progress associated with modernization. Thus, not only are sociologically different actors involved, their historical situation *vis-à-vis* the forces of modernization and thus notion of social progress is also very different from their predecessors who formed the "old" social movements. If the historical situation in which the new social movements have taken form can also be characterized as a period of transition, from modernity to postmodernity, the clashing social forces are no longer centered around the relations of production, with the prospect of integration through the state, except in a negative way. Rather they are centered around issues concerning the quality of life associated with modernization and the notion of progress connected to it (Eyerman and Jamison 1990).

The actively conflicting social forces are currently restricted to a rather narrow configuration: intellectual labor employed largely in the public sector and, in labor market terms, marginalized social categories – the young, the old, and the female. However, the wider basis of support for these movements, especially as they have evolved into green political parties and a wide range of interest groups and organizations, is largely unknown. Regarding our current theme, at stake are two conflicting notions of progress, which include alternative visions of the future: institutionalized progress unfolding in a lawlike manner, and progress founded upon a new consensus which would include a "green" worldview. Thus, the extent of support for either of these "futures" is still an open matter; it depends upon the mobilizing potential of the conflicting visions. Here lies the significance of the classical movement intellectuals that re-emerged in the public spaces opened by the new social movements.

Contemporary movement intellectuals are neither the *déclassé* visionaries claiming insight into the path of history who joined the newly forming working-class movements of the nineteenth century, nor are they their classically educated liberal counterparts armed with moral example and a notion of the progressive public, although traces of both can still be found. Today's movement intellectuals come from the ranks of intellectual labor and appear to have a much more modest self-perception and ambivalent relation to social progress. In addition, their formation as "intellectuals" occurs largely within the publics created by new social movements, rather than established intellectual traditions or institutions. They are thus "organic" intellectuals in the Gramscian sense, who, for the moment at least, appear to have rejected the privilege of being part of a new class formation. That this has occurred, even temporarily, may very well be taken as an achievement of the "education revolution" heralded by modernization theorists. In this sense, modernization has indeed brought progress, for it has helped produce the grounds for its own critical transcendence.[11]

What will constitute "progress" in the final decade of the twentieth century is an open matter. As it was earlier, the very idea of progress is a matter of conflict and political struggle. Progress, like so many other terms, is a contested concept. If no longer its self-appointed bearers, intellectuals, seen as an emergent group, are again at the very center of this conflict. However, times are different and so are intellectuals. Progress today is certainly not what it used to be.

Notes

1. These notions conflicted of course with conservative ideas, often rooted in religious thought. At a later historical moment than that discussed here, one of the greatest intellectual critics of American progressivism was the Christian theologian Reinhold Niebuhr (1932) who attacked John Dewey amongst others for the belief that ignorance was at the basis of social injustice and that progress could be achieved through education. For Niebuhr, who also

attacked preachers of a progressivist "social gospel" amongst his own Christian clergy, sin and predatory self-interest were fixed characteristics of human nature and thus not amenable to either progressive education or religion. This is discussed in detail in Branch (1988) in connection with Martin Luther King, Jr. and the American civil rights movement.

2. Here it can be seen that scientific knowledge and a recognition of the necessity for socialism develop together with an intellectual culture that is separate and distinct from that of the working class. It is important to note, in addition, that the claim being made here is not only an historical one, i.e., that in historical fact such a distinct development was the case, but rather the much stronger claim that the working class could not develop such an understanding from within the confines of its own culture and daily life. It should also be noted that there may indeed be a difference in the views of Kautsky and Lenin on the role of intellectuals, which is not apparent in this citation. Lenin was never comfortable with "intellectuals" as a distinct group, rather he restricted the role of carrier of correct consciousness to individual intellectuals, as organized in tightly controlled settings, party newspapers, and organizations. For a fuller treatment of these issues, see Eyerman (1981) and van den Berg (1988).

3. The concept of "movement intellectual" is elaborated and discussed in connection with the new social movements in Eyerman and Jamison (1990).

4. Daniel Bell (1980) quotes from a letter written by William James in the year following the Dreyfus letter (1899) which contains the passage: "We 'intellectuals' in America must all work to keep our precious birthright of individualism, and freedom from those institutions (church, army, aristocracy, royalty). *Every* great institution is perforce a means of corruption – whatever good it may also do. Only in personal relation is full ideality to be found" (121).

5. In the essay "Traditional and critical theory," Horkheimer (1972) laid out the politically grounded research programme for the Frankfurt School. The idea that workers had a "natural consciousness" is something which post-Lenin western Marxism developed and refined.

6. An exception was the romantic ideas attached to the engineer, especially in North America, in the early part of the twentieth century. In a sort of transitory position between the classical intellectual and the professional, the engineer mediated modernist utopia and reality with his "gear and girder" technology. On this and the links between technical and literary modernism, see Cecilia Tichi (1987).

7. There were exceptions of course, no social theory can achieve complete dominance, even where it seems to have the support of history. Especially amongst European refugees to England and the US, the classical idea of the intellectual and the intelligentsia survived and still lives on.

8. In the United States, Marxist and liberal intellectuals were not transformed in the same way as their European counterparts. Redbaiting, McCarthyism, and the complicity of the American Communist Party, its tail wagging for Soviet foreign policy, all contributed to the defeat of the classical and Marxian notion of the intellectual. "The end of ideology," and along with it the decline of the intellectual, did not arrive by consensual agreement or blind social force.

9. As president of the University of California and thus counterpoint of the first revolts, Clark Kerr wrote "What the railroad did for the first half of this century may be done for the second half of this century by the knowledge industry: that is, to serve as the focal point for the national growth. And the university

103

is at the center of the knowledge process" (quoted in Wini Breines 1982: 99–100). Both Breines and James Miller (1987) stress the emerging new left's critique of the role given to the intellectual in modern society. Miller goes even further in this regard, suggesting that this critique, along with the concept of participatory democracy, were the main contributions of the American new left.

10. Environmentalism developed in the early 1960s primarily as a movement within the scientific community, a revolt of generalists critical to the incorporation of science and its uses in the productive system of modern society. For a discussion of environmentalism from this point of view, see Cramer, Eyerman, and Jamison (1987).

11. Despite claims to the contrary the alternative visions competing within the new social movements lend themselves to right and left-wing interpretations: the left-wing critique sees state sponsored institutionalized progress as leading to new totalitarian forms of government, as in the notion of the atom-state; the right wing sees such "progress" as going hand in hand with a general cultural and moral decline. For the latter, institutions like the family and the state have the moral mission to preserve the dignity of the nation and the individual, with public education playing a critical role. The left-wing critique has a very different idea of public education and of the role of the state. There are also traces of a pre-industrial romanticism in the new social movements which reach back to rural-urban, rather than class-based tensions and traditions. Ironically, urban intellectuals have played the classical role in helping articulate these traditions, making them relevant to contemporary conflicts and movements (Eyerman 1983).

Bibliography

Bauman, Zigmunt (1987) *Legislators and Interpreters* (Oxford: Polity Press).

Bell, Daniel (1980) *The Winding Passage* (Cambridge: ABT Books).

Bloom, Allan (1987) *The Closing of the American Mind* (New York: Simon & Schuster).

Branch, Taylor (1988) *Parting the Waters. America in the King Years* (New York: Simon & Schuster).

Breines, Wini (1982) *The Great Refusal. Community and Organization in the New Left: 1962–1968* (New York: Praeger).

Cramer, Jacqueline, Eyerman, Ron, and Jamison, Andrew (1987) "The knowledge interests of the environmental movement and its potential for influencing the development of science," in Stuart Blume *et al.* (eds) *The Social Direction of the Public Sciences. Sociology of the Sciences Yearbook* (Dordrecht: Reidel).

Eyerman, Ron (1981) *False Consciousness and Ideology in Marxist Theory* (Stockholm: Almqvist & Wiksell International).

Eyerman, Ron (1983) "Intellectuals and popular movements," *Praxis International*, 3 (2): 185–98.

Eyerman, Ron (1985) "Rationalizing intellectuals," *Theory and Society*, 14: 777–807.

Eyerman, Ron, and Jamison, Andrew (1990) *Reading Social Movements* (Oxford: Polity Press).

Fiori, Giuseppe (1973) *Antonio Gramsci. Life of a Revolutionary* (New York: Schocken Books).

Gouldner, Alvin (1985) *Against Fragmentation. The Origins of Marxism and the Sociology of Intellectuals* (New York: Oxford University Press).

Gramsci, Antonio (1971) *Selections from the Prison Notebooks* (New York: International Publishers).

Habermas, Jürgen (1962) *Strukturwandel der öffentlichkeit* (Neuwied: Lichterland).

Habermas, Jürgen (1974) "The public sphere: an encyclopedia article,"*New German Critique*, 3: Fall.

Hohendahl, Peter Uwe (1982) *The Institution of Criticism* (Ithaca: Cornell University Press).

Horkheimer, Max (1972) *Critical Theory* (New York: Seabury Press).

Jacoby, Russell (1987) *The Last Intellectuals* (New York: Basic Books).

Lenin, V. I. (1977) *Selected Works. Volume 1* (Moscow: Progress Publishers).

Marx, Karl and Engels, Frederick (1976) *Collected Works. Volume 6, 1845–1848* (Moscow: Progress Publishers).

Michels, Robert (1959 [1911]) *Political Parties* (New York: Dover Books).

Miller, James (1987) *Democracy is in the Streets* (New York: Simon & Schuster).

Niebuhr, Reinhold (1932) *Moral Man and Immoral Society* (New York: Scribner).

Tichi, Cecilia (1987) *Shifting Gears: Technology, Literature, and Culture in Modern America* (Chapel Hill: University of North Carolina Press).

van den Berg, Axel (1988) *The Immanent Utopia* (Princeton: Princeton University Press).

6

Progress in the distribution of power: gender relations and women's movements as a source of change

DIETRICH and MARILYN RUESCHEMEYER

The idea of progress and the problem of this essay

Twentieth-century history – as well as twentieth-century social theory – makes it dubious to try to "read off" positive goal states from the actual record of history. There is little reason to look for long-term developments that led to a better or even an acceptable world with any inherent necessity. At the same time, there is reason to view the historical process as less determined by unchangeable factors and therefore as less predictable than much of nineteenth-century social theory held it to be.

That means that a reasonable discourse about progress may contain again a strong normative component, setting out goal states that are desirable on value principles. At the same time, such discourse about progress should not be utopian in a literal sense of the word: its designs have to be based on arguments about realistic historical possibilities, they have to show that the normative premises are also likely to be accepted as valid in the anticipated future, and they have to identify forces that have a chance of bringing the identified goal state closer to realization.[1]

This is a chapter advocating as well as anticipating progress in the distribution of power. Normatively we claim that less power inequality and more democratic participation are major features of a desirable future. Predictively we claim that changing gender relations will continue to transform all industrial societies and that these processes of eroding male domination and privilege have a good chance of contributing substantially to an extension and a deepening of democracy. This contribution to further democratization is more likely under some contingent conditions and parallel developments than under others.

106

In the following comments, we first consider the desirability and the realism of further democratization. Then we turn to the likelihood of advances in gender equality. The next (and central) tasks are to discuss the effects of increased gender equality on democratic participation and to consider whether greater participation of women is likely to change the quality of politics. Finally we examine some conditions that make the discussed outcomes more or less likely.

The problems of this essay grew out of work on changing gender relations on the one hand, and on power and democracy on the other.[2] In its present form, the essay is not a report on completed research. Rather, it outlines problems and anticipated results, and it does so in woodcut fashion and without carefully developing alternative positions or their critical evaluation. The resultant simplicity may be deceptive, however. Some not very surprising propositions have to be spelled out because they contain important truths; at the same time, the argument as a whole is perhaps not as obvious and uncontroversial as it may appear at first sight.

Progress in democracy: what is desirable, what is possible?

". . . Democracy is not only or even primarily a means through which different groups can attain their ends or seek the good society; it is the good society." This proposition of Seymour Martin Lipset (1963: 439) will appeal to many, but it will mean quite different things to those who agree. And there are others who disagree: at the one end of a continuum of opinion, because they see democracy as an instrument of human freedom that may or may not perform well and that must be rejected if it infringes on individual liberty (e.g., Hayek); at the other end of that spectrum, because it is doubted that democracy can ever approximate in substance what it promises in form – a determination of collective decisions in which all participate as equals – and because it is argued that democracy will inevitably be just a deceptive device protecting objectionable concentrations of private power (the classic Marxist position).

The contrast roughly indicated by these two positions – dividing also the conceptions of democracy embraced without reservation as an end in itself – has a long history in democratic theory (Locke, Madison, Bentham, J. St. Mill, Rousseau, Marx). Radical proposals for democratic participation and political equality were countered by arguments for stable and efficient government, and a primary concern for protecting individual liberty against state intrusion, whether democratic or not. In the twentieth century, empirical democratic theory – initiated by Max Weber and Joseph Schumpeter and developed in American political science and political sociology after the Second World War – gave strong support to the position that rather modest forms of democracy (protecting individual liberties quite

107

effectively, however) were all one could hope for. This was, in fact, the conception of democracy Lipset had in mind when he wrote the words just quoted.

This position of modest skepticism, which supported its prescriptive implications with the authority of empirical social science, accepted a number of features of "really existing democracies" as inevitable in complex industrial societies. A simplified model of this conception can be stated as follows: rather narrow political élites make a few "oligopolistic" offers on the political market among which the many choose in periodic elections. Lack of participation must not be viewed with too much alarm – it serves stability, and for most people politics is not very important anyway. Substantial socioeconomic inequality and its impact on political decision-making are facts of life that must be accepted (aside from marginal change) lest one invites tyranny. If this political order does not come very close to equality in collective decision-making, it does protect rather efficiently individual civil liberties.

This position drew additional support from the experience of twentieth-century totalitarianism. The denaturation of socialism under Lenin and Stalin discredited more radically egalitarian democratic ideals in the eyes of many. And Nazi as well as Salinist rule made individual liberties far more precious than they had ever been before.

Yet the consensus around the position of modest skeptics was shattered in the late 1960s. If the early iconoclasts – like Marcuse, Goodman, or Zinn – were not exactly a match for empirical democratic theorists in rational argument and responsiveness to empirical fact, they did expose the normative component of "empirical" democratic theory. And they were followed by others (including, one might note, a partial convert like Robert Dahl (1956, 1971, 1985, 1989), in addition to C. B. Macpherson (1973, 1977), Carole Pateman (1970, 1983), or Nicos Poulantzas (1980)) – others who made far more sophisticated and complex arguments about the possibilities of advances in democratization. The question of the quality of democracy in the future has been reopened.[3]

What are the chances of a deepening of democratization, of participatory democracy? We can here only give the briefest sketch of our position, but a few basic points must be made in order to give some substance to our conception of a desirable, as well as possible future.

Radical democracy – in the sense of a roughly equal influence on collective decision-making through the participation of all – is impossible in societies of any complexity. Social and political theorists (not exactly rich in propositions that are both powerful and commonly accepted) virtually agree on a number of propositions that spell out the obstacles. Since they are well known, a few reminders will suffice. The most important theorems concern the exclusionary role of expertise and systematic administration, the difficulty of the many to come to collective goals and co-ordinated collective action, the oligarchic tendencies that emerge once collective organization is achieved, the likelihood that oligarchic élites of weaker groups are co-opted by the agents of more resourceful and powerful ones, and finally the fact that many people have little interest in a participation that shapes in a more or less infinitesimal way larger collective decisions (even if these decisions affect the structural conditions of their lives).

It is of course these propositions that underlie the position of skepticism regarding more than very modest progress toward more democratic forms of social and political life. Yet such a conclusion overlooks the considerable variability of the phenomena invoked. State and other administrative machineries do not all have the same degree of autonomy. The relations between experts and citizens are by no means uniform, varying for instance with the level of general education and with political splits among the experts. Even very large and socially weak groups did achieve collective organization. Not all organizations have stable oligarchies. There is great variation in patterns of co-optation. And the interest in participation in public life also varies with resources, chances of success, and the urgency of need. In short, all of the problematic outcomes are *variable and contingent outcomes*, contingent on conditions as yet only partially understood.

The different outcomes seem interdependent. Thus low levels of public participation correlate more or less closely with a lesser sense of efficacy as well as with lower socioeconomic status and in particular with low levels of education.[4] Greater participation could make democracy more "real" in a number of ways. First, it could reduce oligarchic tendencies at least at the base of interest organizations and parties. Second, an increased capacity and willingness to shape one's own life through active participation would transform authority relations in a variety of institutions and social contexts – especially in family and neighborhood and at work, but also in schools, in various voluntary associations, and in religious organizations. Success in participating in these different social arenas would reinforce participation in politics and vice versa. Third, successful participation entails the learning of social and political skills as well as the acquisition of a lay capacity to judge the advice and the work of experts. This has powerful potential consequences for an increased control of administrators and experts in interest organizations, parties, and state institutions.

Such changes may not usher in the good society in any comprehensive sense. But they would constitute progress, however partial and incomplete. This for three reasons. First, a spreading commitment to active participation beyond the sphere of immediate self-interest would improve the quality of public life. Since it would create new "habits of the heart" (Bellah *et al.* 1985), it would make possible common undertakings that now all too easily fall victim to the pervasive appeal of "free riding." Second, active participation in matters that concern one's own life is a value in itself and thus a basis of self-respect. The changes in question would make such participation more meaningful and effective at the grass roots level but also, if to a lesser extent, at more distant levels of collective decision making. Third (and only third), such changes would increase (if only somewhat increase) the chances of the many to pursue their interests effectively with political means.

From where should the impulse for such increased participation come? Why should we expect that under certain conditions participation will make more sense, thus become more widespread, and then engender at least some of the democratizing consequences indicated? It is possible but unlikely that those in power have reason to promote an expansion of effective participation. Gorbachev's policies illustrate the underlying mechanism: a minimum of autonomous participation is necessary in order to maintain the efficient management of even a highly centralized political economy.[5] Still, beyond rather circumscribed limits, those in power will hardly contribute to real advances in democratization.

One might plausibly hypothesize that the vast expansion of leisure time in industrial societies over the last two generations would generate a greater readiness for active participation in public life. But whatever the potential of more free time as a supporting condition, it has not as yet been associated with notable developments towards democratization. Graeme Duncan (1983: 202) seems right when he notes that "the rivers which feed contemporary liberationist thought, which challenges deeply entrenched interests and practices, appear to flow less towards a fuller democracy than towards a hedonistic utopia of leisure and indulgence."

Responses to the threats of technological advance – the peace movements and the ecology movements – have a better claim to having contributed to active democratic participation and to innovations in the form of democracy. At present it is hard to judge whether these movements are born of temporary fear, destined to decline when their themes are absorbed into regular political channels, or whether technological developments will persistently run ahead of the steering capacity of regular governmental institutions and thus continue to foster such movements.

It is our claim in this chapter that the drawn-out process in which gender relations are being transformed in the direction of equality constitutes a quite likely source of substantial advances toward participatory democracy (in the sense skeched above). We turn first to a brief characterization of the basic causes underlying the slow advance toward gender equality.

Gender equality: underlying factors and long-term chances

However one wants to date the beginning of the process of women's emancipation, it has been in motion for a good deal more than a century. And it is far from having spent its force. It has been – and it is likely to be – accompanied by feminist movements; though these push the process forward, they are at the same time symptoms of the underlying forces eroding gender inequality. These underlying factors are of lasting importance and they make for a secular trend of change that may be slowed, interrupted, and even temporarily reversed, but that in the long run is likely to continue ineluctably until a rough equality (or at least a much lower level of inequality) between men and women is reached.

It is possible to imagine different outcomes of this process, but past work on differentiation and inequality suggests that a rough equality has stable structural foundations only if the gender division of labor is radically reduced. This means that women's emancipation points to a social order fundamentally different from all known social orders. It not only entails radical changes in the positions of women and men. It also means that the most central institutions of the social order have to be reshaped – the institutions of government and religion and, above all, the institutions of family and work, the two arenas in which people spend most of their everyday life. In its most elementary aspect, radically reducing the gender division of labor means that men and women will have a roughly equal involvement in family affairs and domestic work and in occupational work outside the house.

The secular process of eroding gender inequality rests on a number of underlying developments that – for the first time in human history – may come close to eliminating the basic structural causes of male domination and an unequal gender division of labor.[6] We list in particular five such factors:

(1) The decline in the number of pregnancies and desired children frees women for other life tasks.

(2) The role of family and kinship – and therefore of gender relations – as a construction module in social organization of every kind has been radically reduced in modern industrial societies and replaced by relations based on voluntary agreement and legal guarantees.[7]

(3) Changes in the nature of work have reduced or eliminated the premium on overwhelming body strength and on the use of violence, the dimensions in which men – on average – have an advantage over women.

(4) Cultural changes in the west (individualism, liberalism, egalitarianism) have made ascriptive disadvantages of any kind profoundly problematic. These ideas have spread successfully into other cultures

111

and activate everywhere the readiness of the disadvantaged to embrace the promise of equality.[8]

(5) Increases in productivity in the industrially advanced countries lift the standard of living – in principle for all – beyond the minimum for survival. This can compensate for – temporary or permanent – productivity losses should the reduction (and ultimately the virtual elimination) of the division of labor by gender entail such disadvantages.

The elimination of male domination and privilege encounters very powerful obstacles. This is, first, a correlate of the fact that no previous society has existed without a gender division of labor as a major structural feature. The absence of any historical precedent for social life without a gender division of labor makes experimentation necessary, and much of that experimentation is likely to be unsuccessful. Furthermore, deep-seated and change-resistant ideas and values surrounding gender-roles (as well as the sheer contrast of gender roles independent of content) are shared by both women and men. They profoundly shape personality formation, the legitimation of established institutions, and even the paths of behavioral and institutional innovation.

Finally there are, last but not least, powerful vested interests defending the status quo, in particular the very strong interests in reproducing positions of domination and regulating access to them. These exist in the family, in work organizations, in associational life, in religion, and in political and state systems of rule. Even where these vested interests are not directly and consciously antagonistic to new chances for women, they often in effect turn antagonistic because rearrangements favoring women disrupt the established order and may at least temporarily interfere with established institutional goals – be they economic, social, political, or religious.

These adverse conditions explain why social change toward gender equality is such a slow and protracted process. In fact, in advanced capitalist economies recent progress in reducing the gender division of waged labor, in improving the relative earning power of women, and in engaging men in household and family activities is so limited that some observers will dismiss our anticipations about the future as hollow optimism.

It is of course true that one can stipulate assumptions about the relative weight and the interaction of different strands of social change that lead to conclusions contrary at least to the strong version of our proposition – that in the long run gender division of labor will virtually disappear and gender equality will be closely approximated. In particular, it seems possible that important elements of gender difference will remain salient features of social life and that such differences in gender roles will be affirmed by both men and women even if that retention of gender

112

difference lends some support to old forms of gender inequality and interfere with egalitarian developments.[9] However, we submit that current levels of gender inequality will be very hard to stabilize in the long run and, furthermore, that compromises between demands for equality and an appreciation of gender difference will be stable only after profound change in the character of gender roles and in the level of inequality.

Women's participation in public life and progress in democracy

Has woman the same rights in the state which man has? This question may appear ridiculous to many. For if the only ground of all legal rights is reason and freedom, how can a distinction exist between two sexes which possess both the same reason and the same freedom? Nevertheless, it seems that, so long as men have lived, this has been differently held, and the female sex seems not to have been placed on a par with the male sex in the exercise of its rights. Such a universal sentiment must have a ground, to discover which was never a more urgent problem than in our days (quoted in Pateman 1983).

Carole Pateman considers these words of J. G. Fichte typical of the prevailing approach to the position of women since "the time, three hundred years ago, when the individualist social contract theorists launched the first critical attack on patriarchalism" (ibid.: 206). Clearly this is not the case any more. The principle of equal rights is generally accepted except in the most traditional countries. Yet this is a recent development.

Voting rights stood at the center of the early women's movement. Only in the twentieth century (in Switzerland as late as 1970), did women nearly everywhere gain suffrage rights equal to men. But the formal right to participate stands in stark contrast to continued underrepresentation of women in positions of political power. Less than 10 percent of the members of national parliaments in the United Kingdom and the United States are women, while in Sweden, one of the most progressive countries for women's issues, the proportion is a little more than a quarter. Generally, the proportion of women is – in the east and the west – lower the higher one moves up in the hierarchies of state and politics.[10]

The causes of this state of affairs are largely found in the gender division of labor outside of politics, though sex discrimination in the political sphere also plays a role. First, the central life activities of many women are still confined to family and domestic work. This often has disabling consequences for their interest in politics as well as for the development of skills that make political participation effective. Since the Second World War, however, we can observe in all advanced countries a steady increase in the labor force participation of women as well as in their level of education.

113

Second, many women who do work outside the house find themselves carrying most of the burden of housework as well. This not only limits their career commitment, but also makes it very unlikely that they will actively engage in politics. The dual burden of job and housework is not merely the result of cultural lag, though that is a factor, too (M. Rueschemeyer 1981). A thorough-going change requires – in addition to adequate childcare facilities and similar public aid – that men get equally involved in domestic work and family affairs. This would be a major change in gender roles. It would not only involve a transformation of life plans and gender identities, but it also requires radical changes in the employment systems of economy and state.

An alternative to an equal sharing of occupational and familial responsibilities is the delayed entry into one's career – usually the woman's career. That entails substantial disadvantages in later advancement and in the possible conversion of occupational experience and success into political assets.

Partly due to these conditions rooted in the linkage between family and work and partly due to the strong reproduction tendencies of occupational and economic power structures, women end up more often in less powerful occupational positions than men. The same holds for those positions that have more or less close links to politics and therefore in a particular way make political participation easier – such as positions in unions as well as civic, religious, and other voluntary associations.

These problems must not only be seen as individual issues. They acquire their greatest significance on the aggregate political level. There is little doubt that women will not attain a substantial share of political power unless they gain a substantial share of economic power.

It is conceivable – especially if one focuses only on individual life plans and decisions – that women's emancipation could leave politics virtually untouched and primarily play itself out in the arenas of work and family. That is, however, extremely unlikely, because in all modern societies the state has become a – if not the – main agent of deliberate social change. Persistent politicization of women's issues is likely precisely because the emancipation process encounters so many obstacles. The repetitive and manifestly structural character of individual difficulties systematically converts private problems into public, political issues. Therefore, while women's movements in different countries and time periods may run different courses and take on different political colorations, they will not turn away from politics. And in continuous political systems they are likely to crystalize stable political orientations that are progressive in terms of women's causes.[11]

How will all this advance the cause of democratization? To begin with the most elementary target of transformation, approaching real equality in the gender roles in marriage and the family must, in itself, be considered an advance of democracy broadly conceived.

Such equality in the family is not possible without a transformation of work roles. The greater frictions between family obligations and the occupational employment system, which arise from the participation of virtually all adults in the labor force, will engender pressures for change in occupational roles and work organization. It is possible, and even likely, that this will come about only with powerful pressure from employees and that – wherever such pressure is exerted – it will also strengthen industrial democracy.

Advances in the direction of gender equality in family and work that do not leave women with vastly increased task burdens will enable women to participate more in political life. For these developments will increasingly give them the time as well as the abilities and the social power necessary for equal participation in various interest organizations as well as in politics proper. Whether such participation is also attractive and meaningful to them depends on other features of state and politics as well. Yet wherever continued gender inequality is a persistent concern of women, it will create strong incentives for political participation. Women's political participation, then, is likely to be strongest where change in gender relations has removed some of the obstacles to participation but has not eliminated major features of gender inequality and strong feelings of injustice.

Increasing social and political participation of women is in itself a significant advance of democratization. In addition, the influx of new people, new concerns, and new styles is likely to make encrusted organizations and institutions more open, flexible, and responsive, and to engender experimentation with new institutional and political forms (such as extraparliamentary citizens' initiatives or class actions in court, to cite only two examples of the recent past).

Democratizing transformations of the mechanisms of politics – of tendencies toward oligarchy in associations and parties, of administrative decision-making being exempt from democratic guidance and control, of deference toward an expertise that is never impartial toward contending interests – transformations of these mechanisms are not necessarily associated with increased political participation of women. Whether they are, depends to a large extent on the particular constellations of emancipatory demand and resistance as well as on other, not directly related developments. However, the increased participation of women in politics does seem to make such democratizing transformations more likely, especially at the grass-roots base of politics.

Women's participation and the quality of politics

Will increased participation of women make a difference in politics? Once the 40 percent women's quota for all offices in the German Social democratic party is voted in, argued Heidemarie Wieczorek-Zeul, one of the woman leaders of the SPD, "it won't be the same party, comrades. You will notice that." The style of work and interaction would change, and the "endless speeches of some men" would soon be a thing of the past, once a certain number of women is involved (*Der Spiegel*, June 20, 1988: 40).

There is likely to be more than a change in style. This prediction is quite safe for the protracted periods of transition. One can show now that women have political concerns that are distinctive from those of men. They center around problems with which at the moment women are more concerned than men – school and children's problems, drugs, and the friction points between work and family obligations – as well as around such issues as peace and environmental concerns (Lee 1976, Skard 1983). That women's current concerns – held distinctively now even under the hegemony of male politics – would gain more prominence with greater political participation of women is very likely indeed. It is the substantive reason why one must judge the sheer fact of an increased participation of women significant progress in democratization.

Whether there will be differences in the nature of politics in the long-term future that can be attributed to the fuller participation of women is a far more speculative question. It may well be that women have universally a lesser inclination toward violence and aggression than men (Sanday 1981). A plausible explanation of this phenomenon – assuming it were well established – could be derived from women's universal role in the nurturance of children. We are inclined to adopt this position.

On these assumptions what would be the consequence of new patterns in which women and men equally share familial and domestic tasks as well as occupational work? The conservative answer invokes the potential losses that may derive from the changes in the (middle-class) roles of housewife and mother. It would make good theoretical sense to expect on the contrary that the roles and orientations of men would be far more significantly transformed through the adoption of nurturing responsibilities. This could have subtle but far-reaching consequences for the treatment of conflict and the display of aggression in politics.

However, it seems wise to break our speculations off at this point. To anticipate with any plausibility changes in the quality of political life due to changed gender relations and increased participation of women is far more hazardous than to develop reasonable scenarios for a reduction in gender inequality, increased political participation of women, and a deepening of the democratic character of political life.

Modifying conditions and parallel developments

The consideration of other developments and of their impact on the process of woman's emancipation and its potential/likely democratizing consequences opens an impossibly wide field of questions and problems. That means, among other things, that all of the above must not be understood as a prediction of the future, which inevitably would require the determination of all significant interaction effects as well as a prediction of all the possible modifying developments and their contingent conditions. Our argument rather must be understood as the explication of one plausible strand of future developments.

Yet interactions with various other developments that have in turn their own contingent conditions are of special interest for the particular approach we have taken, because we might find here especially clear illustrations of opportunities for historical choice.

A rather simple example concerns the increase in leisure time. Only two or three generations ago, a limited work-day and secure vacations were an upper-class privilege. The tremendous increase in free time clearly could aid the developments envisioned. It eases the transformation of gender roles as well as greater political participation if other conditions foster such developments. Yet this positive contribution is radically curtailed by present trends in the west, where the most qualified professions experience very little release from work and its time pressures while the least qualified 10 to 20 percent are periodically forced into unemployment. Any policy measures that would equalize somewhat the burdens and the attractions and rewards of work would also make a positive contribution to women's emancipation because they would improve the conditions for the transformation of gender roles.

Much more complicated issues are raised by environmental concerns and the call for steady-state economies. Among many other requirements, the latter goal would presuppose a transformation of the systems of inequality, because continuous growth serves at present as one of the major mechanisms preserving social peace (it is easier to lose in comparison to others when one still gains in absolute terms). Reduced social inequality and a no-growth economy may be very desirable, but they are perhaps even more difficult to approximate than the transformation of gender relations and the attendant deepening of democracy sketched earlier. Still, it may be worth pointing out that these different goal states would not only be quite compatible with each other, but actually increase each other's chances of realization – a quite remarkable constellation, since so often different desirable goal states are at odds with each other so that their realization involves difficult choices.[12]

Conclusion: changing gender relations and democratization

Our argument can be restated in a nutshell. We anticipate as a plausible and desirable long-term development that open political systems will

117

experience a deepening of democracy that is due to changes in gender relations and the activities of feminist movements. Modern societies lack the structural foundations of gender inequality that have characterized all previous forms of social life. At the same time, change in gender relations encounters powerful obstacles. It is this tension that has repeatedly given rise to women's movements, and it will continue to do so in the future. Any success in transforming gender relations in the family and at work can be considered a deepening of democracy in the broad conception of that term. Such advances would also enable women to participate more frequently and more effectively in various interest associations and parties as well as in political decision making proper. While this influx of new participants and interests may make the working of political organizations more responsive and less oligarchic, the very attainment of a rough equality in political participation between men and women must be considered a major advance in democratization.

Acknowledgments

We wish to thank Jesse Biddle, MariJo Buhle and Ellen Douglas for helpful comments. The Institute of Advanced Study, Berlin provided ideal conditions for our work and we are very grateful for that.

Notes

1. There are other problems involved in such discourse about progress that will not be treated here. We may mention just one complex of issues. Long-term change is not very likely to result from the intentional action of some organized groups. Even where it is substantially affected by intentional collective action, the outcome may not be intended by any one collective actor. Unintended consequences are much more likely. What, then, is the role of normative discourse about the future? In the best of circumstances it may – in conjunction with empirically oriented theories and anticipations – somewhat improve some of the intentional actions. More important, it may help shape value orientations that transcend narrow sets of collective actors as well as short historical time spans. Nevertheless, these considerations suggest that the value of theorizing about progress may be quite limited even with a rehabilitation of normative designs.

   Our position sketched in the text is based on Rueschemeyer (1986) as well as Giddens (1981, 1985).
2. Marilyn Rueschemeyer's work on marriage, work and community participation in the German Democratic Republic (Rueschemeyer 1981, 1982, 1988) was especially important even though East German political life does not come close to our conception of democracy. Dietrich Rueschemeyer is working with Evelyne and John Stephens on a comparative analysis of the conditions of democracy (Rueschemeyer, Stephens, and Stephens forthcoming).

3. See Held (1987) for a careful review of classic and contemporary conceptions of democracy.

4. Education has a number of relevant effects. It may not only increase one's status, earning power, and influence but also widen horizons beyond the realm of personal interaction and enlighten about the structural conditions of one's more immediate experience.

5. For discussions of the complex interrelations of participation, grass roots influence, and central control in the more circumscribed arenas of workplace and residential area in a state socialist society see M. Rueschemeyer (1982, 1988).

6. We acknowledge that there is disagreement on what constitutes gender equality and consequently on whether gender equality existed in any earlier circumstances (see, e.g., Rosaldo 1974 and Sanday 1981). The discussion of the causes of male domination and the gender division of labor has been conducted primarily by anthropologists. While it is in a narrowly specific sense inconclusive, there is a convergence on a range of relevant factors. For overviews and substantive contributions see Rosaldo (1974), Rosaldo and Lamphere (1974), Hartmann (1976), Sanday (1981). Hartmann (1976) and Boeserup (1970) offer important historical analyses of the impact of capitalist industrialization in England and economic development in Third World countries, respectively.

7. Here, in the importance of family and the exchange of women for the construction of society, lies for C. Lévi-Strauss the point of origin for the gender division of labor and male domination.

8. Sanday (1981), turning away from an earlier materialist position, emphasizes the ideological foundations of a culture as a condition for modifying the impact of other factors shaping gender relations. While there is little doubt that patriarchal traits dominate in the Judaeo-Christian tradition, this tradition has drawn its vitality from the fact that it was able to embrace and accommodate also the opposites of its main themes and to shift the weight given to certain values with changing conditions. The values of European modernity have deep roots in this tradition, but also represent a major redefinition of Judaeo-Christian culture – so much so that some would prefer to think of them as post-Christian.

9. Karen Offen (1988) has argued persuasively for the strength of what she calls "relational" in contrast to "individualist" feminism in the continental European women's movements of the nineteenth and early twentieth centuries. She also argues that relational feminism, which accepts greater gender difference and emphasizes familial and other social responsibilities, would appeal to many women who today take their distance from current, more strongly "individualist" forms of feminism.

10. See, e.g., Epstein and Coser (1980), Lee (1976), Meyer (1986), Skard (1983), and Stacey and Price (1981). Lee (1976) reports one very revealing study in Westchester County, New York, on "why few women hold public office." Beckwith (1986) found in the United States few differences between men and women in voting and other non-élite forms of political participation; but women showed a consistently lower sense of political efficacy. Useful reviews of how women's participation is treated in political studies are given by Evans (1980), Goot and Reid (1975), and Wally (1988).

11. The politics of women's issues took a very different course in the industrialized west and the state socialist east. In Eastern Europe state policy strongly encouraged women's participation in the labor force and developed a series of important support measures including a system of childcare, a paid

baby year with guaranteed return to one's job and other measures. This has led especially in the younger generation to far reaching changes in gender relations. At the same time, women's movements are tiny if they exist at all, and the official women's organizations are weaker than other mass organizations. The industrialized west has seen since the late 1960s a resurgence of women's movement. It was this development that has succeeded in securing a series of favorable political and judicial decisions, and it probably accelerated the increase in the labor force participation of women. The public policy measures supporting women are, however, considerably weaker than those in Eastern Europe.

This difference between a state-induced development and one in which the yeast of a grass-roots movement (if largely a middle and upper middle-class movement) played a central role, raises interesting comparative questions about fundamental aspects of the long-term emancipation process.

12. This compatibility is not accidental. Reduced social inequality is a common feature of the goal states of environmentalism, women's emancipation, and participatory democracy. C. B. Macpherson (1977) argues that a transformation of politics towards participatory democracy (which he defines in more demanding terms than we did) depends on two prerequisites. "One is a change in people's consciousness (or unconsciousness), from seeing themselves and acting as essentially consumers to seeing themselves and acting as exerters and enjoyers of the exertion and development of their own capacities." "The other prerequisite is a great reduction of the present social and economic inequality, since that inequality, as I have argued, requires a non-participatory party system to hold society together" (Macpherson, 1977: 99, 100).

Bibliography

Beckwith, Karen (1986) *American Women and Political Participation: The Impacts of Work, Generation, and Feminism* (New York: Greenwood Press).

Bellah, Robert N., Madsen, Richard, Sullivan, William M., Swidler, Ann, and Tipton, Steven M. (1985) *Habits of the Heart. Individualism and Commitment in American Life* (Berkeley: University of California Press).

Boeserup, Ester (1970) *Woman's Role in Economic Development* (London: Allen & Unwin).

Dahl, Robert A. (1956) *A Preface to Democratic Theory* (Chicago: University of Chicago Press).

Dahl, Robert (1971) *Polyarchy: Participation and Opposition* (New Haven: Yale University Press).

Dahl, Robert (1985) *A Preface to Economic Democracy* (Cambridge: Polity Press).

Dahl, Robert (1989) *Democracy and Its Critics* (New Haven: Yale University Press).

Duncan, Graeme (1983) "Human nature and radical democratic theory," in G. Duncan (ed.) *Democratic Theory and Practice* (Cambridge: Cambridge University Press, 187–203).

Epstein, Cynthia F., and Coser, Rose L. (eds) (1980) *Women and Power. Cross-National Studies of Women and Elites* (London: Allen & Unwin).

Evans, Judith (1980) "Attitudes to women in American political science," *Government and Opposition*, 15 (1): 101–14.

Giddens, Anthony (1981) *A Contemporary Critique of Historical Materialism* (London: Macmillan).

Giddens, Anthony (1985) *The Nation-State and Violence* (Berkeley: University of California Press).

Goot, Murray, and Reid, Elizabeth (1975) *Women and Voting Studies: Mindless Matrons or Sexist Scientism?*, Sage Professional Papers in Contemporary Political Sociology, 1 (Beverley Hills, CA: Sage).

Hartmann, Heidi (1976) "Capitalism, patriarchy, and job segregation by sex," *Signs* 1, 3 (2): 137–69.

Held, David (1987) *Models of Democracy* (Cambridge: Polity Press, and Standford: Stanford University Press).

Lee, Marcia Manning (1976) "Why few women hold public office: democracy and sexual roles," *Political Science Quarterly* 91: 297–314.

Lipset, Seymour Martin (1959) *Political Man* (New York: Doubleday).

Macpherson, C. B. (1973) *Democratic Theory: Essays in Retrieval* (Oxford: Clarendon Press).

Macpherson, C. B. (1977) *The Life and Times of Liberal Democracy* (Oxford: Oxford University Press).

Meyer, Gerd (1986) "Frauen in den Machthierarchien der DDR," *Deutschland-archiv*, 3: 294–311.

Mill, John Stuart, and Mill, Harriet Taylor (1970) *Essays on Sex Equality*, edited and with an Introductory Essay by Alice S. Rossi (Chicago: University of Chicago Press).

Offen, Karen (1988) "Defining feminism: a comparative historical approach," *Signs* 14 (11): 119–57.

Pateman, Carole (1970) *Participation and Democratic Theory* (Cambridge: Cambridge University Press).

Pateman, Carole (1983) "Feminism and democracy," in Graeme Duncan (ed.) *Democratic Theory and Practice* (Cambridge: Cambridge University Press, 204–17).

Poulantzas, Nicos (1980) *State, Power, Socialism* (London: Verso/New Left Books).

Rosaldo, Michelle Z. (1974) "Woman, culture, and society: a theoretical overview," in M. Z. Rosaldo and L. Lamphere (eds) *Woman, Culture, and Society* (Stanford: Stanford University Press).

Rosaldo, Michelle Z., and Lamphere, Louise (eds) (1974) *Woman, Culture, and Society* (Stanford: Stanford University Press).

Rueschemeyer, Dietrich (1986) *Power and the Division of Labour* (Cambridge: Polity Press, and Stanford: Stanford University Press).

Rueschemeyer, Dietrich, Stephens, Evelyne Huber, and Stephens, John (forthcoming) *Capitalist Development and Democracy* (Cambridge: Polity Press).

Rueschemeyer, Marilyn (1981) *Professional Work and Marriage: An East-West Comparison* (London: Macmillan, and New York: St. Martin's Press).

Rueschemeyer, Marilyn (1982) "The work collective: response and adaptation in the structure of work in the German Democratic Republic," *Dialectical Anthropology*, 7: 155–63.

Rueschemeyer, Marilyn (1988) "Participation and control in a state socialist society: the German Democratic Republic," University Center for European Studies Working Paper 17.

Sanday, Peggy Reeves (1981) *Female Power and Male Dominance* (Cambridge: Cambridge University Press).

Schumpeter, Joseph (1942) *Capitalism, Socialism and Democracy* (New York: Harper & Row).

Skard, Torild (1983) "Women in political life in the Nordic countries," *International Social Science Journal* 35: 639–57.

Stacey, Margaret, and Price, Marion (1981) *Women, Power, and Politics* (London: Tavistock).

Wally, Sylvia (1988) "Gender politics and social theory," *Sociology*, 22 (2): 215–32.

Weber, Max (1958 [1919]) "Politics as a Vocation," in *From Max Weber*, edited by H. H. Gerth and C. W. Mills (New York: Galaxy Books, 77–128).

Weber, Max (1978 [1922]) *Economy and Society* (Berkeley: University of California Press).

7

The end of western trade unionism?: social progress after the age of progressivism

DAVID KETTLER and VOLKER MEJA

Contemporary sociological theory, like contemporary politics, is marked by the somewhat paradoxical conviction that progressivism is out of date. Social change cannot be denied as a reality, but its coherent, cumulative, developmental character is frequently called into doubt. No cause, moreover, can plausibly justify itself today simply by claiming to be "in the line of social development." The paradox involved in social or political analyses which conclude, in effect, that it is no longer progressive to be progressive points to a needless confusion. First, then, it is perfectly possible and often valuable to retain an analytical concept of social progress in order to maintain critical contact with the sophisticated tradition of social theory that emphasizes the importance of irreversible experiential learning in the development of vital congeries of social relations over time (Luhmann 1981, 1984). This conception need not assume that all social phenomena can be referred to as social progress or that disruptions and radical discontinuities cannot occur, because it need not imply that social progress is the only subject matter for social theory. And it certainly does not commit the analyst to a normative progressivism, the second context in which progress is a key term. The abandonment of progress as a criterion for evaluating social achievements and projects does not, however, imply the rejection of everything done earlier and justified in the name of progress, but only their reanalysis and reassessment. Because political life does not necessarily benefit from nominalist clean sweeps, it may even be justifiable to continue referring to such achievements and projects as "progressive," so long as it is made unmistakably clear that the progress here intended is a project, political in the broad sense, and not a process in the sense of the analytical concept.[1]

This essay is about trade unions, an institution that arose to play an important part in relation to the social progress characterizing much of the present century and that served as an important reference point for several varieties of normative progressivism. The past two decades of social progress in the most prosperous established nations appear to be rendering the institution obsolete. The objective of the essay is to reject all progressivist interpretations of this trend – neither condemning the development as a regressive obstacle to progress nor welcoming it as a normal part of the developmental process. The aim is to inquire anew into the historical project of trade unions and the interplay between this project and the processes of social progress, past and prospective. The analytical thesis is that the institution has been multi-dimensional, serving in one of its dimensions as an important political response to social progress. The normative problem is whether the unions' political contribution to a socially conscious political democratization can be revived or transferred, when the unions' constitutive adaptations to past stages of social progress appear to be failing so badly in the present.

After a brief overview designed to show that analytical awareness of social progress has been historically linked to critical politically-minded theoretical currents as well as to progressivist theories, and that it has been the ideology-process that has tended to smudge this distinction, we briefly outline three alternative progressivist approaches to unionism. Next comes a review of the contemporary state of the problem and a proposal for an analytical approach that avoids the holistic errors of progressivist analyses and lets the political issues be properly posed. In this approach, unions are situated in the context of labor regimes, an historical concept that highlights the dual character of unions, between social progress and political constitution. The contemporary decline of unions is then analyzed in relation to both levels of analysis. The political dimension poses questions of strategy for unions, and the chapter closes with a critical assessment of strategic alternatives generated by the progressivist alternatives. The conclusion is skeptical and political rather than programmatic, but that illustrates the social-theoretical point of the exercise. The demise of progressivism does not automatically condemn either its contributions to social theoretical analyses of social progress or its political projects.

Progress and politics

The perception of social progress enters into Enlightenment thought in the context of political theory, before the emergence of social theory as such, and the phenomena intended by the concept are by no means universally or uniformly accepted as unconditional benefits. At this point, social progress is often acknowledged as a reality that challenges the continued timeliness of established political doctrines but that does not necessarily show the way to a satisfactory new alternative. Although Rousseau's paradoxically artful challenge to the progress of the "arts and sciences" in his First Discourse was doubtless an idiosyncratic provocation, his Second Discourse claim that a scientifically-grounded conjectural reconstruction of social development would explain why modern humanity must formulate its political designs without hopes of achieving classical excellence touches a far more common chord (Rousseau 1973).

In his pioneering venture in social theory, Adam Ferguson identifies "progress" as a central feature of the main processes that constitute the history of civil society, but he insists that each stage in this composite progress poses a characteristic complex of difficulties for political action and that these difficulties are more vexing and dangerous at higher stages than at lower. There are doubtless steady improvements in the arts and sciences that put external nature increasingly in the service of humankind, on this view, and there are stadial advances in the civil pacification of human relations, but there are also debilitating distortions in human capacities consequent on these changes, as well as mounting threats to collective capabilities for self-mobilization and action (Ferguson 1966, 1975, Kettler 1965, 1977, 1978). Condorcet's rhapsodic invocation of linear progress as the guarantee of secular salvation is perhaps the more eccentric conception until late in the nineteenth century, not least because of the events that brought his speculations to a violent halt (Condorcet 1955). Fifty years later, de Tocqueville (1987 [1835]) never doubts the social reality of the progressive movement towards equality, but his analysis is dedicated to the search for political strategies to tame and manage this development. As John Stuart Mill's generous borrowings from de Tocqueville (Mill 1977 [1835], 1977 [1840]) show, this complex attitude to social progress cannot simply be equated with conservatism. For an important current in social thought, characterized above all by a thematization of problematic relationships between social and political theory, progress has been as much a part of the problem as it has been the precondition for any possible solutions.

The claim that processes of inevitable social progress have only to be unchained in order to bring rational solutions to all difficulties has figured more clearly in the simplified rhetorical constructs of political ideology than in self-reflective theoretical designs. "Progressivism" more properly pertains to such formations. But even where theories can be said to be premised on an "idea of progress" that is thought to legitimate the direction as well as to uncover the tendencies of social change (Bury 1920, Nisbet 1969, Hayek 1952), in the progressivist manner, they share at least one common preoccupation with the more critical, political current. The perception of social progress poses fundamental questions about organization. Social change brings with it a critical disorganization of established institutions for collective purposive action, most strikingly in government and religion, and it provides both resources and needs for new organization.

Progressivist thinkers like Saint-Simon and Comte stress the organizational resources engendered by progress; critical thinkers like Durkheim and Weber equally stress the sometimes contradictory needs. For the one group, progressive increments of social knowledge among progressively potent social actors generate social diagnoses and organizational engineering technologies to obviate political operations of choice, power, conflict-management, and coercive co-ordination. For the others, the new developments bring new powers and disabilities requiring uncertain reconstitutive organization and political management, in the face of forceful oppositions and difficulties. During the early decades of the twentieth century, the ideologized expressions of the two currents were often allied against hostile and defensive old power structures, but even then the internal tensions within the resulting progressive political movements were often manifest.

Urban progressivism arises as a political tendency at the end of the nineteenth century above all in conjunction with a perception of "the social question." This referred to challenging, irresistibly emerging phenomena of both social disorganization and social organization. The new disorganization was epitomized by threats from dangerous slums and abusive workplaces; the new organization, in turn, by state formation, legal differentiation, reform organization, capitalist concentration, and collective action by workers. Progressives agreed in understanding both complexes as aspects of progressive transition, mandating responses that went beyond the political alternatives thought possible by liberals and conservatives. The social question called for a social answer – from social responsibility, social work, and social legislation to social democracy. And conflictual, interest-generated politics had to be replaced by social science, yielding social technologies, social awareness, and problem-solving social action (Dewey 1935).

Those were the general terms of progressivist discourse, but the range of interpretative and policy responses to the dis/organizational developments hints at the theoretical fault-lines within the progressivist consensus, revealing the movements as being in effect a coalition between a tendency to presuppose progress as holistic process and a tendency to treat it as a project. Numerous issues could be cited to illustrate this point, but none is more central or revealing than the range of responses to the conflicts attending workers' self-organization. Simply stated, the division appears as one between those who view the growth of a new power center as a transitional symptom of a problem to be overcome in the course of social progress, and those who accept it as the beginnings of a new departure in the political constitution of social life. Since coalition-forming ideologies leave a lot of room for ambiguities and coalitional politics strive to blur internally divisive issues, the historical evidence of inner tension is often indirect, articulated in terms of detailed questions of tactics and policies.

But a retrospective view undistracted by the ideological dynamics of self-confident progressivist political campaigning will see the patterned differences in emphasis and will thus be able to weigh the elements of the progressivist project without being deluded by indefensible assumptions about a progressivist process. The contemporary crisis of progressivism makes it easier to see the horizontal division between the two analytical tendencies that had been bound together in political coalition. We think that this development can be especially productively studied at the instance of the debate occasioned by the many signs of decline in trade unionism in the west.

Unions and progress

Even at the level of political ideology, it is of course oversimplified to speak of only one form of progressivism. And the theoretically reflected thought that was adapted by progressivist ideology must certainly be analytically subdivided. We propose a threefold vertical division to complement the principal horizontal division that we have been discussing, conventionally accepting Marx, Weber, and Durkheim as emblems for the three. Each category is distinguished by a characteristic conception of the central dynamics of social progress: (1) class conflict grounded in a depth-structure of lawful economic development, (2) rationalization as a function of cumulative, institutionalized individual acts of transactions, and (3) collective integration of ever greater social differentiation. A systematic treatment would work out the importance of our horizontal divide within each of these theoretical approaches, but our present special interest will lead us to concentrate principally on the progress-as-process side, since this is the side most evident in the most influential subsequent social-scientific theories. The progress of sociology has been largely a matter of disencumbering these theoretical models from their seemingly under-theorized recognitions of discontinuities not readily subsumed under the laws of social progress. This disciplinary progress, most would agree, has now reached an impasse. The difficulties posed for all three traditions by such developments as the abrupt decline of unions open us to a reappropriation of their potentials for comprehending political complexity. We shall attempt to indicate the nature of those difficulties and to illustrate the possibilities for such reappropriation, remaining within the comparatively manageable limits of the theme we have selected. This will quickly move us from the level of grand theory, introduce a measure of problem-specific eclecticism, and consequently leave us with future tasks for theoretical reflection upon our evolving intellectual strategy. Our present objectives do not require us to pretend to more; theoretical reconstruction is a long-term, collective enterprise, and its starting point, we are told, is typically a concern with concrete anomalies.

127

Marx and Engels both began their distinctive theoretical departures with attempts to comprehend collective movements among the working class, including the organization of such movements in trade unions (Marx 1975 [1844]: 189–206, Engels 1975 [1845]: 295–583). But their need to specify the place of trade unions within the broader pattern of social progress gained new urgency with the formation of the First International. In his 1866 "Instructions for the delegates of the Provincial General Council," Marx clearly formulates his conception of the unions' dual role, as essential function of the present state of the social process and as integral to the inherent dynamics of change:

> Trades' Unions originally sprang up from the *spontaneous* attempts of workmen at removing or at least checking that competition [i.e. the unavoidable competition among the workmen], in order to conquer such terms of contract as might raise them at least above the condition of mere slaves. The immediate object of Trades' Unions was therefore confined to everyday necessities, to expediencies for the obstruction of the incessant encroachments of capital, in one word, to questions of wages and time of labour. This activity of the Trades' Unions is not only legitimate, it is necessary. It cannot be dispensed with so long as the present system of production lasts. On the contrary, it must be generalised by the formation and the combination of Trades' Unions throughout all countries. On the other hand, unconsciously to themselves, the Trades' Unions were forming *centres of organisation* of the working class, as the medieval municipalities and communes did for the middle class. If the Trades' Unions are required for the guerilla fights between capital and labour, they are still more important as *organised agencies for superseding the very system of wage labour and capitalist rule*. (Quoted in Lapides 1987: 64)

This remains Marx's theoretical account of unions, carried forward by Engels after Marx's death and by orthodox Marxism.

At a more concrete, practical level, however, Marx and Marxists are plagued by the all but universal tendency of unions to perform the first function at the cost of the hypothesized second. Most Marxist analyses of actual unions, accordingly, follow the pattern also laid down in 1865 by Marx in "Wages, price, and profit" (quoted in Lapides 1987: 95):

> Trades Unions work well as centres of resistance against the encroachments of capital. The fail partially from an unjudicious use of their power. They fail generally from limiting themselves to a guerilla war against the effects of the existing system, instead of simultaneously trying to change it, instead of using their organised forces as a lever for the final emancipation of the working class, that is to say, the ultimate abolition of the wages system.

Marx's consequent injunctions to unions have appeared no less appropriate to Marxists in the present century:

> Apart from their original purposes, they must now learn to act deliberately as organising centres of the working class in the broadest sense of its *complete emancipation*. They must aid every social and political movement tending in that direction. Considering themselves and acting as the champions of the whole working class, they cannot fail to enlist the non-society men into their ranks. They must look carefully after the interests of the worst paid trades, such as the agricultural labourers, rendered powerless by exceptional circumstances. They must convince the world at large that their efforts, far from being narrow and selfish, aim at the emancipation of the downtrodden millions. (Quoted in Lapides 1987: 65)

Equally common in the subsequent history of Marxism, – and fatefully so – are the following sentiments in an 1871 letter by Engels:

> The trade-union movement, above all the big, strong and rich trade unions, has become more an obstacle to the general movement than an instrument of its progress; and outside of the trade unions there are an immense mass of workers in London who have kept quite a distance away from the political movement for several years, and as a result are very ignorant. But on the other hand they are also free of the many traditional prejudices of the trade unions and the other old sects, and therefore form excellent material with which one can work. (Quoted in Lapides 1987: 81)

Marxist progressivism, in short, is distinguished by clear expectations about the important place of unions, as well as by a constant need, at another level, to deal with the disappointment of those expectations. The result has been a rich, complex, and ingenious literature, setting the agenda for most interpretations of the phenomenon. The present question, however, is whether the progressivist theoretical underpinnings must not simply be put aside as mistaken.

While unions do not figure so centrally in the other two types of progressivist thought, they do appear historically as progressive organizations strategically important to the forward movement implied by the emergence of the social question. Weber's German editors place Weber's reflections on the rationalizing contribution of trade unions, specifically in Germany, in the last paragraphs of the text that is published as *Wirtschaft und Gesellschaft* (Weber 1976 [1922]: 868). He is speaking of dangers implicit in the general progressive development towards democracy, especially the possibility that the mass might be driven towards an emotionalist politics of the streets. He sees the decisive counter to this in rational organizations within democracy. Citing institutional parliamentary features in several countries, he concludes that the equivalent function is performed by working-class organizations in Germany, specifically the unions as well as the Social Democratic Party. The corresponding passage in his political essay on "Parliament and government in a reordered Germany," published in May 1918, after the strike wave of January, 1918, predicts that the unions will have a difficult disciplinary task in the immediate postwar period, as they attempt to cope with a "syndicalism of immaturity" which will afflict the adolescents who had been drawn into the production process by wartime conditions and had become accustomed to unparalleled wages and bargaining power. In that context, he implicitly specifies the kind of extra-political organizational contribution that unions make: the young, war-recruited workers will not have been educated to "any feelings of solidarity and any sort of usefulness for and adaptability to an orderly economic struggle" (Weber 1958 [1921]: 392). For Weber, unions appear economically as interest-generated class formations under certain conditions of competition in the labor market, in the context of the basic power asymmetries involved in the labor contract. Workers under capitalism share the experience of being systematically disadvantaged in the employment contract, due to the power disparities between themselves and their employers, both at the time of contracting and in the conditions of dependent work, and they may well unite for collective bargaining where their individual market positions do not open preferable ways of serving their individual interests. Subsequent analyses of unions in the Weberian tradition have tended to generalize further on the place of unions in the political as well as economic rationalization process, in line with the general systematizing of his more historically differentiated (horizontally unintegrated) thinking. Unions came to appear central to the progressive integration of the working class into a procedurally rational pluralistic process of political interest adjustment (Bendix 1976, Schumpeter 1976), and to the rational ordering of both internal and external labor markets (Dunlop and Galenson 1978). Like Marx, Weber himself feared that actual working-class organizations – parties perhaps more than unions – were in fact constantly prone to pursuing developmentally irrational policies. He worried especially about their inclinations towards legislative challenges to the formal rationality of law, their weakness for substantively rational renderings of the law of contract, in the vain hope of using law to provide "fair" wages or guarantee against exploitation of superior bargaining power. These misgivings merge with his general distrust of socialism as a political movement.

They also point to the fundamental contrast between the Weberian and the Durkheimian currents in progressivist thinking about the significance of unions in the course of social development. For the latter tendency, the emergence of coalitions among employers and employees and the conflictual relations between them presage new corporate institutions regulating their collective interrelationships and having as their eventual legal expression a supercession of consensual contracts (and the morally objectionable property system corresponding to them) by "just contracts" wherein "the sole economic inequalities dividing men are those resulting from the inequality of their services" (Durkheim 1957 [1950]: 214f.). On unions in the evolutionary process, Durkheim writes in *The Division of Labour*:

> The only groups which have a certain permanence today are the unions, composed of either employers or workmen. Certainly there is here the beginning of occupational organisation, but still quite formless and rudimentary. For, first, a union is a private association, without legal authority, and consequently without any regulatory power. Moreover, the number of unions is theoretically limitless, even within the same industrial category; and as each of them is independent of the others, if they do not federate or unify there is nothing intrinsic in them expressing the unity of the occupation in its entirety. Finally, not only are the employers' unions and the employees' unions distinct from each other, which is *legitimate and necessary*, but there is no regular contact between them. There exists no common organisation which brings them together, where they can develop common forms of regulation which will determine the relationships between them in an authoritative fashion, without either of them losing their own autonomy. Consequently, it is always the rule of the strongest which settles conflict, and the state of war is continuous. Save for those of their actions which are governed by common moral codes, employers and workers are, in relation to each other, in the same situation as two autonomous states, but of unequal power. They can form contracts, as nations do through the medium of their governments, but these contracts express only the respective state of their military forces. They sanction it as a condition of reality; they cannot make it legally valid. In order to establish occupational morality and law in the different economic occupations, the corporation, instead of remaining a diffuse, disorganised aggregate, must become – or rather, must again become – a defined, organised group; in a word, a public institution. (Durkheim 1972: 186–7)

Durkheim, like Weber, rejects revolutionary theories of socialism. But he is quite content to accept the concept as a projection of the next step of social development: "It is a question, in the end, of knowing whether socialism is miraculous, as it imagines, whether it is contrary to the nature of our societies, or whether it accords with their own natural evolution, so that it does not have to destroy them in order to establish itself. It is to this latter view that history seems to me to point" (Durkheim 1958 [1928]).[2] The subsequent Durkheimian tendency of progressivist thinking was more uncertain about the socialist label, given its widespread political identification with Marxism, and it gave a more subtle sense to the way in which relations between coalitions of employers and employees were progressively becoming "public institutions," with the development of conceptions of collective bargaining labor regimes and neo-corporatist intermediations. But it retains the strong emphasis on the profoundly integrative functions of unions and their central bearing upon the ethical quality of social relations, as well as an almost Aristotelian sense of the causal interlinkage between these two dimensions (Selznick 1969).

The Marxist, Weberian-rationalist, and Durkheimian-integrationist theoretical tendencies have been mingled and meshed and refined in various ways during the twentieth century, of course, but they variously contributed to a consensus after the Second World War that trade union participation in political and economic designs was a settled and, in principle, progressive feature of the institutional makeup of a progressive modernity. Marxists objected to trade unions that failed to subordinate themselves to the larger strategic objectives of class struggle; Weberians continued to worry about irrationally ideological modes of unionism; and Durkheimians likewise attacked the notion of socialism as "miracle" born of warlike conflict. But none expected unions to enter into a period of continued and seemingly accelerating decline. Theoretical ingenuity being what it is, all three tendencies have in fact developed analyses of the present arguably symptomatic downturn of unionism in many places where they had earlier considered it impregnable. Our thesis is that an adequate encounter with these changes must call into question the whole idea of a progressivist theoretical strategy comprehending the relationship between social progress and political issues, rather than adaptations in progressivist theories.

The tendential decline in trade unionism

For the past decade or longer, trade unions have been measurably in decline in a number of the industrially advanced, predominantly capitalist nations with comparatively stable liberal-democratic political systems, where progressivist ideologies and the social theories upon which they selectively draw had held them to be not only secure but also integral to social development. This decline has not been universal or uniform, by any means, but it is substantial, sustained, and widespread enough to raise serious questions about established progressivist expectations, and the analyses upon which they rest. We will draw on some comparative analyses of deviant cases in the attempt to derive theoretical lessons from the general tendency. We will also look briefly at the corresponding rise and strategic importance of trade unions in several authoritarian states with comparatively advanced economic systems, in order to test our approach against progressivist claims that these developments can serve as models for revival in the nations where unions are in decline. Our own claim overall is that unions can be best understood as strategic political entities operating within interdependent but distinct action contexts of polity and economy whose constitutional and systemic features they can variously influence but never unilaterally control. Our normative premise is that the political argument on behalf of unions that is hidden within the progressivist theories is eminently defensible and that any conclusion that unions may in fact no longer be adaptable to the emerging state of social progress (analytically understood) would pose a serious political problem, from the standpoint of the progressive project. If social progress no longer causes unions to exist, we might say, it may be necessary to invent them – or a functional equivalent.

The tendential decline in union power has been widely observed in nations with both of the principal types of industrial relations systems commonly distinguished in the disciplines of industrial sociology and industrial relations. Specialists broadly distinguish between systems where autonomous trade union organizations attempt to shape the terms and conditions of employment through adversarial collective bargaining at the level of firms or industries, relying on strikes and similar job actions as principal sanctions, and "neo-corporatist" or participatory systems, where union influence is exercised through autonomous co-participation, as legitimate partners of associated employers and state agencies in planning and regulatory institutions at various levels of economic organization. Despite important exceptions, at least at the present time, the most common observations are of drastic losses of power, under circumstances where prospects for recovery appear uncertain and obscure. The indicators of decline are different in each context. Unions operating in adversarial collective bargaining systems depend for their power first of all on the proportion of the labor market that is unionized, at least in decisive sectors, for which union density, i.e., the proportion of the non-agricultural labor force that is unionized, is a reasonably reliable measure. In neo-corporatist contexts, union density is less directly indicative of power, not least because measures to stabilize less than voluntary memberships are a common starting point for neo-corporatist arrangements. In these settings, union decline is measured, first, by policy failures within neo-corporatist processes. Second, and more importantly, it is measured by the reduced saliency of those processes within the decision-making system: decisions are pre-empted by actions beyond its bounds and the institutions in which unions play a central part are marginalized without necessarily being changed.

The most widely noticed sharp drops in union density have been recorded in the United States (from a high of 36% in 1945 to 19% in 1984 and estimates closer to 12% at the present time), Japan (from 56% in 1949 to 28% in 1986), and Britain (from 55% in 1979 to 37% in 1987). Despite all that has been said about the unique organization and discipline of the Japanese labor market, its unions nevertheless are oriented to adversarial collective bargaining, like the other two.[3] Britain had been a classical case of union strength, where the basis in adversarial collective bargaining appeared for a while strong enough to open the planning and regulatory process to unions, without requiring them to accept the measure of accommodation that more commonly goes together with the neo-corporatist pattern. Strategic efforts to marginalize collective bargaining within firms and industries, accompanied by state actions inimical to former bases of union strength appear to be important aspects of union density decline in these adversarial collective bargaining contexts, and quite possibly a cause of such declines in unionization. The prime factors do not appear to be simple labor market transformations. Such extra-market explanations are suggested by studies of present-day exceptions to the trend. Canada's situation, greatly resembling that of the United States and subject to most of the same economic factors, has largely held gains made while American density rates were in precipitous decline. Australia too displays a collective bargaining oriented system where unions remain strong.[4] Progress in the political economy, and especially in the world market, is doubtless extremely important; but the inclusion or exclusion of unions in the organized responses to these changes depends on additional social-political factors, according to most specialist studies.

The decline of unions oriented to neo-corporatist relations has been especially marked in the Netherlands, where it also manifests itself in steady, serious membership losses, and in several of the Scandinavian countries, except Sweden, although membership rates have remained relatively stable. Striking neo-corporatist experiments in Italy, Spain, and Belgium have also fallen on hard times, with a corresponding marginalization of trade unions and their increasing recourse to improvized adversarial measures with comparatively little impact under the institutional circumstances, except in narrow sectors where market power is exceptionally strong. West Germany is a disputed case: union membership losses have been slight and important co-participation institutions appear intact, but unions have lost influence in several of these institutions, and decisions characteristically central to union concerns are being shifted to workers' councils at enterprise levels, where union voices are becoming weaker. Little important leverage is exercised by agencies with an autonomous strategy process (e.g. centralized unions) and with an independent coercive power resource (such as the strike). The development of labor relations into a kind of firm-level "producers' syndicalism" implies *de facto* deunionization, many observers conclude, even if this is temporarily masked by government legislation facilitating continued union membership.[5] As in the adversarial collective bargaining systems, there are good reasons for emphasizing the strategic actions of unions, employers, and public agencies as well as wider systemic changes, especially in view of the exceptions found in Sweden and Finland.

In an illustrative case study of the contrast between the United States and Canada, Kettler, Struthers, and Huxley (1989) have approached the wider problem as a study in comparative labor regimes, rather than drawing on the older, process-oriented theoretical conceptualizations of industrial relations and related sociological treatments. By the concept, also adopted here, we mean the power-constrained but inwardly contested range of rules, practices, and expectations that organizes the labor market. The concept attempts to integrate the elements of the industrial relations system with the elements of its public policy environment, treating the whole as a partially-integrated, conflictual, sectorially diversified, and provisional historical formation, produced and reproduced by the interplay among organized economic and governmental actors. The concept illustrates, in our view, the type of complementary conceptualization which we believe necessary in order to acknowledge the horizontal division between social progress and progressive projects that progressivist theoretical formulations obscure.

As employed here, the term "regime" draws on two distinct usages. While lawyers often use it to refer to the complex of juridified regulations governing some issue domain, recent international relations theory has broadened and deepened the concept. The distinctive feature of "regime" in the latter conext, and the feature that makes this conceptualization of interest to us, is that it comprehends not only the quasi-legalistic "principles, norms, rules, and decision-makers" (Krasner 1982: 185) around which the expectations of the relevant political actors converge in a given issue area over an identifiable period of time, but also the power constellations that condition the effectiveness of the institutionalized order in question. The institution is not reduced to the power factors and the power factors are not idealistically denied. Among students of international relations, the point of the concept has been to qualify the monistic "realism" that has dominated their study during the past generation, to facilitate inquiry into the causal importance of quasi-legalized institutions where and when they can be discerned, without denying the general force of power-oriented systemic theory (Keohane 1986).

In adapting the concept of the constitution and development of institutions in certain intranational issue-areas, the point is rather to help conceptualize institutions that have an irreducible legal component but that are shaped in important measure by the non-legal power resources that participants bring into play. There are similarities between this conceptualization and Max Weber's treatment of constitutional law. More immediately to the point, in the application that we are making here, is the parallel between such "regimes" and the collective agreement that forms so characteristic a feature of the employment domain during the period when awareness of industrial relations as a distinctive issue-domain and object of analysis grew in importance (Kettler 1987: 9–47). In our work, then, the lawyer's "regime" provides the starting point for analysis, but the complex of norms and regulations is understood "realistically," in conjunction with the competing political designs and clashing power resources at work in the field. A regime is a response to social progress, not simply a manifestation of it.

As a constituted pattern, a regime embodies a measure of resistance to disruptive change; it places constraints upon the forms and exercises of power deployed; but both of these identity-forming characteristics differ significantly in degree from regime to regime and from time to time in the life of a regime. A regime may be said to intend a preferred type of outcome, but this teleological design will be manifested in a structural tendency, subject to even quite important exceptions, and not in a purely instrumental machinery. To function as a regime, it must be accorded a measure of legitimacy by all participant actors, and this is rarely consistent with transparently one-sided utilities. Regimes differ as to complexity, flexibility, and tolerance for inner inconsistency or conflict. But they all display that visible blend of legal manner and power factors that mark international law, which was the paradigm for the international relations theorists' version of the concept, and which has, in fact, been earlier used as a model for the analysis of labor law, realistically understood in its social effectiveness (Korsch 1972: 142ff.).

In the study of labor, then, regime refers to the institutionalized political organization of labor markets (Offe 1984: 95ff.), comprising the patterned interactions among state (and possibly other legal and administrative) agencies, employment-dependent labor, and employers, however severally articulated. The degrees and forms of organization of the latter two types of actors will obviously make a decisive difference for the shape of the regime concerned. Our proposed conceptual shift is designed to facilitate inquiry into the political dynamics of any such regime as well as into its historical sources and competitors. In locating legal and administrative designs within regimes, in short, we mean to emphasize their direct relationships with the patterns of practice by the principal parties in the industrial relations interaction, to show that these are integral to the patterns, as well as their relationship with the political constellations constituted by the direct involvement of these parties in political life (see, for example, the treatment of the "organizational practice" of the West

German labor movement in Loesche 1982). The differences in governmental policies and practices must be seen in conjunction with differences in the outlooks and activities of unions and employers, for example, serving as factors in the political makeup of the regimes. Kochan and his associates have recently developed valuable materials for the United States, especially for the study of "strategic choices" by employers (Kochan *et al*. 1986a and b). For obvious reasons, our present analysis will concentrate rather on the regime-constitutive politics of unions.

For purposes of the present theoretical exercise we should be prepared to conceive of the possibility of declines in unionization and union power so drastic that unions are almost everywhere marginalized in the labor regime – in the public ordering of the labor market – and reduced to ghettoized interest groups in the political field. Our present theoretical objective requires neither a demonstration that the phenomenon of decline is universal nor does it require a universal explanation for it. But we consider it theoretically instructive and practically important to know whether and how it matters that such a development is occurring in important places. What would it mean if there were no more unions? We take issue with Alain Touraine's contention that "the loss of strength of American and French unions, the serious problems met by British and Italian ones, are in the end no more significant than the effectiveness of the Swedish and West German labor organizations, the current expansion of Brazilian unions, and the central role play by the *Solidarnosc* union in the Polish democratic, social, and national liberation movement" because unions have ceased to be a "social movement" and have become merely a "political force" with contingently changing fortunes" (Touraine 1986).

This is a major critical issue that is, in our view, so poorly served by analyses derived from progressivist Marxist approaches oriented to the central problem of relating unions to a schematic conception of the destined place of workers' self-organization in the movement towards revolution, or to a schematic conception about the revolutionary vocation of class-conscious workers. A prominent theme in contemporary Marxist or quasi-Marxist analyses has been the claim that union decline can be traced to a dissipation of radical class-mobilization capabilities through the organizations' complicity in the juridification (*Verrechtlichung*) of collective labor activity.[6] Our analysis assigns a politically significant constitutive role to the regime developments that are stigmatized in this way. They have been essential contributions to the formation of the politically democratic welfare states of the past generation, many of them at least tendentially socially democratic as well, and there is no reason for confidence in what might take their place (see Offe 1984: 95ff. Cf. also Streeck 1987a and b and Müller-Jentsch 1987). Precisely because the Welfare State may have been rendered obsolete as it is so intimately tied to an unsustainable (and unconscionable) exploitation of ethnic or national privilege and of the eco-system, the possible demise of a prime historic resource of democratic politics and collective self-management must be discussed without the constraints of schematic scenarios of a fixed order of social change.

An interesting light is thrown upon union decline in representative countries of the First World by the bursts of union strength in other kinds of countries, as will be shown below. Illustrative cases are the rise of black unionism in South Africa, massive protests on behalf of independent unions in South Korea, and *Solidarnosc* in Poland. Although these are often dealt with in Marxist terms, especially the first, the juxtaposition of all three and the problem of relating them to the larger discussion required by the situation of unions noted above combine to make such an approach implausible. Such instances of unions that flaunt some of the ideological signs that Marxist and Marxist-derived progressivism take as emblematic of the undistorted progressive functions of the institution must rather be understood in the context of their struggles against repressive states and the quasi-unions that are their creatures. Such unions, we will try to show below, are attempting to secure collective-bargaining-oriented labor regimes that will allow them to play precisely the kinds of constitutive roles that are now in trouble in the richer countries and that Marxist analysts deprecate, and their attempts must be understood in the context of the obstacles and opportunities provided by the labor regimes in place.

While Marxist progressivism responds to the present situation with its characteristic ambivalence, fluctuating between a satisfied registration of the failure of a unionism to meet its revolutionary developmental task, and a misjudged surge of approbation for a unionism that appears to be sufficiently universalistic in its designs, Weberian and Durkheimian progressivist social theory are more inclined to accept the apparent verdict of the present stage of social progress. In the Weberian tradition, rationality is increasingly seen to stand against collective action in the labor market. Unions are declining, according to this view, above all because they no longer contribute to the rational pursuit of workers' interests and because they are harmful to the rationality of economic organization and public policy (Olson 1982, Rogers 1988). The Durkheimian line of progressivist thinking is more divided, as might be imagined, with some writers anticipating a further adaptation of unions to the new integrative requirements of emerging highly differentiated organizations of social reproduction (Teubner 1978) and others accepting the growing obsolescence of unions as these new organizations develop more adequate novel normative institutions. Since all three of these traditions embody irreplacable strands of analytical insight into social progress, they clearly have important contributions to make to an understanding of the developmental tendencies that militate against unionism. Nevertheless, we find that these insights cannot be rendered productive in isolation one from another, and we propose to give them their place within our study of transformations in labor regimes. Insisting upon the horizontal division introduced above, regime analysis complements analytical study of social progress with diagnosis of political possibilities and assessment of political objectives. Its perspective is strategic. That does not mean that we absolutize the value of unions or guarantee recipes for their revival. Our analysis will have a far more indeterminate outcome, leaving much for informed political choice and leaving much to unpredictable political conflicts. But we will not let presumed laws of social progress pre-empt those choices or obviate those conflicts.

The decline of labor unions, where it is most marked, is a concomitant of what is variously called the "crisis of the Welfare State" or the "end of the century of social democracy" (Kettler 1987). From the standpoint of economic analysis, the central phenomenon is said to be the contradiction between contemporary market imperatives and unions' inherent preoccupation with shopfloor due process, job protection, and increments in labor's distributive shares across the market. All three of these preoccupations made eminent sense to the Weberian and Durkheimian types of theoretical approach, understood either as a structural contributor to the rationalization of internal labor markets and expansionary factor in aggregate demand, quite apart from its latent political function, or as a qualitative contributor to the co-operative ethos of productive units, notwithstanding the conflictual motif, and as contributor to a self-regulating situationally adequate complex of integrative social institutions. From a Marxist perspective, as noted, the normalization of trade union-oriented labor regimes represented an obstacle to the formation of a revolutionary class-conscious proletariat – a pattern earlier denounced by Lenin as "economism" and imperialist opportunism by labor élites, and later, more subtly, analyzed as integral to an extended phase of "corporate liberalism" – although the conflictual component in the regime also appeared as a constant reminder and possible regenerator of the ultimately generative class conflict upon which the progressivist model rests.

The most powerful social progress elements in the explanation of this decline refer to production and labor market changes inimical to historic patterns of unionization and union action. The rise of service industries and the technological transformation of production industries shift the labor force into occupational groupings, work structures, and geographical settings where the characteristic contractual patterns and implementation techniques of historic unionism are comparatively alien. Comparatively high unemployment and the tendency towards a large minimum-wage ghetto in tendentially dualized labor markets multiply this deunionization effect (Berger and Piore 1980). Intense international competition from the co-operation with nations with labor regimes antithetical to unionism increases the demand for "flexibility" in the organization of work in nations with union traditions and largely dissipates former economic or organizational benefits that resulted from industrial relations oriented to collective bargaining, especially in the design of internal labor markets and the stabilization of domestic markets (Piore and Sabel 1985).

But the differential rise and decline of unions in economically comparable nations, as well as more general theoretical considerations, make us question the sufficiency of such analyses at the level of economic development alone. Organizational and political factors shape the capacity of union-oriented labor regimes to manage the new economic developments. These must be examined in order to explain the widespread reorientation away from unions. From the standpoint of regime analysis, the massive socioeconomic changes schematically surveyed above appear as powerful reasons for changed patterns of action and powerful explanations for changed patterns of consequences; they don't suffice as determinants. Labor regimes are constituted by patterned interplay among three categories of collective actors: employees, employers, and state agencies. For present purposes we must disregard the important fact that each of these categories is by no means homogeneous or undivided, a radical simplification since the very concept of labor regime points to the sectorially differentiated character of the institutionalized relationships comprehended by the concept. Speaking generally and concentrating on the sectors where unions have been most important, we can nevertheless avoid egregious error. Characteristic changes affecting each of the three actors help to explain the present changes in the pattern to the detriment of unions.

State agencies active in the labor regime are changing their pattern of conduct in a number of ways in response to political redirection from government leaders committed to business-led economic restructuring. Some influential observers trace these shifts to ideological changes in public opinion, but such analyses appear seriously overstated in view of the fact that unions are no more popular in many of the nations where they have retained their comparative strength than they are in those where they are in rapid decline. More to the point, no doubt, are such factors as élite perceptions of failures in the "policy-ideas" historically linked to unions (Vallelly 1989); delegitimations of existing regulatory patterns in the course of the 1960s; the dramatic shifts in the balance of power between "economy" and "polity" resulting from the internationalized economy and the enormous scale and power of capital combines; the weakening of state revenues and apparatuses attending the demands of the institutionalized Welfare State under conditions of massive unproductive military investment for many of them; and the immeasurable investments required by contemporary means of production. New state actions in the interactions constitutive for labor regimes include express interventions to weaken existing union organizations (and their material and ideological power resources), as in Britain, or easing of enforcement against violators of regulations designed to uphold the regime, as in the United States. In both kinds of labor regimes, an important development is the shift in the constitution of public policy so that key matters are no longer decided in the context of the labor regime. The shift is especially easy to observe where the labor regime tends towards the neo-corporatist model, as in the Netherlands, because there the consultative bodies are quite visibly not consulted. It is no less important, however, in the other model, as when trade regulations pre-empt the field of decisions affecting the labor market – a present prospect in Canada and an impending prospect throughout the European Economic Community after 1992.

The actions of employers cannot be understood simply as a parallelogram of economic forces. The exceptional cases, whether national units like Sweden and Australia or sectorial exceptions like the American native auto industry or the Canadian steel industry, indicate that the market-impelled productivity-enhancing adjustments can even be furthered by collective bargaining arrangements under certain circumstances. But the widespread strategic design is to regain intra-organizational control and especially to bound and internalize the communications system, disencumbering it from the uncertainties of power-constrained negotiations, which always carry the risk of requiring the internalization of externalities that can otherwise be shifted elsewhere. The new concerted widespread resistance to unionism and unionization in a number of nations must be seen as a result of strategic decisions (Kochan *et al.* 1986a and b, Fiorito *et al.* 1987), frequently involving considerable short-run costs in new social technologies of human resources management, as in the United States, or material inducements to bring co-participation mechanisms out of union control, as in West Germany. In Weberian terms, these are investments in power rather than direct exercises in economic rationality, collective goods purchased at immediate cost, on the basis of historical experience and imprecise prospective calculations (Hardin 1982).

In trying to understand the changing role of unions it is important to consider questions of their organization and strategy. Their weakening within the labor regime is not a matter of declining memberships alone, because membership levels are quite commonly a function of the importance assigned to unions within the labor regime. Their future power depends on the uses they make of the power they have. This is evident from the record of mass unionization, which did not begin in Germany, Britain, and the United States, for example, until it was either promoted by government labor force planners during the First World War or by postwar successor states as organizing devices amenable to exchanges helpful to demobilization and reconstruction, and which was similarly served by the Second World War and its aftermath. It is also suggested by the deviant cases at the present time. But in all these cases, the point is not simply that "the state" wanted unions for its own purposes; rather, it is that unionism as an institution appeared effective enough to be so wanted. Nor should it be thought that governmental designs invariably achieved their purposes without major costs. This particular occasion is clearly not the place for political commentary on the makeup and policies of unions throughout the First World. We simply want to register our conviction that such commentary is not at all beside the point, that the strength of unions within the labor regime depends in some significant measure on what they in fact do (Huxley *et al.* 1986).

Wolfgang Streeck (1981) has clearly formulated the central organizational problem confronting unions: they must somehow deal, under ever more differentiated circumstances, with their dual nature as organizations that must simultaneously make good as rational actors in complex rationalized relationships and as inspirers of solidaristic enthusiasm among their actual and potential members. Formulated in Weberian language, Streeck's thesis is that they must constantly reproduce both rational-legal and charismatic legitimacy, although we might prefer to say that they must combine the characteristics that have been singled out respectively by the Weberian and Durkheimian theoretical models. All labor regimes are importantly conditioned by the unions' needs in these respects, since the other two actors control resources that may be vital to unions in their struggle for organizational effectiveness (or survival). This is an important source of that obsessive preoccupation with the organization and those compromises for the sake of the organization that are the despair of radical opponents and observers, and that too often are interpreted (and denounced) in purely moralistic terms, especially in the Marxist tradition.

Cella's and Treu's typology of union formations can help us to distinguish the factors that inhibit the strategic responses of different kinds of unions under present conditions and appear to increasingly limit their abilities to protect union-supportive labor regimes under so many emerging conditions. Of five types of unions distinguished by Cella and Treu, three models are principally represented in the adversarial and neo-corporatist labor regimes now under consideration: business unionism, competitive unionism, and participatory unionism (Cella and Treu, 1982: Ch. 10).[7] This first type is distinguished by its narrowly economic objectives, its comparative distance from stable political commitments, and reliance on workplace organization; the second type is marked by wider social objectives, more conflictual orientations, and closer ties with political organizations; and the third type is geared to neo-corporatist participation in designs for public economic policy. We shall equate each type with a characteristic strategic pattern and indicate difficulties confronting each of the strategies in question.

142

Business unions depend on collective bargaining results to legitimate themselves as rational guardians of members' interests and on adversarial mobilization, especially through strikes, to provide for solidarity. They are dramatically weakened in regard to the rational-legal dimensions of legitimacy by unfavorable developments in labor markets and public policy and by employer deployment of full powers of resistance; they can be decisively undermined in their principal source of charismatic legitimacy by the adjustments they make to respond to the former problem, as well as by shifts in the ideological field importantly affected by state actors.

Competitive unions depend to a considerable extent on the vitality and loyalty of the political parties with which they are typically allied, commonly labor or social democratic parties. Party leaders, ideologies, and mobilization campaigns can reinforce the solidaristic components of their inner legitimacy. As factors in government, in competitive opposition, or as coalition-members, the parties are also their principal levers for securing support from state agencies within the collective interchanges constituting the labor regime, thereby strengthening their capacity to meet members' interests. Although there is clearly a great measure of reciprocal dependency, the strength of the relevant parties is by no means exclusively dependent on the independent strength of unions. A central feature of several of the exceptions to the phenomenon of general decline is the exceptional continuing strength of the allied political parties, as has been true of the Swedish and Finnish Social Democrats, as well as the labor parties in several of the historically white Commonwealth nations, where these parties have not bought their continuing strength, as in Southern Europe, by substantially downgrading their alliances with unions. The more general trend away from social democracy and laborism in the political domain (and the renewed militancy against them) is a key problem for the competitive unions (Dunn 1984).

Participatory unions have historically relied on alliances in government, whether through parties or other routes of access, to give them sufficient leverage to count independently in the comparatively non-adversarial dealings with employers that are characteristic of the neo-corporatist designs in which they take form. Their legitimacy depends on their evident functional efficacy, but their quasi-official status also makes them organizationally less dependent on legitimacy. They are being seriously harmed in many places by an abrupt and continuing loss of governmental allies and by an appropriation of their functions by competing agencies fostered by employers, as exemplified by the widening split between unions and co-participation institutions in West Germany.[8] Under these circumstances, their attempts to retain neo-corporatist linkages may also jeopardize the loyalty and discipline of their membership, leading to wildcat direct actions by groups advantageously situated in narrow labor market niches, as illustrated by the case of air traffic controllers in Italy.

Such actions further undermine the co-participatory institutions upon which this strategy depends.

If the labor regime is the provisional institutionalization of these interrelationships, embodied in broadly legalized designs, as well as policies, we can speak of a tendential deunionization of labor regimes and inquire into the importance of such a development not only with regard to the presumed processes of social development but also with regard to the repertory of political responses to these processes. Our argument is that failure to appreciate the political importance of unions and the importance of strategies for affecting that importance leads to misleadingly progressivist ideological interpretations of our times.

Unions and the progressive project

Once the complementarity between the social progress and political project dimensions of unionism is recognized, the problem moves out of the contexts of industrial relations or labor economics as well as Marxist social theory. At issue is the political significance of labor regimes centered on labor market conflict-resolution mechanisms involving collective actors – trade unions and employers of dependent labor – that are more or less autonomous. The contingent, political relationships to the state are not peripheral to the theoretical treatment of the social interactions mistakenly comprehended as elements of a progressivist movement (Cf. Erd and Scherer, 1985: pp. 115ff., esp. 128–31). Labor regimes oriented to unions, we shall argue, have made a vital and distinctive contribution to the constitution of dynamic democratic constitutions, even where the unions pursued quite narrow programs. Unions in labor regimes that perpheralize or ghettoize their activities, on the other hand, may be positively harmful to social justice or other objectives of social democratization, unless they make the reconstitution of the labor regime central to their strategy. Political judgments concerning unions, in short, are difficult, uncertain, and context-dependent. But they cannot be made on the basis of progressivist social theory.

Turning first to the historical contribution of trade unions during the struggle for trade-union oriented labor regimes, we want to emphasize two kinds of contributions to the production and reproduction of working democratic orders, one relating to the generation of political conflict and the other relating to the transformation of the legal order. Unlike Marxist analysts, our interest here is concentrated in the first place on political effects that are arguably concomitants of the minimal designs of unionism rather than on political effects that depend on express political projects oriented by egalitarian political ideologies, although we do not deny contingent positive correlations between the two. We want generalizations that apply to the founder years of Samuel Gompers' AFL as well as Carl Legien's social democratic trade union federation (ADGB), generalizations that cover business, competitive, or participatory unions alike, during the organizing period prior to the labor regime crisis that has been spreading since the late 1960s.

First, then, unions have served to activate and reproduce democratic politics because their activities institutionalize the political agenda items of power sharing and economic distribution. This does not mean that they have been necessarily or even commonly dedicated to egalitarian objectives in these regards. The point we are making need not be harmed by the recognition that unions have often pursued quite particularistic policies under these regimes, seeking privileged access to privileges rather than the abolition of privileges. As principal players in a labor regime, their activities and conditions of existence have nevertheless implied generalizable politics forming issues that ramify beyond the unions' manifest purposes or those of their competitors or antagonists, rendering all settlements provisional, while reproducing contests and choices. The Marxist tradition of commentary has misconstrued this, taking it as a developmentally determined imperative to transcend particular interests and to attain to universality; but it is time to conclude that there has never been such a univocal logic. The unified labor movement has always been more a matter of internal collective bargaining than solidaristic common consciousness, notwithstanding periods during which the bargaining was conducted in a shared ideological vocabulary. Although there is a record of affinity between unionism and mass democratic parties in many places, the politics of those parties has been a matter of cultural history and changing situational patterns.[9]

In this connection, we are not arguing merely, with S. M. Lipset, that unions have contributed to a pluralistic political field that limits the powers of all. Twentieth-century democracy, in our view, is about economic distribution and power sharing, not about effective system maintenance and limitations of governmental power. Unions in union-oriented labor regimes have not been simply one of a multiplicity of interest groups. By virtue of their projects, they have been structurally linked to the generation of the distinctively democratic issues. The rise of nineteenth- and twentieth-century democracy is inseparable from the emergence of the "social question," and unions have given organizational expression to that question, forcing it onto all political agendas, whether or not their own strategy has addressed it in an effective or defensible way.

Second, unionism has contributed to democracy because it initiated and occasioned changes in the legal system that make the law less subordinate to the demands of property and more open to democratically generated demands and self-regulation. The characteristic institutions relevant here are the collective agreement and other quasi-juridified multi-partite negotiating frameworks, "reflexive law" (Teubner 1983) that regulates by fostering self-regulation, and new types of arbitration mechanisms. Philip Selznick's classical *Law, Society, and Industrial Justice* (1969), itself formulated in terms of a progressivist theory with Durkheimian inclinations, lays out a brilliant analysis of these legal developments within the American labor regime that continues to have analytical value, notwithstanding its shortcomings as prophecy. His main objective is to show that the institutions of collective labor law displaced the uncontrolled powers of command grounded in property that had gone with the contract of employment under industrial conditions, and that this displacement has had paradigmatic as well as direct impact on the legal order. Socialist precursors of this analysis during the Weimar years, expressly stressing the horizontal dualism in Marxism, emphasized the wider constitutional ramifications of this type of collective bargaining regime, crediting it with complementing democratic parliamentary institutions with institutions for social parity and co-participation between primary social contestants (cf. Kettler 1984: 278–303, Luthardt 1986).

A more cautious legal political analysis nevertheless acknowledges the formative demands made on the wider system of law, especially on the property regime, by the legal aspects of the labor regimes which were devised to accommodate unionism (Görlitz and Voigt 1987). That the labor regimes are by no means unilateral creations by unions, and that the law often serves to manage unions for the sake of objectives which unions do not share is not decisive here, where the principal questions concern the reflexive effects of changes in labor law on the legal system, as well as reflexive effects of changes in the legal system on the political system. Our thesis is that unionism has been conducive to democracy: the "push" towards the Welfare State and its consolidation, which are the marks of twentieth-century democracy in the wealthier countries, cannot be easily imagined without the impact of unions on politics, law, and constitution (Habermas 1981, 1985).

Yet we have noted the massive developmental tendencies which collaborate with strategic shifts by primary actors in the labor regime to render the future of union-oriented labor regimes increasingly uncertain. Under these pressures, surviving unions are often challenged by their own members to pursue the narrowest, most exclusivist, and most defensive policies, regardless of their impact on those who are relegated to other, undefended sectors of the labor regime, too often inimical to persons in the burgeoning underclass as well as to the wider, ethical, internationalist, and ecological concerns that contemporary democracy must address if it is to retain its legitimacy. Exceptional positions giving bargaining power within some narrow sectors of the labor market are exploited without any reference to strategic responsibilities. As a result, unions are increasingly isolated and rejected among those whose alliance and movement would require for a renewal of labor regime and gives them a place of right. We

146

conclude our analysis with a respectful but critical review of the orientation to this present situation offered by representatives of the three principal progressivist approaches. The review is respectful because we are indebted to much in the analyses of social progress found here. It is critical because we cannot, of course, accept the progressivist depoliticization implicit in the conclusions.

Some of the outstanding commentators in the Marxist tradition complement their critiques of what they have always taken to be the self-defeatingly narrow labor regimes correlative to the activities of business, competitive, and participatory unions with the example of burgeoning militant unionism in several important poorer nations, exemplifying what Cella and Treu call "oppositional unionism." In the militancy of their styles, the openness to radicalization of their tactical demands, and the express links between their stated programs and political programs for comprehensive social change, oppositional unions more nearly fulfill Marxist hopes for unions as schools for working-class revolution. Yet historically they have always disappointed social revolutionaries.

In briefly reviewing recent developments in South Africa, South Korea, and Poland, we want to show that union movements are structurally inclined towards labor regimes giving them an independent bargaining role and permitting political democratization, and that such a conception provides superior orientation even where appearances support Marxist expectations. In South Africa, South Korea, and Poland, oppositional unions arose against a scheme of state-supported unions and in some measure, paradoxically, with the help of opportunities provided by the old labor regime. The regime analysis makes possible a more accurate understanding of developments as well as shielding us from unargued progressivist standards of political judgment. Such a shift in perspective allows a more realistic appraisal of the actual capabilities of unions as well as of long-term designs. Our argument is not intended as a critique of radical unionists' ideologies in any of these nations. Problems of ideological symbolization are different from problems of social analysis, and the relationships between them do not concern us here. The narrow focus of our present interest, of course, inevitably yields a rather abstract picture of the massive socio-political events in which unionism forms only a part. There is a matter-of-factness in most union development, except for flashes of intense drama during certain strikes, not least because the people always have to go back to work in order to live. But this is precisely why unionism resists romanticization.

South African unions for blacks operated as illegal "unregistered" unions until 1979, but they were dealing with employers oriented to a collective bargaining regime with regard to white employees. White unions were state supported against blacks, through job reservation and residential apartheid schemes, but otherwise functioned within a labor regime resembling that familiar to business unions in other industrialized nations. The recognition of black unionism through the qualified extension of that regime (with certain racist restrictions) came after an upsurge of black unionism in the early 1970s had dramatized the issue of black wages and black labor conditions. The political events of 1976, in particular, constituted a degree of crisis the government had never seen before and which could not simply be "fixed" by repression. But the recognition of black unionism was also conditioned by employers' susceptibility to international pressure and by the government's determination to put hitherto prohibited organizations with considerable power in special labor markets and with disciplined solidarity under controls more subtle and effective than pure police measures. The unions have stretched and sometimes defied the limits placed on them by the labor regime, especially the attempts to render them unpolitical, and they have increased black membership many times over since legalization, notwithstanding coercive sanctions by both employers (through mass dismissals of strikers) and state authorities. There is no doubt that new consolidations of scattered black union organizations and widespread urban political leadership by unionists make the black unions central actors in militant campaigns for black rights far beyond the objectives of business unionism. But there is also no doubt that these political roles are grounded in union functions and in the unions' partial institutionalization as collective bargaining agents in several industrial sectors. The wider political struggle is indispensable for black trade unions in South Africa, but it is a mistake to suppose that the concurrent struggle to reconstitute the labor regime so as to strengthen the unions' abilities to exercise trade union functions is merely a means to the end of political mobilization. The organizations depend upon the conjunction of both campaigns. The government strategy of suppressing the political action of unions by offering collective bargaining rights in exchange for abstention from the fight against apartheid clearly failed. The new black unionism had learned the lessons of repression and recognized this strategy as a fraud. While unions cannot legitimate themselves before their memberships in anything but the dramatic short term, if they do not show themselves to be serious about collective bargaining objectives – and this is our principal point – they cannot also pretend to seriousness if they agree to such political terms, under the conditions that prevail in South Africa.[10]

The South Korean independent union movement has mobilized mass actions against a labor regime that parodies those oriented to independent unions in form but actually restricts union rights to yellow unions controlled by government agents who are either simply in the service of employers or deferential to the informal subservient labor regime. The independent unions are allied to antimilitarist oppositionists, in defiance of prohibitions on union political action, but are hardly free to initiate or sustain a radical course. Their organizational base, so far as we can tell, depends on the promise of achieving traditional trade union gains. Because of the depth of economic deprivation and the unifying effects of opposition to a harsh government, such organizations do not have serious legitimacy problems. But they are vulnerable to coercion (and, in many places, to state-supported terror). They are also poor in organizational resources. Accordingly, compromises to protect organizations are inevitable.[11]

The history of *Solidarnosc* is even less satisfactorily compressed within the present narrow perspective. Nevertheless there is something to be gained by thinking of it from the perspective of our thesis about the structural bias of the historical institutions of unionism. Many might consider it a sacrilege or betrayal to think of incremental improvements in the labor regime as fulfilling the historical purpose of this movement, as witness the internal debates within the organization in early 1989. But the more modest view is a useful corrective, we think, to dramatizations of human actions that ultimately denigrate the actual achievements of those who must work with little. Many active leaders of Solidarnosc units appear to agree. Union accomplishments are almost always in bitter disproportion to the hopes of those who sacrificed most for them, but they are nevertheless real.[12] To denigrate such organizational efforts because they aspire to a civilizing and democratizing labor regime rather than acting for some total transformation as "social movements" (Touraine) or "revolutionary centers" (Marx) must do is to permit a misleading theory to contribute to needless human pain.

The Weberian tradition of commentary has always assigned a more modest and more ambiguous position to the self-organization of labor. With interesting and important exceptions, whose theories tend to integrate Durkheimian elements as well (or to fit awkwardly within the schematic trifurcation of our analysis), these analyses have concluded that unions are anachronistic reminders of a rationalizing function that is now played by quite different institutions, a form of collective action that is irrational for evolutionary social progress but kept barely alive by a mix of ingenious, self-interested leadership that is able to manipulate the power resources that remain at their disposal together with essentially irrational and harmful action by certain specially-placed members in privileged economic niches (Olson 1982). Our objection is not so much to the political balancing of economic developmental interests against the other interests subservable by the labor regimes we have been reviewing. Our objection is rather to an approach that obviates the need for such balancing, on the premise that the argument from presumed social progress completes the tasks of social thought.

Olson stresses the polarization and conflict that accompany union-oriented labor regimes. We do not deny the conflictual moment, but we believe that democracy requires a mode of civility that accommodates such tensions because we think that the alternatives devitalize the political institution. To justify this later claim, we turn to the concept of civilized order. The problem of civilized order (and we count political democracy as a central constituent) is not progress but the reproduction of civility. This problem confronts the *Gesellschaft*-sphere itself, and not a special *Lebenswelt* (Habermas 1981). The available answers are all radically imperfect and constantly provisional. We think that the ethics of the collective agreement – which is very different from a "social contract" – is not only an apt figure for democratic civility but an element that has to secure its institutionalized place. Hence our concern about union decline. This is an ethics that conjoins utilitarian and solidaristic considerations in an always unstable whole, having to be held together by political power in a mediated constitutional form – a political power that the parties must somehow generate themselves. This constituting activity is what we call the union-oriented labor regime. Such considerations are not alien to Weber's own thought, of course, but they are lost when that thought is construed as progressivist, without regard to the horizontal line that runs through his actual work, his awareness of the distinction between process and agency.

Among non-Marxist analysts closest to the exceptionally prosperous union-oriented labor regimes, a variant of Durkheimian progressivism occupies a central place. Such commentators find that the course of development implies a shift in organizational design towards the participatory model, claiming that adversarial unionism in either its business or competitive forms has become obsolete and noting that density figures suggest comparatively higher resilience for participatory unions operating within neo-corporatist settings.[13] Taken as political counsel, the argument has much to recommend it. But taken as a dictate of progressivist analysis, it runs the grave risk of neglecting the political presuppositions and consequences of the labor regimes that such cooperative union strategies in fact may foster. The question is whether a shift to the "new production-oriented" unionism may not defunctionalize autonomous unions altogether, at the cost of the political functions that the progressive project requires them to perform.

Günther Teubner offers a unique perspective on the supposedly firm links between trade unionism and neo-corporatist institutions in the German Federal Republic. This is a noteworthy case because its stable, comparatively high union membership figures are often cited as proof that non-adversarial union strategies are best.[14] Teubner finds a development away from the macro-corporatist institutions in which national trade unions play a decisive role towards a "micro-corporatism" at the level of firms and enterprises, a "producers' coalition" comprising capital, labor, management, and state officials. In his view, this tendency accords with the evolutionary requirements of the kinds of systems exemplified by productive enterprises and generates an organization optimally capable of the learning needed for its functioning.

When considered from the political perspective of paramount present interest, however, the development appears to undermine a vital source of union legitimacy and membership strength, the unions' place in a centralized labor regime. The enterprise-centered organizations of labor need not be tied to unions, although they have been so to a large extent, and in any case they lack the power to strike or to compel management to adhere to agreements by other legal means. The development converges with complex new forms of representation devised by numerous sophisticated American corporations expressly in order to fight unionization. Such uncertain prospects in the nation with one of the most firmly established union movements make it a questionable model for others (Kochan 1985).

We conclude then with a plea for respect for the principal secular institutional creation of the working class and recognition for its modest but substantial contributions to democratization. We cannot question that there may be a strong economic logic at work upon the structure of the labor market, making it ever more difficult to rely for its organization on the kinds of collective bargaining mechanisms which have historically sustained unionization. Nor can we deny that union malfeasances and misfeasances have contributed to their own decline. But our analysis leads us to emphasize the costs of any further weakening of unions. From the standpoint of political democracy, an end of trade unionism in the west might be a severe and perhaps irreplaceable loss. That loss can be hastened and intensified by modes of social theory that militate against its assessment and against the reconceptualization of the project in which they have played a central role. The widely proclaimed end of progressivism in social theory can only be welcomed, but not the thoughtless dismissal of the social developments and social actions that progressivism taught us to recognize and value.

Notes

1. Jürgen Habermas has proposed a difficult, more dialectical statement of the relationships among conceptions of progress, as part of his impressive grand theoretical design (Habermas 1970: 112–26, 1976: 173–94, 1981: 145–56, 1985). We continue to see the relationships between theoretical and practical discourses more dualistically, but we do not imagine that we have refuted Habermas (cf. Dallmayr 1988). We are pursuing our independent, far more modest experiment, in the hope that development of our model can also contribute to the ongoing collective theoretical effort (Kettler and Meja, 1988).
2. Durkheim also writes: "[Put] this way, the social question would present itself in an entirely different manner. It no longer opposes the sources of technic to that of power, as two antagonists who exclude each other in such a manner

that the process of successive reorganization presupposes prior destruction. But one is only the continuation of the other. It does not awaken for everything that is or was a feeling of subversive hatred. It incites only to seek the new forms which the past should take today. It is not a matter of putting a completely new society in the place of the existing one, but of adapting the latter to the new social conditions" (Durkheim 1958 [1928]: 246–7).

3. On union density figures in the US see Lipset (1986: 118). On Japanese union density figures see *The Japanese Times* of January 19, 1987 cited in *Social and Labour Bulletin* (1986), and Walkom (1988b: A8). On British density rates see Tower (1987: 239ff.), and Lohr (1988, 3: 1, 7). The most sweeping statement of decline can be found in Troy (1986).

4. For Australia see Hill (1984), Niland (1986: 37–9; 129ff.). For Canada see Kumar (1986: 95–160), Lipset (1986a and b) and Husley, Kettler, and Struthers (1986), Meltz (1985: 315–34), Rose and Chaison (1985: 97–111).

5. On West Germany see Bergmann (1971), Däubler (1976), Streeck (1981, 1987a and b), Markovits (1986), Teubner (1986b: 261–73). On the Netherlands see Albeda (1985: 49–60). On Sweden see Martin (1987: 93–128).

6. For West Germany see Erd (1978), cf. Simitis (1985: 73–165). For the United States, see Rogers (1984) and Tomlins (1985). For Canada, see Panitch and Swartz (1985).

7. The other two types of unionism are oppositional and state-sponsored, both of which will concern us below. Oppositional unions, for reasons that will concern us in somewhat more detail below, are under less strain in these respects; for that reason, it is a fundamental mistake to treat them as models. The legitimacy of state-supported unions shares the fate of other state agencies, although they are especially vulnerable to challenges from oppositional unions, when these can generate the resources for visible resistance.

8. In West Germany, for example, Oskar Lafontaine, a prominent SPD member and possible 1990 candidate for chancellor, recently proposed the creation of new jobs by reducing work hours without full wage compensation – a position that is now more widely shared within his party. As a result, the specter of an increasing cleavage between the unions and the Social Democratic Party is being raised. Cf. the article by the chairman of the Metal Workers' Union (Steinkühler 1988: 13, Blanke 1987).

9. For the historicity of working class "consciousness" see Jones (1983).

10. For a general discussion of the South African labor situation see, for example, Adam and Moodley (1986: Ch. 6), Saul (1986), Plaut (1984: 116–23), Braun (1985: 21–44), Vose (1985: 447–64). On union sizes see Piron and le Roux (1986). On recent attempts to weaken black labor unions, see Schuster (1988: 6ff.).

11. On the labor situation in South Korea see, for example, Sunkim (1985), which also gives union membership figures (1985: 153ff.), Bognanno and Kim (1981), Launius (1984: 2–10), Walkom (1988a: A8). Cf. also the statement by Herman Rebhan, General Secretary of the International Metal Workers' Federation (1987): "We are seeing in Korea the same kind of explosion that was witnessed in Poland at the beginning of the 1980s, and can be seen today in South Africa, namely a desire of workers to be treated fairly and have their own democratic trade unions."

12. On the Polish labor situation see, for example, Pravda (1986), Keenoy (1986), Touraine *et al.* (1983), Minc (1982). Cf. also Karatnycky, Motyl, and Sturmthal (1980).

13. See, for example, the studies prepared for a recent Canadian Royal Commission, especially striking because of the comparative success of Canadian unions in maintaining their membership numbers: Bernier and Lajoie (1986).
14. Praise of the West German model is combined with a fervent argument that it is also better for democracy than unions adapted to the Canadian labor regime in Beatty (1987).

Bibliography

Adam, Heribert and Moodley, Kogila (1986) "Industrial relations, unions, and employment," in *South Africa Without Apartheid* (Berkeley, Loss Angeles, London: University of California Press: 170–95).

Albeda, W. (1985) "Recent trends in collective bargaining in the Netherlands," *International Labour Review* 124 (1) January–February: 49–60.

Beatty, David (1987) *Putting the Charter to Work. Designing a Constitutional Labour Code* (Kingston and Montreal: McGill-Queen's University Press).

Bendix, Reinhard (1976) *Building Citizenship: Studies of Our Changing Social Order* (2nd edn) (Berkeley: University of California Press).

Berger, Suzanne and Piore, Michael (1980) *Dualism and Discontinuity in Industrial Societies* (Cambridge: Cambridge University Press).

Bergmann, Joachim (ed.) (1971) *Beiträge zur Soziologie der Gewerkschaften* (Frankfurt: Suhrkamp).

Bernier, Ivan, and Lajoie, André (Research coordinators) (1986) *Labour Law and Urban Law in Canada*. Volume 51 of the Research Studies prepared for the Royal Commission on the Economic Union and Development Prospects for Canada (Toronto: University of Toronto Press).

Blanke, Thomas (1987) "Rechtsmissbrauch und Rechtsfortbildung im Arbeitsrecht," *Kritische Justiz*, 20 (3): 351–63.

Bognanno, Mario and Kim, Sookon (1981) "Collective bargaining in Korea," in B. Dennis (ed.) *Proceedings of the 34th Annual Meeting*, International Relations Research Association Series, Washington, DC.

Braun, Gerald (1985) Modernisierung weisser Vorherrschaft und gewerkschaftlicher Widerstand in Südafrika," *Afrika Spectrum*, 20 (1): 21–44.

Bulletin of Comparative Labour Relations 16 (1987) (Deventer, Netherlands: Kluwer).

Bury, J. B. (1920) *The History of the Idea of Progress* (London: Macmillan).

Cella, G. and Treu, T. (1982) "National trade union movements," in R. Blanplain (ed.) *Comparative Labour Law and Industrial Relations* (Deventer, Netherlands: Kluwer).

Condorcet, M.-J. (1955) *Sketch of an Historical Picture of the Progress of the Human Mind* (London: Weidenfeld & Nicholson).

Dallmayr, Fred (1988) "J. Habermas and Rationality," *Political Theory*, 16 (4) November: 553–79.

Däubler, Wolfgang (1976) *Das Arbeitsrecht* (Reinbeck-Hamburg: Rowohlt).

Dewey, John (1935) *Liberalism and Social Action* (New York: Putnam).

Dunlop, John T. and Galenson, Walter (1978) *Labor in the Twentieth Century* (New York: Academic Press).

Dunn, John (1984) *The Politics of Socialism* (Cambridge: Cambridge University Press).

Durkheim, Emite (1957 [1950]) *Professional Ethics and Civic Morals* (London: Routledge & Kegan Paul).

Durkheim, Emile (1958 [1928]) *Socialism*, edited by Alvin Gouldner (New York: Collier Books).

Durkheim, Emile (1972) *Selected Writings*, edited by Anthony Giddens (Cambridge: Cambridge University Press).

Engels, Friedrich (1975 [1845]) "The condition of the working-class in England," in Marx and Engels, *Collected Works*, Vol. 4 (New York: International Publishers: 294–583).

Erd, Rainer and Scherer, Christoph (1985) "Unions – caught between structural competition and temporary solidarity: a critique of contemporary Marxist analysis of trade unions in West Germany," *British Journal of Industrial Relations*, 23 (1) March.

Erd, Rainer (1978) *Verrechtlichung industrieller Konflikte: Normative Rahmenbedingungen des dualen Systems der Interessenvertretung* (Frankfurt am Main/ New York: Campus Verlag).

Ferguson, Adam (1966) *An Essay on the History of Civil Society* (Edinburgh: Edinburgh University Press).

Ferguson, Adam (1975) *The Principles of Moral and Political Science* 2 vols (New York: Hildesheim).

Fiorito, Jack, Lowman, Christopher, and Nelson, Forrest D. (1987) "The impact of human resource policies on union organizing," *Industrial Relations*, 26 (2): 113–26.

Görlitz, Axel and Voight, Rüdiger (eds) (1987) *Grenzen des Rechts. Jahresschrift für Rechtspolitologie* (Pfaffenweiler: Centaurus Verlag).

Habermas, Jürgen (1970) "Verrufener Fortschritt – Verkanntes Jahrhundert. Eine psychoanalytische Konstruktion des Fortschritts," in J. Habermas, *Arbeit, Erkenntnis, Fortschritt* (Amsterdam: de Munter: 112–26).

Habermas, Jürgen (1976) *Zur Rekonstruktion des historischen Materialismus* (Frankfurt: Suhrkamp).

Habermas, Jürgen (1981) *Theorie des Kommunikativen Handelns*, Vol. 1 (Boston: Beacon).

Habermas, Jürgen (1985) "Der normative Gehalt der Moderne," in J. Habermas, *Der philsophische Diskurs der Moderne* (Frankfurt: Suhrkamp: 390–425).

Hardin, Russell (1982) *Collective Action* (Baltimore: Johns Hopkins Press).

Hayek, F. A. von (1952) *The Counter-Revolution of Science* (Glencoe, IL: The Free Press).

Hill, John D. (1984) "Australian density rates 1976–1982," *Journal of Industrial Relations* 26 (4) December.

Huxley, Christopher, Kettler, David, and Struthers, James (1986) "Is Canada's experience 'especially instructive'?" in S. M. Lipset (ed.) *Unions in Transition* (San Francisco: Institute for Contemporary Studies).

Japanese Times, The (1987) Tokyo, January 19, cited in *Social and Labour Bulletin* 3 (September) (1987).

Jones, Gareth Stedman (1983) *Languages of Class, 1832–1982* (Cambridge: Cambridge University Press).

Karatnycky, Adrian, Motyl, Alexander, and Sturmthal, Adolph (1980) *Workers' Rights, East and West* (New York: League for Industrial Democracy and Transaction Books).

Keenoy, Tom (1986) "Solidarity: the anti-trade union," in A. Pravda and B. A. Ruble (eds) *Trade Unions in Communist States* (Boston: Allen & Unwin).

Keohane, Robert O. (ed.) (1986) *Neorealism and its Critics* (New York: Columbia University Press).

Kettler, David and Meja, Volker (1988) "The reconstitution of political life: the contemporary relevance of Karl Mannheim's political project," *Polity* 20 (4) Summer: 623–47.

Kettler, David (1965) *The Social and Political Thought of Adam Ferguson* (Columbus, OH: Ohio State University Press).

Kettler, David (1977) "History and theory in Ferguson's *Essay on the History of Civil Society*. A Reconsideration," *Political Theory*, 5 (4): 437–60.

Kettler, David (1978) "Ferguson's *Principles*: constitution in permanence," *Studies in Burke and His Time*, 208–22.

Kettler, David (1984) "Work community and workers' organization: a central problem in Weimar labour law," Economy and Society, 13 (3): 278–303.

Kettler, David (1987) "Legal reconstitution of the Welfare State: a latent social democratic legacy," *Law and Society Review* 21 (1): 9–47.

Kettler, David, Struthers, James, and Huxley, Christopher (1989) "Unionization and labour regimes: a comparison between Canada and the United States since 1945," (forthcoming in *Labour/Le Travail*).

Kochan, Thomas A. (ed.) (1985) *Challenges and Choices Facing American Labor* (Cambridge, MA: MIT Press).

Kochan, Thomas A., Katz, Harry C. and McKersie, Robert B. (1986a) *The Transformation of American Industrial Relations* (New York: Basic Books).

Kochan, Thomas A., McKersie, Robert B. and Chalykoff, John (1986b) "The effects of corporate strategy and workplace innovations on union representation," *Industrial and Labor Relations Review*, 39 (4): 487–501.

Korea Herald, The (1987) August 13.

Korsch, Karl (1972) "Jus belli ac pacis im Arbeitsrecht," *Kritische Justiz*, 5 (2).

Krasner, Stephen D. (1982) "Structural causes and regime consequences: regimes as intervening variables," *International Organization* 36 (Spring).

Kumar, Pradeep (1986) "Union growth in Canada: retrospect and prospect," *Canadian Labour Relations* (Research Coordinator: W. Craig Riddell). Vol. 16 (Toronto: University of Toronto Press: 95–160).

Lapides, Kenneth (ed.) (1987) *Marx and Engels on the Trade Unions* (New York: Praeger).

Launius, Michael A. (1984) "The state and industrial labor in South Korea," *Bulletin of Concerned Asian Scholars*, 16 (4): 2–10.

Lipset, Seymour Martin (ed.) (1986a) *Unions in Transition* (San Francisco: Institute for Contemporary Studies).

Lipset, Seymour Martin (1986b) "North American labor movements: a comparative perspective," in Seymour Martin Lipset, *Unions in Transition* (San Francisco: Institute for Contemporary Studies).

Loesche, Peter (1982) "Über den Zusammenhang von reformistischen Sozialis-mustheorien und sozialdemokratischer Organisationspraxis in der Weimarer Republik," in H. Heimann and T. Meyer (eds) *Reformsozialismus und Sozialdemokratie* (Berlin, Bonn: J. H. W. Dietz Nachf).

Lohr, Steve (1988) "In Britain, renewed labour unrest," *The New York Times*, February 14, section 3: 1, 7.

Luhmann, Niklas (1981) *Politische Theorie im Wohlfahrtsstaat* (Munich: Günther Olzog Verlag).

Luhmann, Niklas (1984) *Soziale Systeme* (Frankfurt: Suhrkamp).

Luthardt, Wolfgang (1986) *Sozialdemokratische Verfassungstheorie in der Weimarer Republik* (Opladen: Westdeutscher Verlag).

March, James G. and Olsen, Johan P. (1984) "The new internationalism: organisational factors in political life," *American Political Science Review* 78 (3) September: 734–49.

Markovits, Andrei S. (1986) *The Politics of the West German Trade Unions* (Cambridge: Cambridge University Press).

Martin, A. (1987) "The end of the 'Swedish Model?' recent developments in Swedish industrial relations," *Bulletin of Comparative Labour Relations* 16: 93–128.

Marx, Karl (1975 [1844]) "Critical marginal notes on the article 'The King of Prussia and social reform'. By a Prussian," in Marx and Engels, *Collected Works*. Vol. 3 (New York: International Publishers: 189–206).

Marx, Karl (1976 [1847]) "The poverty of philosophy," in Marx and Engels, *Collected Works*, Vol. 6 (New York: International Publishers: 105–212).

Meltz, Noah M. (1985) "Labor movements in Canada and the United States," in T. Kochan (ed.) *Challenges and Choices Facing American Labor* (Cambridge, MA: MIT Press: 315–34).

Mill, John Stuart (1977 [1835]) "De Tocqueville on democracy in America," in *Collected Works*, Vol. 18 (Toronto: University of Toronto Press: 47–90).

Mill, John Stuart (1977 [1840]) "De Tocqueville on democracy in America [II]," in *Collected Works*, Vol. 18 (Toronto: University of Toronto Press, 153–204).

Minc, Bronislaw (1982) "The reasons for the Polish crisis of 1980–81," in *Economic and Industrial Democracy*, Vol. 3 (London and Beverly Hills: Sage).

Müller-Jentsch, Walther (ed.) (1987) *Zukunft der Gewerkschaften* (Frankfurt: Campus).

Niland, John (1986) "How do Australian unions maintain standing during adverse periods?" *Monthly Labour Review* 109 (6) June: 37–9.

Nisbet, Robert (1969) *Social Change and History* (New York: Oxford University Press).

Offe, Claus (1984) *Contradictions of the Welfare State*, edited by John Keane (Cambridge, MA: MIT Press).

Olson, Mancur (1982) *The Rise and Decline of Nations* (New Haven and London: Yale University Press).

Panitch, Leo and Swartz, Donald (1985) *From Consent to Coercion. The Assault on Trade Union Freedoms* (Toronto: Garamond Press).

Piore, Michael and Sabel, Charles (1985) *The Second Industrial Divide* (New York: Basic Books).

Piron, J. and le Roux, P. A. K. (1986) *South Africa* (Deventer, Netherlands: Kluwer).

Plaut, Martin (1984) "Changing perspectives on South African trade unions," *Review of African Political Economy*, 30 (September): 116–23.

Pravda, Alex (1986) "Poland in the 1970s: dual functioning trade unions under pressure," in A. Pravda and B. A. Ruble (eds) *Trade Unions in Communist States* (Boston: Allen & Unwin).

Riddell, W. Craig (research co-ordinator) (1986) *Canadian Labour Relations* (Toronto: University of Toronto Press).

Rogers, Joel (1984) *Divide and Conquer: The Legal Foundations of Postwar US Labor Policy* (Princeton University PhD dissertation).

Rogers, Joel (1988) "Divide and conquer: further reflections on the distinctive character of American labor laws" (unpublished).

Rose, Joseph B. and Chaison, Gary N. (1985) "The state of the unions: United States and Canada," *Journal of Labor Research*, 6 (1) Winter: 97–111.

Rousseau, Jean-Jacque (1973) *The Social Contract and the Discourses* (London: Dent).

Saul, John (1986) "South Africa: the question of strategy," *New Left Review* 160 Noevember–December.

Schumpeter, Joseph (1976) *Capitalism, Socialism and Democracy* (5th edn) (London: George Allen & Unwin).

Schuster, Lynda (1988) "Black labor lost in legal web," *The Christian Science Monitor, World Edition*, 18 (79) March 21–7.

Selznick, Philip (1969) *Law, Society, and Industrial Justice* (New York: Russell Sage Foundation).
Simitis, Spiros (1985) "Zur Verrechtlichung der Arbeitsbeziehungen," in F. Kübler (ed.) *Verrechtlichung von Wirtschaft, Arbeit und sozialer Solidarität* (Frankfurt: Suhrkamp: 73–165).
Social and Labour Bulletin 1 (1987) (March): 181–2.
Steinkühler, Franz (1988) "Angst vor Freunden. Zerbricht das Bündnis von Gewerkschaften und Sozialdemokraten?" *Die Zeit* (overseas edition) 43 (12) (March 25).
Streeck, Wolfgang (1981) *Gewerkschaftliche Organisationsprobleme in der sozialstaatlichen Demokratie* (Königstein/Ts.: Athenäum Verlag).
Streeck, Wolfgang (1987a) "Industrial relations in the Federal Republic of Germany, 1974–1985: an overview," *Bulletin of Comparative Labour Relations*, 16: 151–66.
Streeck, Wolfgang (1987b) "The uncertainties of management in the management of uncertainty: employers, labor relations, and industrial adjustments in the 1980s," *Work, Employment and Society*, 1 (3).
Sunkim, Chi (1985) *South Korea* (Deventer, Netherlands: Kluwer).
Teubner, Günther (1978) "Mitbestimmung – Gesellschaftliche Steuerung durch Organisationsrecht?" *Arbeit und Gesellschaft* 26: 296.
Teubner, Günther (1978) *Organisationsdemokratie und Verbandsverfassung* (Tübingen: Mophr and Siebeck).
Teubner, Günther (1983) "Substantive and reflexive elements in modern law," *Law and Society Review*, 17 (2): 239.
Teubner, Günther (1986a) "Industrial democracy through law?" in Terence Daintith and Günther Teubner (eds) *Contract and Organisation* (Berlin/New York: Walter de Gruyter).
Teubner, Günther (1986b) "Unternehmenskorporativismus: new industrial policy und das 'Wesen' der juristischen Person," 2 *Kritische Vierteljahresschrift für Gesetzgebung und Rechtswissenschaft*.
Tocqueville, Alexis de (1987 [1835]) *Democracy in America* (2 vols) (New York: Alfred A. Knopf).
Tomlins, Christopher (1985) *The State and the Unions, Labor Relations, Law, and the Organized Labor Movement in America, 1880–1960* (Cambridge: Cambridge University Press).
Touraine, Alain et al. (1983) *Solidarity. The Analysis of a Social Movement: Poland 1980–1981* (Cambridge: Cambridge University Press).
Touraine, Alain (1986) "Unionism as a social movement," in S. M. Lipset (ed.) *Unions in Transition* (San Francisco: Institute for Contemporary Studies: 151–73).
Tower, Brian (1987) "Trends and developments in industrial relations," *Industrial Relations Journal* 18 (4).
Troy, Leo (1986) "The rise and fall of American trade unions: labor movement from FDR to RR," in S. M. Lipset (ed.) *Unions in Transition* (San Francisco: Institute for Contemporary Studies).
Vallelly, Richard M. (1989) "Responding to Reagonomics: the politics of policy ideas and the democratic-labor alliance" (unpublished).
Vose, W. J. (1985) "Wiehahn and Rieckert revisited: a review of prevailing black labour conditions in South Africa," *International Labour Review*, 124 (4): 447–64.
Walkom, Thomas (1988a) "Labor's voice becoming louder," *Globe and Mail* (Toronto), January 7: A8.
Walkom, Thomas (1988b) "On the horns of a dilemma," *Globe and Mail*, Toronto, January 18: A8.

Weber, Max (1958 [1921]) *Gesammelte Politische Schriften* (2nd edn) (Tübingen: J. C. B. Mohr (Paul Siebeck)).
Weber, Max (1976 [1922]) *Wirtschaft und Gesellschaft* (5th edn) (Tübingen: J. C. B. Mohr (Paul Siebeck)).

PART III

Rethinking the mechanisms of progress

8

Secularization and sacralization

KENNETH THOMPSON

Introduction

The first question that has to be asked about the concept of "secularization" is whether it continues to serve any useful purpose for sociological theory at the end of the twentieth century. Despite numerous criticisms of its assumptions and inherent ambiguities (Shiner 1967, Martin 1969, Luckmann 1977), its usefulness has been defended on the grounds that it acts as a "sensitizing concept," giving the user a general sense of reference and guidance in approaching empirical instances (Dobbelaere 1981). Whilst accepting that it may have been a useful sensitizing concept for analyzing the passage from traditional to modern society, it can be argued that the collapse of the meta-narratives of "history as progress" and "progressive rationalization," of which it was a part, renders that usage redundant in the analysis of culture in the period of late or postmodernity. If the concept is to serve any useful function it needs to be redefined as an on-going cultural process in a dialectical relationship with its opposite – "sacralization," rather than equating it with the decline of the influence and scope of religion as an institution.

The focus should be on the sacred/profane couplet, as suggested by Durkheim, rather than on secularization as the inevitable decline of religion in the face of institutional differentiation. Durkheim may have shared some of the assumptions of contemporary theories of progress as they related to religion, but he also stressed that the sacred would be transposed into new cultic forms. Correspondingly, his methodology included not merely the sort of social evolutionary approach to the analysis of structural-functional differentiation adopted by most of the early sociologists, but also a structuralist method of analysis that anticipated the "linguistic turn" taken by Saussure, Lévi-Strauss, and other contemporary analysts of culture. It is these newer perspectives and methods – structuralist and post-structuralist – that have rejuvenated the study of ideologies, "imagined communities," discourses, regimes of truth, symbolic codes, and all the other aspects of culture that are structured by differences such as that represented by the sacred/profane couplet. Viewed in this light, contemporary phenomena such as the workers' movements to defend their communities or secure their freedoms (as demonstrated by miners and shipworkers in Britain and Poland), and religious nationalisms, can be seen as evidence of continuing elements of *Gemeinschaft* and sacralizing tendencies in tension with the profane-rationalizing tendencies of a *Gesellschaft* sort being promoted by the managers of the state and the economy. Examples of similar reactions and tensions can be found in many societies, not simply in the form of religious institutions – churches, sects, and cults – but within other institutional spheres and in various forms of popular culture and subcultures.

Secularization and history as progress

Both sociology and Marxism as heirs of the Enlightenment theories of progress shared the assumption that social progress entails a process of secularization. Sociology, as conceived by Comte, was itself to be a science of social progress. It was scientific because it dispensed with previous methods of gaining knowledge based on reference to transcendent laws, states, or beings (Wilson 1975: 9 and Thompson 1975). Its subject matter was social progress, because the history of mankind was marked by increase in knowledge and the capacity to exercise mastery over nature. With regard to both its methodology and subject-matter, therefore, sociology seemed to celebrate secularization and oppose the sacred. Much the same has been said of the method and content of classical Marxism. Sociology and Marxism have been described as documenting a secularizing process (Wilson 1985).

As Robertson puts it: "there can be little doubt that the general *Gemeinschaft* to *Gesellschaft* perspective of classical sociology itself hinged largely on the idea of the secularity of modern societies" (Robertson 1985: 355). In the most forceful and explicit expression of this standpoint by the sociologist of religion, Bryan Wilson, he defines the shift from *Gemeinschaft* to *Gesellschaft* as a process of *societalization*, involving the rejection of religion, which is largely defined as "the ideology" of the communal social formation (*Gemeinschaft*). In that scenario, society – as opposed to community – is bereft of other than peripheral religiosity (Robertson 1985).

As Robertson points out with regard to the implications of this perspective for processes of globalization and the world system, it follows that the world as a whole stands on the threshold of complete secularization: "For not merely has there been a globewide *series* of processes of societalization, the global circumstance *itself* hinges increasingly upon

'agglomerations' of states, the relationships *among them* being characterized by the societal principles of 'rationality' " (Wilson 1982: 158).

The skeptical observer of the intense rivalries between nation-states and
of the heightened sense of nationalism and ethnicity in many countries,
might be forgiven for questioning whether relationships are becoming
more "rational." The strains generated by economic rationalization and
internationalization frequently have the effect of stimulating nationalistic
or subnationalistic reactions at the level of politics and culture. It should
be noted that even Wilson comes close to conceding that the societal and
global circumstances which he depicts as being governed by entirely
instrumental-rational norms are not permanent and that it may be that
"the virtues nurtured essentially in local communities in religious contexts
(will) in the long run be shown to be as indispensable to the society of the
future as they were to the communities of the past" (Wilson 1982: 52).
Nevertheless, Wilson's view is typical of the dominant reading of the
classic sociological tradition's interpretation of modernity as progressive
rationalization. It is essentially Weberian, although with some reference
to Tonnies' depiction of the transition in social relations from *Gemeinschaft* to *Gesellschaft*. With respect to secularization it seems to echo
Becker's sacred-secular antithesis, except that for Becker there was no
notion of an irreversible process taking place. The primary value of the
Becker polarity lies in its use in getting at the sacred or secular aspects of
a group relationship conceived of as a *system*, and in exposing the process
of secularization or sacralization that might be taking place (Loomis and
McKinney 1963: 17). (For Becker, although the main historical trend had
been toward secularization, it was equally permissible to speak of cases of
sacralization, such as the Nazi movement (Becker 1946).)

The neo-Weberian perspective has been contrasted with the Durkheimian
tradition. According to Seidman (1985):

Neo-Weberian perspectives (e.g. Berger 1967, Fenn 1978, Wilson 1966)
articulated and revised Weber's ideas in terms of the processes of
institutional differentiation, cultural pluralism and privatization –
retaining both Weber's belief in the disintegration of normatively
integrated societal community as well as Weber's anxiety about the
decline of individual autonomy . . . The Durkheimians take issue with
the Weberian claim of the dissolution of sociocultural unity and the
thesis of the secularization, segmentation, and privatization of moral
and existential meanings. The Durkheimians argue that every society
rests upon a religiously based set of shared moral understandings
which, by virtue of integrating the personal and social system provide
a basis for identity and societal community as well as a transcendent
standard of judgement (e.g. Bellah, 1970: 168). Thus, Durkheimians
insist that the Weberian notion of a great transformation from a

163

"religious" to a "secular," or communitarian to utilitarian individualist, society is mistaken. Modernization entails alterations and transmutations in the form of religious and collective life, not secularization, the disintegration of social unity, and a privatized type of individualism. Durkheimians argue, moreover, that the new forms of religious life are continuous with Christianity in that they preserve its transcendentalism, millennialism, and its individualistic yet communitarian ethical core. Finally, these contemporary models of religious consciousness are insinuated into the institutional and cultural system creating stable modes of identity and moral community in modern societies. (Seidman 1985: 110–11)

Whilst agreeing with the contrast between Weberian and Durkheimian views of modernity, I disagree with Seidman's simplification of the Durkheimian position and his tendency to equate it with the views of Parsons and Bellah on societal integration through shared values. I want to suggest that the logical development of Durkheim's view of the persistence of the sacred in modern society involves a perception of the dialectical relationship between secularization and sacralization. The various social processes that have been held to characterize modernization and modernity can themselves generate countervailing tendencies – secularization provokes sacralizing reactions. This argument differs from the conventional sociological and classical Marxist view that the secular progressively eliminates the sacred from the public sphere, and also the view that what is left of the sacred is confined to the private sphere of family life or individual consumer choice between meaning systems.

The notion that, in keeping with changes in social organization, one mentality pushes out another, persists in the face of any evidence to the contrary that there is a tendency for one set of beliefs to dislodge another as though for lack of "mental space" (Cohen 1969: 353 and Thompson 1980: 250). There is plenty of evidence from contemporary societies that the sacred element in culture persists in a dialectical relationship with the secular-profane; it is not simply squeezed out by it. As Durkheim puts it, the sacred and the profane (or mundane) principles within culture constantly alternate with each other and "in the present day as much as in the past, we see society constantly creating sacred things out of ordinary ones" (Durkheim 1965: 243). Durkheim gives various examples, such as the cult of authority: "The simple deference inspired by men invested with high social functions is not different in nature from religious respect" (ibid.: 244); the cult of the nation (ibid.: 245); and the cult of reason, liberty, and progress (ibid.).

In contrast to the treatment of secularization in the Weberian tradition, the Durkheimian tradition is concerned not with the decline of the sacred, but with changes in its cultural manifestations. Durkheim urges us to look for experimental examples of these manifestations and transformations, in the same way that he singled out the French revolution for such treatment, and was in no way embarrassed about the fact that it was short-lived: "But this experiment, though short-lived, keeps all its sociological interest. It remains true that in one determined case we have seen society and its essential ideas become, directly and with no transfiguration of any sort, the object of a veritable cult" (ibid.: 245).

Events such as the French revolution are not the only example we can find of the interplay between secularization and sacralization within the cultures of modernity and postmodernity. Although it may be admitted that there have been many such events in the twentieth century, ranging from the Russian revolution, through Nazism, to contemporary Iran, the tendency is to categorize these as "short-lived" phenomena of an exceptional kind that soon give way to the convergent "real" tendencies of modernity. In fact, I would argue, they are only the "tip of the iceberg" or just one of the many forms of the cultural tendencies towards sacralization. Furthermore, whilst secularization may have been the cultural tendency that characterized modernity in the eyes of the early sociologists, it is the persistence of sacralizing tendencies and of the "irrational" that should engage the attention of theorists of late modernity or postmodernity at the end of the twentieth century. Whilst there are some theorists, such as Habermas, who continue to develop a theory of progress in terms of increasing rationality, Jean-François Lyotard and other theorists of postmodernity have argued that such "meta-narratives" of Enlightenment thought as the idea of progress and its linked ideas of secularization and emancipation, are no longer plausible or useful in the age of the Holocaust and Hiroshima (Habermas 1987, Lyotard 1984).

Even one of the most sympathetic reviewers of theories of secularization admits that they do not give sufficient attention to Weber's distinction between goal-oriented action or functionally rational action (*Zweck-rationalität*) and value-oriented action (*Wertrationalität*) (Dobbelaere 1981: 77). Such theories tend to overestimate the extent to which instrumental-rationality governs thought and action in social relations within various institutional spheres. Indeed, sociologists of religion seem more inclined to accept at face value the ideologies of power élites in various institutions, who seek to give the impression that their organizations' instrumental-rational norms are "functionally" necessary and morally neutral. However, sociologists who study such organizations are more aware of the ideological character of such claims and of the extent to which organizational life contains a variety of logics, values, and symbol systems, and even "imagined communities" (cf. examples discussed in Thompson 1986: 85–93).

Similarly, just as we should be cautious about the secularization theorists' claim that modern society is becoming more and more

165

functionally rational with less and less room for different value-orientations based on different communities of shared interests and experience, so we should beware of the dichotomy between a rational public sphere and an irrational private sphere. Both the public and private spheres contain a variety of symbols, logics, and rationalities, and there are symbolic communities that cut across institutions. The two spheres cannot be dichotomized in terms of their rationality, and even at the level of different forms of social interaction they are not wholly distinct. The different forms of social relations (sociality) as defined by Georges Gurvitch (mass, community, and communion), each favoring a different sort of collective consciousness or mentality, appear in both public and private spheres (Gurvitch 1971).

The early sociologists contrasted modernity with traditional society by employing meta-narrative of progressive rationalization and emancipation from irrational sacred bonds, but this meta-narrative no longer functions effectively to generate sociological insight into the cultural complexity of late modernity or postmodernity. We are faced with a profusion of cultural codes, many centers of cultural production, and competition between them to interpret us as subjects in their discourses, or to integrate us into their "imagined communities" (not necessarily "unreal"; cf. Anderson 1983). In the age of mass media, whilst communication technologies may have the potential to construct a future "global village," the present reality is that there exists a profusion of "imagined communities" which dissolve any simple distinction between public and private. Proponents of the secularization thesis might object that the pluralization of "meaning systems" in modern society supports their thesis because it means that the global, cosmic, claims of religion are weakened, and this "laicization" is precisely what they understand by secularization (Dobbelaere 1981). However, this assumes that religion and the sacred are the same thing and that pluralism weakens not just the authority of religion but also the appeal of the sacred. Against this view, it can be argued that cultural differences lead to an intensification of attachment to those very cultural features which make communities and groups different from each other, and which, consequently, they regard as sacred and of ultimate significance. Ethnic and religious differences often take on this kind of ultimate or sacred significance, particularly when they are threatened by dissolution or absorption into some larger entity.

Community and the sacred

Sociologists of religion tend to explain secularization in terms of the diminishing impact of religion due to the decline of community, as in Wilson's statement: "My thesis is that secularization is the decline of community: secularization is a concomitant of societalization" (Wilson 1976: 265–6). However, there are some sociologists of religion, such as Luckmann who, whilst agreeing with Wilson that "religion is a constitutive element of 'community' " (Luckmann 1976: 277) challenge some of his assumptions and draw attention to the presence of "community" layers in modern life, and to the problems of meaning and of life crises which solicit "religious" answers. For Luckmann, secularization is confined to the institutionally specialized social form of religion and does not necessarily extend to the institutionally non-specialized social form of what he terms "invisible religion." The latter is the individual form of religion, supported by friends, neighbors, and members of cliques – the so-called private sphere (Luckmann 1967). Luckmann maintains that privatization of individual existence and cultural pluralism are the basic social conditions which determine religious consciousness in modern societies, and that this consciousness is characterized by a high degree of "arbitrariness" and "bricolage" (a concept drawn from Lévi-Strauss's structuralist study of myths). Although Luckmann probably concedes too much to the privatization of religion aspect of secularization theories, his stress on the "bricolage" character of postmodern culture is welcome.

In his seminal essay on "The structural study of myth," published in the *American Journal of Folklore* (1955), Clause Lévi-Strauss likened the mental operation of mythical thinking to the "bricoleur," the handyman who constructs objects from odds and ends. Before Lévi-Strauss introduced the structuralist analysis of myth, it was generally accepted that, like religion, mythical thinking was destined to die out or be marginalized to a position where it could be dismissed as irrelevant and incongruous when set alongside the formal rationalities of those institutions that were thought to be characteristic of modern society. Even those anthropologists and sociologists who admit that Lévi-Strauss may have made a case for the continuing social usefulness of myths in mediating oppositions or contradictions in society, often do so because they think this is not too great a step away from the structural-functionalist emphasis of Malinowski on the legitimating function of myths in situations where "reason" fails (Malinowski 1926). On this basis they see a continuing function for myths *faute de mieux*, until the remaining contradictions are removed by the spread of more rational systems of thought or changes in the social institutions. (Heirs of the Enlightenment theories of progress, such as sociological theories of modernization and classical Marxism, incline towards this view.) But sociologists and anthropologists inspired by Lévi-Strauss's example have shown that many genres of myth and folklore continue to thrive in the interstices of urban-industrial society (cf. Thompson 1980). Lévi-Strauss's theory provides some of the reasons why: first, because oppositions and contradictions proliferate in *all* societies; second, because the mentality that gives rise to myths, that of the "bricoleur," is likely to continue in the oral culture of face-to-face interactions, such as those studied by ethnomethodologists, and in modern subcultures and popular culture which depend extensively on oral and visual communication (Hebdige 1979). Although such subcultures may not be religious, as in the case of many youth subcultures and, therefore, be dismissed as evidence of "desecularization" (Dobbelaere 1981), their adherents often attach a sacred status to them and will fight to preserve them, so much so that they constitute what Umberto Eco has called "semiotic guerilla warfare" (Eco 1972).

Just as predictions of the demise of mythological thinking were premature, so too were the linked predictions concerning community. It became fashionable during the 1960s for sociologists to talk about the "eclipse" or "end" of community and of ideology, arguing that the convergent tendencies of the spread of mass media, centralized state power, urbanization, and economic development, would eradicate such "irrational" cultural distinctions. By contrast, in the 1970s and 1980s we have witnessed a massive upsurge in nationalism, subcultures, and subnational militancies founded on ethnic and local communities against the homogenizing logic of the national and international political economies. Once this empirical fact is allowed to penetrate through the theoretical barriers set up by the unlinear view of modernization and secularization, then sociologists will be able to turn their attention to analyzing the complementarity of *Gemeinschaft* and *Gesellschaft*, secularization and sacralization, as modalities of behavior within any society at any given period of its history. In Durkheimian terms, mechanical solidarities (complementarily opposed to each other) exist within organic structures. Durkheim recognized the historical compatibility of these supposedly opposite tendencies, although as a believer in progress he regarded the persistence of mechanical forms as a source of difficulty that could only be overcome by restructuring society along more just and communitarian lines (Cohen 1985, Thompson 1982).

Community, as a symbolic assertion of difference over and against some other cultural entity, need not be seen as an anachronism in urban-industrial society. Nor need it be regarded as pathological simply because its symbolic expression is frequently cast in oppositional terms. It can be an example of what Dumont calls "the encompassment of the contrary" in complementary opposition, in which the whole is founded upon the coexistence of juxtaposed parts (Dumont 1980). For, as the anthropologist James Boon has argued, culture is inherently antithetical; just as individuals define themselves by reference to a "significant other," likewise "self-conscious" cultures and communities (Boon 1981). The intimate relationship between community and identity has been described in Durkheimian terms as "cultural totemism" or "ethnogonomy" (Schwartz 1975). These terms suggest that community, and its refraction through self, marks what is not, as well as what is, emphasizing traits and characteristics, "at once emblematic of the group's solidarity and of the group's contrasting identity and relation to the groups within its ambit of comparison" (Schwartz 1975: 108 and quoted in Cohen 1985: 109). In contrast to Talcott Parsons' tendency to discuss culture as socially integrative because of the shared value content or substance of its symbols, this approach emphasizes symbolic forms and their capacity to carry different meanings based on difference and opposition. Thus, in the context of our discussion of the motivation of community assertiveness, it has been commented that this stimulus may not necessarily derive from any articulate and committed sense of the inherent character of a community; but rather, from a felt need to distinguish it from some other entity. This assertion of distinctiveness may resemble the domino theory of politics in that, once one group marks out its distinctiveness, others feel compelled to follow suit.

In this respect community is the compass of individual identity; it responds to the need to delimit the bounds of similarity. Without the benefit of hindsight, Durkheim thought this need would be swept away by the political and economic logic of large-scale systems of production. They would appear to have brought about almost entirely the opposite effect. (Cohen 1985: 110)

Similarly, with regard to the diminution of the geographical basis of community boundaries, there has been a renewed assertion of them in symbolic terms:

Since the boundaries are inherently oppositional, almost any matter of perceived difference between the community and the outside world can be rendered symbolically as a resource of its boundary. The community can make virtually anything grist to the symbolic mill of cultural distance, whether it be the effects upon it of some centrally formulated government policy, or a matter of dialect, dress, drinking, or dying. The symbolic nature of the opposition means that people can "think themselves into difference." The boundaries consist essentially in the contrivance of distinctive meanings within the community's social discourse. They provide people with a referent for their personal identities. Having done so, they are then themselves expressed and reinforced through the presentation of those identities in social life. (Cohen 1985: 117)

These new theorizations of symbolic community and the sacred diverge from the classic theories of progress, modernization, and secularization, which had a mechanical unidirectional character because they sought to understand the newly emerging modern society by contrasting it with premodern "traditional" society. From our vantage point at the end of the twentieth century, that earlier focus may be more of a hindrance than a help. It is for this reason that some of the most lively theoretical debates in recent times have been over "postmodernism," which heralds the recognition of a plurality of cultures and the collapse of the grand narratives of modernism in the face of cultural fragmentation, marked by cultural and political reaction and revival of old forms (ICA 1986).

Once we get away from the assumption that community has to be defined by stable face-to-face social relations and accept the notion of symbolic community, and that the sacred need not refer to a religion which posits a supernatural being or force, then sociology is free to analyze the cultural dynamics involved in the relations between the principles of *Gemeinschaft* and *Gesellschaft*, sacred and secular/profane. Both symbolic community and the sacred are founded on difference over and against a significant other category; community identity is sacred to the extent that members regard it as of ultimate and transcendent significance. This is the starting point of Durkheim's theory of the sacred, and of its binding effect on those who consider themselves to share a common bond, a kinship not based on blood but on a shared symbolic identity. His subsequent definition of religion, which is secondary to this concept of the sacred bond, entails reference to "a unified system of beliefs and practices relative to sacred things . . . which unites into one single moral community called a Church, all those who adhere to them" (Durkheim 1965: 62). The extent to which a sacred community develops a unified system of beliefs and practices, with a moral and normative basis, may affect its prospects for longevity and whether it qualifies as a "religious" or "quasi-religious" institution. But these are secondary matters and should not divert attention from the essential characteristic of the sacred community being founded on symbolic difference which members regard as of fundamental significance.

Desecularization through symbolic community and sacralization

The implication of Durkheim's discussion of new cults of the sacred was that modern society contains a variety of discourses that could serve as the basis of symbolic communities. Whilst some social bonds would be based on routine and custom, and an increasing number of others on complementarity of functions and exchange of services, there would always be some that resulted from the awe and reverence that were inspired by symbols and ceremonies expressive of the experience of the transcendence and power of the collectivity itself (deriving from both real and imagined social relatedness). Such symbolic communities could draw on a variety of discourses, of which religion and ethnicity are two that articulate together most powerfully. It should not be surprising that nationalism and subnationalisms continue to attract greater allegiance than many more formally "rationalized" ideologies, such as socialism, capitalism, or even the doctrines of Catholicism, Protestantism, or Islam. The potency of nationalism derives from its combination of two discourses – religion and ethnicity. Thus, it is an Islamic Iran that attracted widespread support in that country, not pure Islamic ideology stripped of national embodiment; similarly with respect to Polish Catholicism, or Zionism. This capacity for symbolic community and sacralization to be generated by the combination of discourses indicates why theories of secularization based on the decline of a single discourse (religion) may be mistaken. As Benedict Anderson is careful to point out, it is not that nationalism somehow supersedes religion, but that "nationalism has to be understood by aligning it, not with self-consciously held political ideologies, but with the large cultural systems that preceded it, out of which – as well as against which – it came into being" (Anderson 1983: 19). The two relevant cultural systems were religious community (e.g. Islam, Christianity, Buddhism) and the dynastic realm (such as, in Europe, the Habsburgs, Stuarts, Bourbons, etc.), which in their heyday were the taken-for-granted frames of reference that nationality is today. With the pluralization of religions and the breakup of dynastic empires, the nation emerged as the ultimate symbolic or ideological community for most people, the one with the strongest imagined sense of timelessness, disinterestedness, and naturalness. A symbolic community is ideological to the extent that its systems of representation interpellate people ("hail" them) as subjects of the single or combined discourse, and give them an identity as subjects (members) of the imagined community. In analyzing nationalism within a concrete social formation, such as America, Britain, or Poland, these general ideological processes have to be translated into the particular forms in which they occur in each instance. This entails examining the articulation of the various discourses that support each other in producing the actual character of that specific imagined or symbolic community – such as that "nation" – at different points in time.

Articulation of discourses

There is an important difference between this analysis of the articulation of discourses in each specific case and the more blanket and mechanical theories of ideology and secularization, which posit a universal and unilinear development. We cannot depend on a neo-functionalist theory, whether Marxist or Parsonian, which explains ideology as an automatic response to the needs of a social system, so that a common culture or set

171

of values by definition is bound to exist: for Parsonian functionalism there is an assumed homology between social and cultural systems, just as in economistic Marxism the cultural superstructure must correspond to the economic base. Such theories offer little guidance for analyzing how particular symbolic communities such as nationalisms are symbolically constructed and socially mobilized through active processes of persuasion, contestation, and resistance. The sense of being a people is no doubt rooted in elements of shared characteristics and common history, but these are frequently matters of dispute and contestation, linked to power struggles. Territory, language, religion, race, and so forth, are all sources of dispute and have to be ideologically constructed or interpreted in order to produce a sense of belonging to a national community, as a glance at the history of the peoples living in the British Isles illustrates. How else can we understand the conflict in Northern Ireland, or the preference of some people for Welsh or Scottish nationalism over British nationalism? A variety of discourses and sets of differences have been articulated to construct the imagined community of the British nation at different times. Some of the most interesting are those in which there were struggles over the competing religious and political discourses that were combined together to produce an ideologically unifying nationalism. Thus, in the period of internal upheaval and class conflict that accompanied the Industrial revolution at the end of the eighteenth century, such a combination occured in response to the perceived threat posed by revolutionary France. New politically conservative theories of the nation were developed by Burke, Coleridge, and others, drawing on religious as well as political discourses. Public opinion was mobilized against the alien threat and British national characteristics were rediscovered or invented. Many of the shared symbols were drawn from discourses such as political liberalism, where they had a different meaning, and emerged from the ideological struggle inflected in a conservative direction. Indeed, Burke's *Reflections on the Revolution in France* (1790) provides a fascinating example of the rearticulation of existing political and religious discourses and the redefinition of historical events in order to construct a new ideological community – in this case the conservatively defined nation, Britain (Thompson 1986: 52). A similar process of rearticulation of discourses – religious, political, economic, and familial – has been underway to produce the current ideology of Thatcherism, which also gives us a conservatively imagined community of the British nation, although from a different mix to that of Burke.

It is to the analysis of such rearticulations of discourses, religious and non-religious, that we must turn in order to make sense of the various striking revivals of cults of sacred community in the modern world, and in order to understand their causes and conflictual effects. Some theorists of secularization have begun to accept the need to turn their attention to these seeming deviations from the course of progressive rationalization in the process of modernization. Thus, Bryan Wilson, in his most recent writings, takes care to point out that the concept of secularization need not imply that "the process by which religion loses influence is a regular, uninterrupted decline," and "any idea of a unilinear development must be at once rejected" (Wilson 1988: 958–9). However, he tends to imply that religion "prevails only at the margins and in the interstices of an increasingly rational structure," usually for marginal groups, and that an example like Iran "scarcely exemplifies a reversal of secularization" (ibid.: 959–60). But his own review of contemporary examples of religious vibrancy suggests that, not only are they not examples of the marginalization of religion in the private sphere, but that cumulatively they could illustrate the variety of forms in which religion combines with other discourses to produce recurrent social responses to the very social processes that are claimed to be characteristic of modernity. In considering the following description of these examples, we might feel inclined to ask the question: at what point do "special factors" and "marginal cases" begin to add up to a case for regarding these phenomena as variations on a common response to modernity – that of sacrilization? He states:

The most conspicuous evidence of the vibrancy of religion come from societies in which social conflict is expressed in religious terms, in which men are, apparently, prepared to lay down their lives for the sake of religious convictions. The conspicuous cases are the civil strife in Lebanon and Ireland; the religious revolution in Iran; and the passive resistance to the communist state in Poland. In each case, special factors are at work.

The first so-called "special" factor is that of *cultural marginality*:

In both Lebanon and Ireland it might not be too much to say that religion here functions as a legitimation of what are tantamount to tribal allegiances of populations which live on the periphery of the religious confessions to which they claim adherence. In such cases, marginal groups frequently over-identify with the values of the tradition to which they belong . . . Over-identification is a well-known ethnic, nationalist, and/or religious phenomenon, particularly among culturally deprived or retarded constituencies.

The second case is that of *resistance to modernization*:

The Iranian case is manifestly a case of resurgent religiosity, but religion proclaimed in an underdeveloped country in which religion is a rallying-ground against modernization, or, perhaps more accurately, against the inequalities, corruption, and social divisiveness which modernization produced. Iran, as a less developed country, scarcely exemplifies a reversal of secularization, although there is no doubt that secularization – diffused from more advanced countries – might be retarded in contexts where external influences can be resisted, as for instance in pre-war Tibet. How long such self-imposed isolation can persist is a matter of speculation.

The third exceptional circumstance is where religion is a *surrogate* for prohibited political expression:

> The Polish case turns on different considerations. The Catholic Church has long been the repository of national identity for a much conquered and long-occupied people, regularly deprived of their national leaders. Religion is here a surrogate for political expression in a context where such expression is prohibited. (Wilson 1988: 959–60)

These supposedly exceptional cases could just as easily be seen as but a few of the many powerful combinations of the discourses of ethnicity, politics, and religion which are stimulated as a response to tendencies regarded as typical of modernity – such as rationalization, societalization, and the homogenizing pressure to dissolve distinct community identities. Cultural marginality is a common characteristic of many minority and ethnic groups in modern societies, and there are many circumstances that can exacerbate that sense of marginality and produce over-identification with their distinctive tradition. Similarly, in a case such as that of religious discourse in Iran, it cannot be adequately understood simply as a temporary resistance to modernization, although there may be some clues to its coding and functioning in terms of a symbolic rallying against "corruption" and "social divisiveness." The sense of fundamental or sacred community identity can be threatened from two directions: the first derives from the fragmenting and corrosive effect of "mundanization" – what Durkheim called the "profane world" where economic activity is the preponderating one and where the sense of community "is generally of a very mediocre intensity" (Durkheim 1965: 246). The second threat is that of "profanization" of the sacred community through its pollution by an opposed entity, such as the "Great Satan America" in the discourse of Iranian demonology. Thus, in the case of Iran, the threat to its sacred identity may be felt to derive from both these sources. The third suggested "exceptional circumstance," where religion functions as a "surrogate" for some supposedly more realistic form of expression, as is posited for Poland, does not seem particularly exceptional in view of the frequency with which religion, politics, and ethnicity combine together. Further-more, pushed to its extreme, such an explanation can seem reminiscent of the now largely discarded Marxist theory of "false consciousness."

As far as advanced western societies are concerned, sections of the population that experience an acute loss of community attachment are frequently subject to the strains of anomie, according to Durkheim. This is more socially significant than might seem to be the case from the description of it as "individual alienation," as in Wilson's description of the revival of religious discourses in advanced western societies:

> In nations more advanced than any of these, there are also instances of religious revivalism. In these, quite different, circumstances, we may suppose that personal discontents with the increasingly impersonal, large-scale, societally-organized social systems, induce a response in which religion – with its emphasis on personal relationships and transcendent values – is a ready-made focus for the expression of contemporary alienation. (Wilson 1988: 960)

The example of the "new American right," the "moral majority," with its associated fundamentalist religion and television evangelism, is not just a case of an inchoate mass of alienated individuals. The fact that they are "principally concerned with the erosion of *American* moral values" (Wilson 1988: 960, emphasis added), suggests that they have been mobilized by a culturally specific combination of political, religious, and familial discourses, forming them into an ideological community which feels its sacred identity is threatened by an alien other (e.g. socialism, secularism, sexual permissiveness, etc.). The social processes giving rise to that reaction have been widely discussed; some of them are those same processes characteristic of modernity mentioned previously, others are historically and culturally specific, such as the Vietnam War, the various civil rights and social movements (e.g. feminism, youth subcultures like the hippies), and political scandals (Watergate and the resignation of President Nixon).

Other modern, supposedly secularized societies have experienced new combinations of religious and other discourses. As Wilson notes:

> Japan is often regarded as one of the world's most secularized countries, yet it is in that country that some of the most successful and vigorous new movements have developed in the decades since the Second World War . . . Religious movements may serve primarily as mediating institutions between the individual and the increasingly powerful state, enclaves in which some vestige of communal association may be sustained. This is particularly evident in Japan, where, in this respect, their functions are of great importance. Religion may still have this significant function in societies which are increasingly impersonalized by formal, rational, bureaucratic structures and technological work operations. In the face of persisting secularization of the social order, we

175

might expect religious movements, and particularly new forms of religion, to arise, perhaps as recurrent phenomena. (Wilson 1988: 965)

And yet, despite all these concessions to the recurrent revival of religious discourses and new cultic forms, theorists of secularization are still inclined to write this off as simply more evidence for the thesis that modernization means decreasing scope and significance for religion. Indeed, religious diversity, particularly diversification for different constituents as specified by age, education, social class, gender, or sexual preference, can lead to the conclusion that: "Religious diversity is quite consistent with secularized society, testifying in its own way to the limitation of what religion can actually do" (Wilson 1988: 966).

Sometimes it is even suggested that there is a "supermarket of faiths" in western societies, which "coexist only because the wider society is so secular; because they are relatively unimportant consumer items" (Wilson 1975: 80; see also Truzzi 1970, and Fenn 1978). This view has been criticized because it makes an assumption about the depth of commitment and authenticity of these religious groups compared with more traditional forms (Stark and Bainbridge 1985: 437). A contrary hypothesis is that secularization itself stimulates religious revival in the form of movements, sects, or cults, which are not trivial, particularly when they are innovative in their content and supply what is lacking in those traditional religious organizations that have become internally secularized, in the sense of losing their distinctiveness from the surrounding world (Stark and Bainbridge 1987: 307). Stark and Bainbridge make the further point that sects and cults can be significant on a national and international level, not just in the personal dramas of private religion:

> Every proposition we have derived concerning sects, except for one or two that include size as a variable, may apply to groups as large as nations. Unless acting as agents for a superpower, radical groups that seize control of nations and experience great *antagonism* toward outsiders will also display other characteristics of the high-tension sect, including *separation* and *difference*. Ideologies promulgated by other nations, especially those broadcast by the superpowers, may draw forth angry sentiments from nationalists of whatever stripe. There will be a tendency for independent revolutionary parties to seek their own national ideologies, perhaps a local brand of socialism but perhaps also a blend of socialism and a revitalized native religion. (Stark and Bainbridge 1987: 306)

Hitlerian paganism is given as an example of a new national cult which, although it was the dominant religious organization and so not deviant with respect to the society's norms, was deviant from those of the surrounding world. Similarly, with regard to the establishment of Shiite religion as the dominant cultural force guiding the state in Iran: from the perspective of the Moslem world as a whole, the Shiite branch is sect-like – relatively high in tension, a minority with more intense practices and deviant beliefs, compared to those of the more numerous Sunni (Stark and Bainbridge 1987: 307). However, the extent to which a sect or cult ideology is in a relation of high tension with the surrounding culture will vary. Stark and Bainbridge assert that many cults are in a relatively low state of tension with the surrounding culture, particularly audience cults which rely on mass media of communication (e.g. pseudo-scientific cults concerning astrology, flying saucers, ESP, etc.), conveying compensations in the form of a "diffuse hope," and offering little sense of community and so attracting low commitment. Others are client cults, offering specific compensations for experiences of relative deprivation, such as non-professional services to alleviate medical or psychiatric disorders. Some of these evolve into more organized cult movements which offer more general compensations and attract a deeper commitment, as in the case of scientology (Wallis 1976). However, whether they evolve into fully-fledged movements based on face-to-face relations, or stay at the level of common interests and allegiances shared at a distance, cults abound in modern societies. Indeed, Stark and Bainbridge, after documenting that abundance, produce a conclusion that is the reverse of that usually derived from the theories of progress and secularization:

> In the future, as in the past, religion will be shaped by secular forces but not destroyed. There will always be a need for gods and for the general compensations which only they can plausibly offer. Unless science transforms humans into gods or annihilates humanity, people will continue to live lives hemmed in by limitations. So long as we exist, we shall yearn for a bounty of specific rewards, rewards that in the mundane world are too scarce to be shared by all, and we shall ache for those general rewards of peace, immortality, and boundless joy that have never been found this side of heaven. Secularization has unchained the human spirit, not stifled it in a rationalized bureaucratic outbox. (Stark and Bainbridge 1985: 527–8)

This new thesis about secularization gives the main emphasis to religion as a source of compensations for relatively deprived individuals, although Stark and Bainbridge do analyze some of the institutional and community implications of the different forms taken by religion – churches, sects, and cults. Essentially, it maintains that secularization weakens the capacity of traditional churches to offer distinctive compensations, because what they have to offer is relatively indistinguishable from that of the mundane/ profane surrounding culture; consequently, sectarian schisms occur, based on a higher level of tension with the surrounding culture, but then their distinctiveness is gradually weakened by secularization. Cults, which are distinguished by their cultural innovativeness (even if it is only new interpretations of old symbols), arise to fill the gaps left by the secularization or mundanization of established religious movements and faiths, and so cults are likely to go on proliferating. Whilst allowing that cults may vary in their scope and the depth of commitment of adherents, the proponents of this thesis rightly reject the implication of theorists of secularization that all cults are trivial or inherently limited in scope compared with "real" religion.

However, despite the attention given to the relationship of religion to the surrounding culture, this thesis still tends to concede that secularization pushes religion into the private sphere becoming a matter of individual consumer choice of meaning systems to satisfy individual needs. In this respect it differs from the critique of secularization theories being offered here, which is that they too easily assume a continuing long-term decline in the activity of the principles of community and the sacred as sources of identity. Our alternative thesis is that the tensions produced by modernity stimulate assertions of total identity grounded in experiences of the socially-transcendent produced by symbolic community. The symbolic community is held to be of ultimate or sacred significance because it sustains a sense of total identity, as opposed to the partial roles and fragmented identities produced by the processes of rational-functional differentiation of modern social systems. For theoretical purposes, it does not matter whether the symbolic community is based on purely religious beliefs and practices, or whether it combines a mixture of discourses focused on the nation, subnation, ethnic group, or some other subculture or ideological cause (including a workers' movement if it attracts total commitment and a belief that their community is threatened or their freedom denied). Communalization and sacralization are fundamental processes in all societies, whether or not we choose to use the term "religion" in that connection. It is this theoretical conviction that leads us to Durkheim's conclusion:

> Thus there is something eternal in religion which is destined to survive all the particular symbols in which religious thought has successively enveloped itself. There can be no society which does not feel the need of upholding and reaffirming at regular intervals the collective sentiments and the collective ideas which make its unity and its personality. (Durkheim 1965: 474–5)

Conclusion

What has been proposed is a neo-Durkheimian reconceptualization of the processes previously designated by the concept of secularization, stressing Durkheim's notions of the binary opposition of the cultural principles of the sacred and profane, and the formation of symbolic community. The opposed cultural principles and processes of sacralization and profanization (including mundanization) should be seen as being in an ongoing dialectical relationship.

The "sacred" is that which is socially transcendent and gives a sense of fundamental identity based on likeness (kinship), constructed and sustained by difference or opposition over and against: (1) the alien other (which may be another culture that threatens takeover or some other danger to the maintenance of its identity); (2) the mundane/profane i.e. the world of everyday routine, particularly economic activity and its rationality.

The community (*Gemeinschaft*) is based on symbolic unity – it is an imagined likeness with limits or boundaries that separate it from a different, alien other. It contrasts with the functionally-specific relations and instrumental rationalities characteristic of societal association (*Gesellschaft*). The contrast between the two social forms was illustrated in Weber's distinction between the nation, as a *Gemeinschaft*, and the state, as an example of large-scale *Gesellschaft*. Thus the legitimation needs of the state are frequently satisfied by cashing in on the surplus legitimacy accumulated through the discourses that have been combined in the cultural construction of the nation (including religious discourses).

Secularization, which has tended to mean decline of religion as an institution (laicization) as part of the modernization process of structural differentiation, is now largely superseded by this recast analytical framework (except in the case of newly-modernizing societies). This is theoretically necessary for the development of a sociology of culture dealing with the articulation of discourses and decoding of symbol systems in the circumstances of late or postmodernity. Concepts and frameworks developed to analyze the transition from traditional to modern society may no longer be adequate for the new tasks unless we are prepared to look at them afresh and undertake radical recasting.

Bibliography

Anderson, Benedict (1983) *Imagined Communities* (London: Verso).
Becker, Howard (1946) *German Youth: Bond or Free* (New York).
Bellah, Robert N. (1970) *Beyond Belief: Essays in a Post-Traditional World* (New York: Harper & Row).
Bellah, Robert N. (1975) *The Broken Covenant* (New York: Seabury).

179

Berger, Peter (1967) *The Sacred Canopy* (Garden City, NY: Doubleday).

Boon, James A. (1981) *Other Tribes, Other Scribes: Symbolic Anthropology in the Comparative Study of Cultures, Histories, Religions, and Texts* (Cambridge: Cambridge University Press).

Cohen, Anthony (1985) *The Symbolic Construction of Community* (London: Tavistock).

Cohen, Percy (1969) "Theories of myth," *Man*, 4: 337–53.

Dobbelaere, Karel (1981) "Secularization: a multi-dimensional concept," *Current Sociology*, 29 (2): 1–213.

Dumont, Louis (1980) *Homo Hierarchicus* (Chicago: University of Chicago Press).

Durkheim, Emile (1965) *The Elementary Forms of the Religious Life* (trans. by J. W. Swain) (New York: Free Press).

Eco, Umberto (1972) "Towards a semiotic enquiry into the television message," *Working Papers in Cultural Studies*, 2 (University of Birmingham Centre for Contemporary Cultural Studies).

Fenn, Richard K. (1978) *Toward a Theory of Secularization* (Ellington, CT: Society for the Scientific Study of Religion).

Gurvitch, Georges (1971) *The Social Frameworks of Knowledge* (trans. by Margaret and Kenneth Thompson, with an introductory essay by Kenneth Thompson) (Oxford: Blackwell, and New York: Harper Torchbooks).

Habermas, Jürgen (1987) *The Theory of Communicative Action*, 2 vols (trans. by Thomas McCarthy) (Cambridge: Polity Press).

Hebdige, Dick (1979) *Subculture: The Meaning of Style* (London: Macmillan).

ICA (1986) *Postmodernism*, ICA Documents 4 (London: Institute of Contemporary Arts).

Loomis, C. P. and McKinney, J. C. (1963) "Introduction" to F. Tonnies, *Community and Society* (trans. by Charles P. Loomis) (New York: Harper Torchbooks).

Luckmann, Thomas (1967) *The Invisible Religion* (New York: Macmillan).

Luckmann, Thomas (1976) "A critical rejoinder," *Japanese Journal of Religious Studies*, 3 (3/4): 277–9.

Luckmann, Thomas (1977) "Theories of religion and social change," *The Annual Review of the Social Sciences of Religion*, 1: 1–28.

Lyotard, Jean-François (1984) *The Postmodern Condition* (trans. by G. Bennington and B. Massumi) (Minneapolis: University of Minneapolis Press).

Malinowski, Bronislaw (1926) *Crime and Custom in Savage Society* (New York: Harcourt, Brace).

Martin, David (1969) *The Religious and the Secular: Studies in Secularization* (London: Routledge & Kegan Paul).

Martin, David (1978) *A General Theory of Secularization* (Oxford: Blackwell).

Robertson, Roland (1985) "The sacred and the world system," in P. E. Hammond (ed.) *The Sacred in a Secular Age* (Berkeley and Los Angeles: University of California Press: 347–58).

Schwartz, T. (1975) "Cultural totemism: ethnic identity – primitive and modern," in G. de Vos and L. Romanucci-Ross (eds) *Ethnic Identity: Cultural Continuities and Change* (Palo Alto, Mayfield: 106–31).

Seidman, Steven (1985) "Modernity and the problem of meaning: the Durkheimian tradition," *Sociological Analysis*, 46 (2): 109–30.

Shiner, Larry (1967) "The concept of secularization in empirical research," *Journal for the Scientific Study of Religion*, 6 (2): 207–20.

Stark, Rodney, and Bainbridge, William S. (1985) *The Future of Religion: Secularization, Revival and Cult Formation* (Berkeley and Los Angeles: University of California Press).

Stark, Rodney, and Bainbridge, William S. (1987) *A Theory of Religion* (New York and Berne: Peter Lang).

Thompson, Kenneth (1975) *Auguste Comte: The Foundation of Sociology* (London: Nelson, New York: Wiley).

Thompson, Kenneth (1980) "Folklore and sociology," *The Sociological Review*, 28 (2): 249–75.

Thompson, Kenneth (1982) *Emile Durkheim* (London and Chichester: Tavistock/ Ellis Horwood).

Thompson, Kenneth (1986) *Beliefs and Ideologies* (London: Tavistock).

Truzzi, Marcello (1970) "The occult revival as popular culture: some random observations on the old and nouveau witch," *Sociological Quarterly*, 13: 16–36.

Wallis, Roy (1976) *The Road to Total Freedom* (New York: Columbia University Press).

Wilson, Bryan (1966) *Religion in Secular Society* (London: A. C. Watts).

Wilson, Bryan (1975) "The secularization debate," *Encounter*, 45: 77–83.

Wilson, Bryan (1976) "Aspects of secularization in the west," *Japanese Journal of Religious Studies*, 3 (3/4): 259–76.

Wilson, Bryan (1982) *Religion in Sociological Perspective* (New York: Oxford University Press).

Wilson, Bryan (1988) " 'Secularization': religion in the modern world," in S Sutherland *et al.* (eds) *The World's Religions* (London: Routledge).

9

The democratization of differentiation: on the creativity of collective action

HANS JOAS

The present crisis of belief in "progress" is not the first in the history of ideas, or even in the history of sociology. People often talk about progress as if there has existed a tradition of unquestioned assumptions about automatic or easily manageable advance since the Enlightenment. To talk like that means to forget that even some contemporaries of the Enlightenment – and not only its conservative opponents – considered the far-reaching changes of their time as being less than progressive in their effect.

Rousseau's critique of civilization was combined for example, in Germany, as we can see in the thought of Herder, with a religiously grounded repugnance for utilitarianism and materialism and led to a deep ambivalence about the changes set off by the French revolution. The course and consequences of the French revolution irritated even its most loyal supporters.

The first symptoms of industrial capitalism caused alarm within the realm of romantic art and writing. The nineteenth century itself, commonly taken as the time of unquestioned belief in progress, shows only a few traces of the original conception of the Enlightenment. In the socialist and anarchist movements this conception was reinterpreted as the idea of history being a permanent struggle involving class and power. It was only the self-confidence of the rising social classes which held out the possibility of evaluating a radically negative present from the standpoint of progress.

Outside of these social movements, but eventually within them as well, Enlightenment philosophy became transformed into evolutionism. This, of course, displays a deterministic certainty about the mechanisms of historical progress. The original ideas of the Enlightenment are rejected here in so far as an automatic (and deterministic) progress no longer depends on the enlightened will of concrete actors. The representative thinkers of the late nineteenth century, however, were neither Marxists nor Hegelian philosophers of history nor were they deterministic evolutionists. Marx and Spencer, in fact, were their "whipping boys" rather than their models.

In the decades prior to the First World War, Germany and France were under the heavy intellectual influence of cultural pessimism. In the Anglo-Saxon countries, where this influence was weaker, the war radically shook the more moderate and optimistic worldview. The belief in a world that had become interdependent and enlightened by science and democracy received a serious blow. The period between the First and Second World Wars, with its permanent economic and political crises, left little opportunity to renew the belief in progress. Thus, the self-confidence of Marxist revolutionary perspectives increased along with the activism and decisionism propagated by fascist movements in order to supersede nihilism as the nadir of the belief in progress.

It wasn't until the end of the Second World War that the notion of progress in the sense of evolutionism or Enlightenment could rise again and gain ground. Several factors played a role in this. The destruction of the worst fascist dictatorships produced the hope that the future might belong to other world powers. There was the enormous economic expansion of the western democracies, and the optimistic self-confidence of "real" socialism, which allowed for the expectation that social problems might be solved gradually through economic growth. The dissolution of colonial empires allowed such hopes to be developed even in those areas of the world which had formerly been seen as impeded in their progress by political, economic, and military power.

Additionally, the expansion of the sciences during this period was supported by a broad public consensus and considered to be part of the preconditions for healthy economic growth. Even the social sciences could count on benevolent sponsorship. They came to be seen as an important factor in the solution of social problems – exploring the possibilities for increasing productivity and growth and in the improvement of government planning. Sociology itself seemed to become a key discipline for the modern state in this regard.

But the origins of sociology are by no means to be found in such a firm belief in progress. The approaches of Comte and Spencer were not merely perpetuated by those classical figures who gave the discipline its intellectual character and institutional profile between 1890 and 1920. It is closer to the truth to see their thought rooted in a polemical attack against an optimistic kind of evolutionism and against the misleading certainties of philosophies of history. The elaboration of their work came at a time when the cultural and moral consequences of the Industrial revolution came to be felt as increasingly problematic. The philosophy of that time dissected the belief in progress in all its aspects, and that dissection permeated the sociological classics.

The most impressive case of this close relationship between sociology and cultural crisis is undoubtedly found in Germany. None of the leading exponents of German sociological thought at the time – not Weber, Simmel, Sombart, or Toennies – were unaffected by the writings of that ambitiously radical critic of progress: Friedrich Nietzsche. For each of them, Nietzsche had definitively destroyed the easy mediation between individual action and historical progress. This does not mean that they accepted Nietzsche's own attempts to cope with the situation he had so convincingly described. All of them, however, were susceptible to Nietzsche's appeals regarding the destruction of illusions and the new self-consciousness of the "vital" élite of genius. At the same time, these thinkers hesitated in being seduced by a vision of history which saw it as a continuum of meaningless struggles, the only possible meaning of which might be found in the production of such genius.

Thus, it was in Nietzsche's tone that Weber characterized the belief in progress as being a dishonest form of coping with the death of God: "The concept of 'progress' is required only when the religious significance of the human condition is destroyed, and the need arises to ascribe to it a 'meaning' which is not only this-worldly, but also objective."[1]

The situation in France was not much different. Bergson's whole thinking was as directed toward the mastering of a cultural crisis as German "Lebensphilosophie" had been. Durkheim's intellectual development was motivated from the very beginning[2] by the question of the presuppositional basis for generating a new morality and new institutions. But this question could only arise from the notion that the foundations of existing institutions were shaky and the uncertainty about whether the division of labor (as an element of progress) would in fact lead to a new "organic" solidarity.

Even American philosophy and sociology during this period, in which historical optimism and reformist self-confidence could be felt, did not derive its character from a naïve ignorance of the ambivalent nature of progress. The American Pragmatist philosophers and the sociologists of the Chicago school, for example, did not see their world as an idyllic place. They believed, however, that scientific method is a procedure that allows for continuing progress – but only if it is fully institutionalized under democratic conditions and applied to problems of social reform. In a certain sense, pragmatism represents an attempt to return to the original notions of the Enlightenment from the realms of evolutionism and "progressive" philosophies of history.

Thus for John Dewey, the First World War was an almost welcome opportunity to leave the fool's paradise of automatic and uninterrupted progress. "We confused rapidity of change with advance, and we took certain gains in our own comfort and ease as signs that cosmic forces were working inevitably to improve the whole state of human affairs."[3]

According to Dewey the time of "laissez-faire" thinking was over, and he extends the meaning of this expression from the trust in the salutary consequences of markets to the trust in nature, providence, evolution, or "manifest destiny" – all these attitudes are opposed to the acceptance of historical responsibility, but only this can guarantee progress. Only the possibility of a rational procedure is grounded in science.

The larger part of George Herbert Mead's postwar philosophy, as it exists in his *Philosophy of the present*, is dedicated to resisting a philosophy of the past, i.e., a mechanical determinism, as well as a philosophy of the future, or a teleological determinism. A philosophy of the present rather has to think the "emergence of novelty" in the universality of determinations. The crisis of the belief in progress is seen here as a chance for the new connection of responsible action to progress.

An idea that is common to all sociological classics is that only the loss of a naïve belief in progress opens up the historical future as well as the risky and responsible character of present action. They differ sharply, however, in their views on the possibility for mankind to shape this open future. We might ask the rather ironic question, therefore, whether there has been any progress in our thought about progress in the generations subsequent to the sociological classics. Do we have better conceptual means today to cope with our present crises, or did the founders of sociology in fact have greater insight than the mainstream of the discipline today recognizes?

What remedy against the darkening future did the sociological classics have? I think it would be wrong to answer this question through the interpretation of their political views. We find a plurality of political options: from Toennies' gradual approximation to the Social Democratic party to Sombart's way to Hitler. It is often hard to distinguish whether these prescriptions originate in pre-scientific attitudes or in the sociological analysis. But these thinkers must not be reduced to their political convictions; their theoretical constructions cannot be fairly judged when reduced to a political diagnosis of their time.

If one inquires, however, into the fundamental theoretical achievements of sociology's founders, then one aims to discover their central assumptions regarding human action and social order.[4] If we put the question in those terms, it becomes clear that it is precisely in the dimension of action theory that we find the conceptual means of the classics to grasp the emergence of something new or better against an imposing future.

As evolutionism and the philosophy of history disappeared as the "last religion of the educated class" (Benedetto Croce) and the retreat into a transcendental constitution of meaning was no longer acceptable, only immanent traits of the human mastering of life could help in imagining the future. In order to find a way out of the cultural crisis, human action and human sociality had to become understood as being resources for (potential) creativity.

The further development of the sociological theory of action did not always assist in this understanding. It was mainly the influence of Talcott Parsons which brought about a dichotomy between rational, e.g. utility-oriented, and normatively-oriented modes of action, making the creative dimension of action inconceivable. The course of the history of ideas about action did not at all force such reflection into this narrow typology. Many theories of action pointed in other directions, from the "practical philosophy" of classical antiquity via the ramified German tradition of "expressivity" to American pragmatism. This doesn't mean that Parsons' dichotomy does not grasp an important distinction or that this distinction was unimportant in relation to the sociological classics.

In fact, the nascent discipline of sociology claimed the tasks and objects of investigation that the economic theory of rational action refused to take over from the provinces of older economic theory and political philosophy. Sociology therefore had a fundamental need for a theory of action that defined different types of action based on their difference from rational action. It required, therefore, a theory of society as a complex of interrelated actions that amounted to more than the unintended interconnection of self-interested actions. It is for this reason that the dimension of normative agreement among social actors played such an important role for the classics. But the problem of the classics was not confined to this opposition to contemporary economics. They also had to confront the field of contemporary philosophy and to demonstrate the ability to master the cultural crisis of progress through their action theory.

A few examples will have to suffice here. In the work of Max Weber there is on the one hand his typology of action, which is certainly developed through the model of rational action; on the other hand, we also have in his work the idea of charisma as the truly revolutionary force in history.

It is difficult to imagine how Weber would have been able to locate the origination of new institutions in the emotional power and creativity of exceptional individuals in his typology of action; to characterize charisma as "affectual" would have been pointless reductionism. Nevertheless, charisma is not a marginal phenomenon in Weber's analysis. If we are allowed to infer *ex negativo* from the critical scrutiny to which he subjected his own era (and in particular from his critique of the pervasive bureaucratization of all spheres of life), we can see that the yardstick of his analysis is a conception of creativity that became increasingly impossible after the end of the heroic age of the bourgeoisie.

In regard to Georg Simmel's writings, one has to see that he continuously pursued a theory of aesthetic creativity in addition to his analysis of the rationalizing tendencies of a money economy within modern culture. Toennies' book, *Community and Society*, meanwhile, is mostly interpreted in complete neglect of the author's search for synthesis: a type of social order providing guild socialism and a combination of *Wesenwillen* and *Kuerwillen* in the personality structure of the gifted genius. If we subtract all the elements of war propaganda from Sombart's book *Heroes and Merchants*, then we can clearly recognize his attempt to oppose to the utilitarian "spirit of the merchants" and its cultural consequences the "spirit of heroes," a militaristic transformation of Nietzschean ideals of personality.

Durkheim's theory of religion can be considered then as an attempt to reflect on the creation of new institutions and interpersonal relationships in unconsciously creative sociality. It remains open, however, what the present-day importance of such an experience of collective ecstasy in rituals might be. It is only clear that Durkheim ascribes to it effects which change personalities. These changes cannot be ascribed by the participants themselves to their common activity, but only to the place, time, or occasion of their assembly and to sources of power outside their collectivity. What sounded like geniality and longing for a leader in Weber's theory of charisma is completely lacking here, and yet the modern equivalent to the creative sociality of totemistic rituals is very unclear.

In pragmatist thinking, a specific understanding of scientific research as the prototype of historical innovation is put into the same systematic place. Dewey and Mead do not want to use the belief in science as the foundation for evolutionism. What they do want is to demonstrate that scientific research is a particularly clear example of action which is characteristic of the human mastery of life in general. They leave behind the idea that action is rational when it is conceived as the realization of preconstituted purposes. A changed meaning of "intentionality" allows them to put the phenomena of experiment and play, or art, into the center of the theory of action.

The experiment was for Dewey and Mead the clearest case of the overcoming of an action problem by the invention of new possibilities for action. For them, the capacity for such invention has as its precondition the self-aware employment of a disposal over the form of action known as play, the conscious "playing through" in imagination of alternative performances of action. They assume a dialogical interaction referring to argument and control between individual creativity and common culture. When they speak of science as the means to the solution of a cultural crisis, this is not a confidence in the comprehensive problem-solving capacity of social technology, but the perspective of a democratic culture in which a maximum of individual creativity is combined with discursive or argumentative procedures to reach agreement.

The founding decades of sociology brought forth great theories containing models of creative action. These models are, however, very different from one another in their emphasis. Whereas Weber focused on prophets, the founders of religion, or the great men of world history, Durkheim had before his eyes the drunkenness of the religious or revolutionary masses. Dewey and Mead's prototype is the genius of the creative scientist, but this conception is embedded within the framework of a democratic culture in which everyone can argue against the experts. Thus, every idea can – through convincing argumentation – become part of the cultural tradition.

These distinctions demonstrate that by merely pointing out the model of creative action we do not yet gain a sufficient characterization of the theoretical perspectives given in the classics. Within the structure of action it is necessary to distinguish the different types of relationships between pre-rational activity, impulse, and normatively institutionalized world orientation. Abraham Maslow's "humanistic" psychology introduces an appropriate distinction here. Maslow distinguishes between primary, secondary, and integrated creativity.[5] Primary creativity is for Maslow the release of "primary processes" of fantasy and imagination, of the playful and the enthusiastic. Secondary creativity is for him the rational production of something "new" in the world, be it technical or scientific. This category may also include problem solutions involving artistic or practical matters.

For our purposes, the crisis of belief in progress can be interpreted as a crisis of secondary creativity. That is, we did not lose our belief in progress as such, for there has been little doubt regarding the continued evolution of the natural sciences, technology, and economic improvement. The important thing is the widespread feeling that this progress in certain sectors of society does not add up to a comprehensive progress throughout the whole that earns the name of progress in the singular. The critique of progress as the result of secondary creativity leads us – if it is not simply condemned in a hyper-rationalist way – to a new evaluation of primary creativity.

At this point we confront two clear alternatives. On the one hand, there can be a longing for primary creativity which overshadows that of the secondary type. This is the way of irrationalism. On the other, there can be the attempt to integrate primary and secondary creativity. This is Maslow's third type: here the concert of primary and secondary creativity leads to a higher form of action which does not refuse the steering provided by rationality and criticism.

> The great work needs not only the flash, the inspiration, the peak-experience; it also needs hard work, long-training, unrelenting criticism, perfectionistic standards. In other words, succeeding upon the spontaneous is the deliberate; succeeding upon total acceptance comes criticism; succeeding upon intuition comes rigorous thought; succeeding upon daring comes caution; succeeding upon fantasy and imagination comes reality resting.[6]

This notion of "integrated creativity" is an expression of an idea that is fundamental also to the pragmatist philosophy of Dewey and Mead. The explicit expansion of pragmatism from the realm of instrumental problem-solutions to ethics, and especially to aesthetics and religion,[7] makes it clear that pragmatism is not a metaphysics of engineering, but a search for values legitimated within themselves: provisionally termed "democracy" and "science." Integrated creativity is not indifferent towards the normative evaluation of the products of creativity. It does not describe moral or political indifference as an achievement, but rather defends a type of personality whose impulses are not hindered in their articulation by moral and political commandments. The openness of self-articulation goes along with the responsibility of self-control.

Sociology under the influence of pragmatism talked about "self-control" and "social control" to express individual or collective self-government – and was promptly misunderstood.[8] Today Cornelius Castoriadis attempts to think through the notions of individual and social autonomy, notions which no longer – as in the Kantian tradition – oppose sharply the spheres of obligation and inclination. Instead, all inclinations are seen as an integrated part of a dialogical autonomy.

The revolts of romanticism and *Lebensphilosophie* can be understood as the mobilization of primary creativity against secondary creativity. None of the sociological classics simply joined the revolt. They were all attempting to reconstruct the heritage of rationalism and not to nihilistically bury it. An important question is how far they succeed in this attempt on the level of axiological foundations as well as on the level of substantive sociological theory. I will restrict myself here to the second of these levels.

To make the formulation of the issue still more narrow: how far do sociological theories succeed in recognizing the creative dimension of action in their analysis of processes of collective action? This formulation implies the presupposition that Weber's insight into the revolutionary force of charisma can and must be reformulated into a theory of collective action.

The European classics of sociology did not contribute much to an explicit theory of collective action. Durkheim's theory of religion, influenced by contemporary crowd psychology as a scientific reaction to social movements, left unexplained the possibilities of periodic collective revitalization in modern societies. That is why the interpretations of this theory differ so widely: from Tiryakian's stress on the experience of fusion/regression and the importance of periodic de-differentiation, to Habermas's thesis of a "linguistification of the sacred."[9] Parsons' theory did not contain the conceptual means to grasp the creative production of historically contingent institutions and worldviews. The idea of a collective actor does not contradict the construction of his theory, but it is not addressed by it either. Parsons speaks, it is true, about the culturally-innovative character of seedbed-cultures. But his analysis does not in fact deal with the constitution of values, only with the internalization and institutionalization

189

of pre-constituted values along with the generalization, modification, or specification.

The great exception to this general neglect is to be found in the sociology of the Chicago school. The "green bible" of American sociology during the interwar period – Park and Burgess's *Introduction to the Science of Sociology*[10] – defined the process of collective action as *the* subject matter to be considered. The central idea of the macrosociological writings of that school was that institutions have to be studied as the temporarily-stabilized result of creative processes of institutionalization. In this way, the perspective of decline and decay that was common in European sociology is superseded: the present is no longer seen merely as a period marked by the dissolution of old communities, but also as containing the emergence of new social forms. Thomas and Znaniecki, for example, saw the migration of Polish peasants to America from the twin perspectives of disorganization and reorganization. The concept of action was not individualistically conceived, but related from the outset to the process of symbolically-mediated co-ordination through mutual interaction.

Unfortunately, these promising ideas in the work of Park and Burgess became subject to the pressure of deterministic conceptions of the "biotic" or "ecological" order and the "natural history" of social movements. This allowed the incorporation into the theory of elements which did not arise from the intentions of social actors. Included were the unplanned and unintended processes of the interconnection between the consequences of action and the selection of functionally suitable alternatives, along with the development of social movements, not dependent on the will of actors. But these parts were not comfortably integrated with the rest of the theory.

Herbert Blumer, who pursued this approach to collective action, escaped from this situation by concentrating almost exclusively on collective action itself and ignoring again the elements that had remained poorly integrated in Park. Thus, the claim of the determination of sociology by collective action developed into a specialty within the discipline. The relationship between a theory of the emergence of norms and institutions and an analysis of the structural effects of existing institutions remained unclear.

It is unnecessary to discuss here the further vicissitudes of pragmatist or symbolic-interactionist approaches on collective action. Instead, we will shift our line of inquiry and ask whether functionalism, wherein the contribution of institutions to the stability and reproduction of societies is considered crucial, has developed a satisfying analysis of collective action.

The most famous attempt here was that of Neil Smelser in the early 1960s. His main achievement is the "normalization" of collective action; that is to say that Smelser removes the tarnish from non-institutionalized action which is considered to be pathological or irrational. The hermetic seal of a world in which all action conforms to institutionalized norms is thus broken. As in the Chicago tradition there is in Smelser's functionalism a theoretical place for the mastery of social strains by outbreaks of spontaneous action. His typology of such outbreaks is developed out of different possibilities to modify one of the components of action. This typology of non-institutionalized collective action is derived from the theory of action in a logically consistent way.

The deficiencies of this theory of action, however, have obvious repercussions in the analysis of collective action. Smelser proposes to use the economic process of gradual value-addition as a model for the progress of collective behavior. This model, though, clearly refers to a teleological process of action, i.e., a process in which every earlier step can be seen as a means to a future goal. But surely this is inappropriate for the dynamics of non-institutionalized collective action. Here, the definitions of the situation and the norms possibly arising from such a process, even the means and goals themselves, are often unclear to the actors involved. They are clarified only in the process as it occurs.

Instead of conceiving of social control as a counterforce, with its own structural laws, Smelser simply includes it as just another phase in his model of collective action. Thus, the tension between the collective outbreak and the ensuing social control which results in struggle remains unrecognized. The empirical deficiency of Smelser's theory is not simply due to the difficulties in the operationalization of his analytical categories. When one tries to explain which type of collective action will arise as a reaction to structural tensions using Smelser's model, we come up with that of "generalized beliefs." But his theory does not thereby explain which generalized beliefs will arise; so that the original explanatory problem is not solved, but only displaced.

All of these deficiencies are ultimately attributable to the transference of a teleological model of action to open processes of non-institutionalized collective action. Thus, even in the functionalist tradition, Smelser's theory did not find many followers. For all of those who made an effort to integrate the analysis of collective action into the functionalist paradigm, the decisive orientation came from S. E. Eisenstadt's substantive contributions.

In the US, Jeffrey Alexander set himself the goal of enriching differentiation theory as the core of the functionalist approach to social change. He did this by incorporating certain ideas from symbolic interactionism with elements from Eisenstadt, so that differentiation theory might take into consideration such contingent phenomena as social movements, singular historical events like wars, and innovative élites. This means that Alexander no longer sees differentiation as a "smooth on-going process"[11] like most of his predecessors, but as a process that is at least partly brought about by social movements and in any case accompanied by them. We then have to evaluate whether differentiation is intended, or the effect of otherwise directed actions.

Uwe Schimank in Germany argues quite similarly without, however, referring to symbolic interactionism, but rather to a utilitarian model of action. His effort to expand functionalism proceeds from his criticism that most of the work in differentiation theory only deals with the effects, not the causes, of differentiation. Causes, he asserts, remain largely unexplored. He thus presents an argument against the attempt to derive differentiation from the necessities of efficiency or from evolutionary mechanisms, so that it is important to distinguish between successful or unsuccessful intentional differentiation policies and unintended differentiation effects. Schimank believes that his concept of an "acting system" (distinct from a mere "action-influencing system") is able to compensate for the lack of actor-relations in theoretical explanations of societal differentiation. This certainly represents progress in so far as groups, social movements, formal organizations, and "interorganizational networks" can play more than a subsidiary role in the process of differentiation.

The primacy of differentiation, though, remains remarkably unproblematic in both Alexander and Schimank. Whatever the contingent processes leading to differentiation may look like, the result – namely differentiation – seems certain. This is undoubtedly true for Alexander; Schimank admits the possibility of de-differentiation, but does not pursue it further. He does not ask whether the result of an improved theoretical relationship to concrete actors could not be that differentiation is no longer seen as the dominant thrust of historical change. Neither poses the question of whether the degree and direction of differentiation could be made the object of collective action and social movement. Differentiation might then be seen as being at stake in the struggles of social movements. De-differentiation would then appear as being more than a mere interlude in the inevitable march of differentiation. If it is possible for these processes to be the object of collective action, then the reasons for assuming that differentiation is a continuing process become weaker. This is independent of how we as researchers positively or negatively evaluate differentiation.

This problem marks the point beyond which even the most advanced attempts to open up the functionalist tradition do not go. Instead, they cling to the primacy of differentiation theory and refuse to consider instead the constitution of society through collective action. This is all the more remarkable because at present a whole group of theoretical endeavors tends toward this direction, beginning from very different points of departure and often ignoring each other. The least spectacular of these may be the attempt to revive the origins of the Chicago school by developing a symbolic-interactionist macrosociology (the so-called "negotiated order approach"). Amitai Etzioni's opening of the functionalist tradition (as in *The Active Society*) received a poor reception and is frequently misunderstood as a document of governmental planning euphoria. Anthony Giddens' efforts to develop a theory of structuration has been more favorably received. There are considerable similarities between Giddens' approach and that of Alain Touraine. Most recently, the Brazilian social philosopher Roberto Mangabeira Unger has outlined a far-reaching theory involving "anti-necessitarian" notions which hastily proceeds into a political program to the detriment of its conceptual elaboration. Jürgen Habermas' monumental *Theory of Communicative Action* belongs here, too, but only with severe restrictions; for some readers it is the successful synthesis of "systems theory" and the "life-world" approach, for others it represents only "an unhappy marriage of hermeneutics and functionalism."[12] These theories cannot be compared and extensively discussed here. The only question we can pose at this point relates to how a theory that takes the creativity of collective action seriously can effectively present the contemporary situation of society in our age characterized by a crisis of the belief in progress.

We will focus on Alain Touraine's sociology since it deals most extensively with the social conflicts currently arising out of the lack of belief in progress. Touraine's work is the most theoretically and empirically sensitive to today's social movements. But first we must briefly consider the political philosophy of Cornelius Castoriadis, which exerts a strong influence on Touraine in its attempt to reinstate the creativity of collective action as the fundamental theoretical dimension.[13]

Castoriadis does not – as does the larger part of western Marxism – follow Max Weber's ideas about action and rationalization, but instead goes back to Aristotelian practical philosophy. He combines this with the pathos of creativity. Social reality is considered in this action-theoretical perspective as "the union *and* the tension of instituting society and of instituted society, of history made and history in the making."[14] The title of his most important book, *The Imaginary Institution of Society*, reflects the idea that for "instituting" a society, human imagination and its creative meaning constitution are essential. Against differentiation and rationalization theory are opposed the emphases on the creation of new cultural values and institutions, cultural diversity, and the connection of discontinuous historical innovations.

Rationalization is considered by Castoriadis not as a comprehensive tendency, but as an imaginary schema of western culture which contributes to the dominance of technology and bureaucracy, economic efficiency, and science in this culture. Castoriadis distinguishes sharply between the constitution of culture-forming principles and gradual processes of adaptation and learning. His politically-aimed scrutinization of the present remains, despite its distance from Marxism, filled with an abstract revolutionary pathos and clearly deficient from a sociological perspective.

Touraine's sociology, meanwhile, provides the sociological concreteness lacking in the work of Castoriadis. His empirical starting point was industrial sociology. In his action theory, a notion of work which had not yet lost its relationship to Marx's ideas of revolutionary potential in the alienated *producers* was crucial. This point of departure was already far away from the hegemonic theory of structural functionalism. Touraine considered this approach as deficient because it assumes much too directly a normative orientation of action and is unable to explain the genesis of value systems. For Touraine the conflict of competing value systems was never a danger for the stability of societies. He articulated this distance from Parsons not only in abstract meta-theoretical debates, but mainly in a concrete diagnosis of the present.

His formula for the historical moment in which we live is the transition to a "post-industrial" or "programed" society. By calling it "programed" Touraine wants to point out that the most important factors for this transition are not to be found in technology or the professional structure (as Daniel Bell had asserted), but in the growing importance of planning and steering in this society. No more than Etzioni does Touraine mean this to refer to a total planning state, but an increase in the self-shaping possibilities of society itself. The increasing separation of society from nature makes it more evident to the members of society that their situation is the product of their own action. The concept of "historicity" grasps this self-"production" or "self-constitution" of societies which Castoriadis refers to as the "imaginary institution." Touraine defines "historicity" as "the capacity of a society to construct its practices from cultural models and through conflicts and social movements."[15]

This implies that the self-institutionalization of a society is not a simple act of creation, but takes place in a network of discussions about new values and changes of consciousness, of social protest and powerful repression. Enlightened by the experience of "totalitarianism," Touraine does not see this self-constitution in terms of society as a macro-actor to which a gigantic creativity is ascribed, but as the conflict and discourse of many actors whose "historicity" often consists in self-restriction and distance. But these achievements are not based on pre-social relics, but on socially constituted openings of the society.

Theoretical primacy for Touraine lies in the constitution of society in collective action, not in differentiation theory. Just as differentiation theory can open itself up to individual and collective actors, so, too, can a theory of the constitution of society accommodate the insight into the existence and the utility of differentiation.[16] Touraine's notion of "programed society" implies that in the present state of modern societies neither economic, scientific, nor cultural situations exist outside of political mediation. The degree and character of societal differentiation themselves become the political battleground within modern societies. Typically,

194

this does not mean that differentiation must be halted or abolished, but rather that because of its constitution in collective action differentiation can itself be at the disposal of collective action.

Touraine draws from this a strategy for his research, namely to proceed from the analysis of the development of modern societies to the study of social movements: "Gradually a theory of a new action system is developed, that is, a theory of cultural projects, social actors, conflict arenas, negotiation mechanisms, political management and the new social and cultural organizational forms that together characterize a post-industrial society."[17]

In studying social movements, Touraine hopes to observe the emergence of new value systems and social forms in *statu nascendi* and to achieve an adequate representation of present societies which are characterized by the existence of social movements which cannot be reduced to the articulation of class interests. It must be mentioned that Touraine sees the present plurality of movements as a preliminary step towards a central conflict which will polarize these movements into a decisive struggle over the future of their societies.

Here we leave open the question of how empirically convincing this perspective is. Above all, it is unclear whether Touraine simply perpetuates the old myth of some kind of revolutionary "ultimate battle," or whether he believes that beyond all the different areas of conflict there is a fundamental split between supporters and adversaries of a *democratization of differentiation*. In his more recent texts, Touraine has emphasized strongly the duration and resultant conflicts involved in the transition to a "programed society." But he does not seem to have any doubts about this transition itself.

This forms a contrast to two influential sociological lines of reasoning. On the one hand, it could be that the same developments which make industrial society obsolete also destroy the conditions for the formation of new social movements:

> We assume that the dissolution of homogeneous class milieux, the growing heterogeneity of social life situations, the individualization of life projects and the process of cultural pluralization have become irreversible to a degree in which the formation of new, structurally clear-cut collective identities as the basis of social movements can no longer be expected.[18]

In this analysis, several empirical tendencies are summarized, which Ulrich Beck has called "individualization."

Beck talks about a rapid process in which "feudally" influenced social milieux and the lifestyles of social classes disappear and are replaced by a socially isolated, highly individual planning of one's own biography.

Mutually supporting elements in this process include the unintended effects of educational expansion in relation to old class-specific lifestyles, of welfare-state bureaucracies, the lower standardization of work, and the increasing institutionalization of biographic patterns.

From a totally different perspective, namely his development of differentiation theory, Niklas Luhmann disagrees with the diagnosis of the future as a battleground for social movements. It is just the advantage of differentiation for varying subsystems of society that prevents them from reacting in a way different from their logic, even when confronted with problems that are dangerous for society as a whole. This is said to be true for politics and economics as well as for law, science, education, and religion:

> It contradicts every principle of societal differentiation to represent the whole of the system once again within the system. The whole cannot be simultaneously a part of the whole. Every attempt of this kind would only be able to produce a difference within the system, namely the difference of that part, which represents the whole of the system within the system to all other parts. The representation of unity is the production of difference. Therefore, even the intention is paradoxical and self-contradictory.[19]

A unitary representation of the whole is said to have been possible only under the condition of a differentiation from an undetermined other world. But this possibility has vanished since the Enlightenment:

> The Enlightenment reflects the transition from stratificatory to functional differentiation. In the new order there are no natural primacies, no positions privileged by the whole system and, therefore, no position *in* the system which could give effect to the unity *of* the system toward its environment.[20]

Nevertheless, the self-observation of a society within and between its subsystems cannot be excluded. Today's terminology in these self-observations is purely negative: post-industrial, postmodern, post-capitalist. The fundamental structure of the ideology contained therein consists in the tendency to express the losses caused by functional differentiation without having clear alternatives to such differentiation: "For a sociological observation of this observation it is an attractive theory to imagine that all this ultimately is a *protest against functional differentiation and its effects.*"[21] This protest, says Luhmann, is articulated in the form of social movements, which try and act upon society from within "as if this happened from the outside."[22] For a successful self-description of the highly differentiated order of modern societies such a pseudo-outsider position devoid of concrete experiences is said to be an utterly insufficient foundation.

Thus, Touraine's assumption of the transition from industrial class society to a post-industrial society of conflicts between social movements is questioned in two respects. On the one hand, it may be that the structural conditions of the new society do not allow social movements to arise: in this case the class society would be replaced by a multiplicity of individualized lifestyle enclaves and by anomie with regard to the question of generally-binding cultural orientations. On the other hand, functional differentiation can be so advanced that no place can be found which allows a perspective on the society as a whole: then protest against this differentiation is probable, but simultaneously condemned to impotence. For the only perspective then lies in a willingness to accept the principles of the differentiated subsystems as a fact, or be repelled by them unless protest leads to a mere interference with their functioning despite all the best intentions. After all, at least, Luhmann interprets the new social movements as a protest against functional differentiation and its effects. In a certain sense, this is quite close to Touraine's assumption that these movements represent what is called here a democratization of differentiation. But unlike Touraine, Luhmann reduces these movements to a protest against functional differentiation *as such*. If we believe him, the opposition is today between the approval of differentiation without illusions and the illusory dreams of de-differentiation.

If we follow Touraine, the conflict is between many voices which vote for different degrees and directions of differentiation. If one wants to talk at all about polarization into two camps, then there is the camp of those who are willing to accept the degree and character of today's "functional" differentiation as an iron law, and those who want to make differentiation itself the object of social reflection and will-formation.

In Ulrich Beck's theory of the "society of risks," Alain Touraine's approach has been further developed in an interesting way. Beck argues that old conflict areas are becoming unimportant because we are facing new and overwhelming dangers from the enormous risks of a highly-developed technology; the prototype of this is Chernobyl. These new dangers differ from the more typical risks of industrial societies in that they cannot be contained either spatially, temporally, or socially. The established rules of attribution and responsibility fail in these cases, the damages caused are mostly irreversible; the imminent dangers can never be excluded, but only made minimal. In addition, they are different from natural risks because they are – like the risks of industrial society – socially constituted. Science, technology, politics and economy are implicated in these new dangers (e.g., nuclear technology, or genetic engineering), as providing the conditions which make such dangers possible.

Beck calls the belief in progress, as well as its cynical destruction, "industrial fatalism." He wants to say that in a culture in which the autonomy of the actors is institutionalized only a very limited range of decisions are influenced by individual choice or political participation. This argument does not simply aim at a democratization of the economy or the subjugation of the economy to state planning. It does remind us, however, of the new questions that the dangers of high-technology pose for self-understanding within democratic institutions. According to Beck, we lie between a technocratic loss of democracy and a non-technocratic Enlightenment. This becomes additionally important because of the considerable dangers now confronting modern civilization.

In facing today's dangers, says Beck, the repressed dynamics of industrial society reassert themselves: "Dangers are also externalized, bundled, objectivated subjectivity and history . . . They are sort of a compulsory collective memory to remind us that in the situations we face our decisions and mistakes are involved." And he concludes that such dangers must force us to reflect on differentiation, since they remind us "that even the highest degree of institutional autonomy is only an autonomy *until revoked*, a borrowed form of action that can and must be changed when it means self-endangerment."[23]

Unlike Luhmann, Beck maintains that the size of today's dangers leads to a consciousness about the reversibility of achieved differentiation. Unlike Touraine, the emergence of social movements is not seen by Beck as providing freedom for the conflict of value systems but rather as a coercion to such conflicts in order to evade the prospective dangers faced by society. In this context he attempts to connect the tendencies of "individualization" with the emergence of social movements when he asserts that such movements recruit their members mostly from those milieux and cohorts in which "individualization" is particularly advanced.

This empirical hypothesis – which cannot be examined here – leads to Beck's notion of a new automatism, namely the generating and mastery of dangers. This sounds like a repetition of old Marxist ideas about the tendencies of capitalism to break down and the prospect of a revolution associated with such a breakdown. The industrial system which permanently produces new risks – according to Beck – leads unavoidably to a questioning of its economic, political, juridical, and scientific structures. The intellectual problematization of this system and the articulation of protest motives in social movements appear in Beck's theory as if they were mere phases in a predetermined process.

We can avoid this deterministic approach and open up Beck's theory by conceiving of its elements as variable dimensions. Then we must ask how probable are the emergence of social movements which address the extent and direction of differentiation in modern societies. The attempt in this essay has been to address this question by making clear the tensions

198

between a functionalistic theory of differentiation and a "creativist" theory of collective action.

To really answer this question, a theory must be developed for the analysis of creativity in individual action. Beck's own theory will not do. His notion of "individualization" is much too crude for a reconstruction of the developmental stages of individual creativity. In spite of Castoriadis' influence on Touraine, the latter's approach does not develop the psychological and microsociological aspects into a full consideration of the creativity of action. This deficiency is also characteristic of other influential social-psychological analyses of the present. Habermas' dualism of "system" and "life-world," for example, is appropriate for articulating the advantages of "systemic" organization in important subsystems of society. But he tends to draw the boundary between these subsystems and the other spheres in which normative agreements among the actors produce structuration, rather than conceiving of the boundary as empirically variable and seeing it as the object of discourse and conflict. The reification of this distinction leads him to subsume the process of macrosocial collective action under the inappropriate category of the "life-world." Because he does not develop this category from a comprehensive theory of action, but instead from his conception of "communicative action" which is separated from all instrumentality, the notion of "life-world" does not grasp the diversity of everyday actions.

In many important analyses, say those of Daniel Bell or Robert Bellah, the conflict between utilitarian and expressive individualism plays the central role in modern societies. The only possible way out of our current cultural crisis seems to be through a normative restriction of both these forms of individualism. These authors do not recognize that the normative critique of expressive individualism remains ineffective as long as the dimension of morality has not been modified through the idea of expressive-creative action. Today, it is mainly Charles Taylor who attempts to elaborate a morality of collective expressive freedom based upon roots in Friedrich Schiller's notions about aesthetic education and the entire German "expressivist" tradition.

One might dare to utter the assumption that the conflict between utilitarian and expressive individualism is itself derived from the long-standing attempt to push tendencies toward "integrated creativity" into the strictly individual realm, where they do not naturally belong. It is the commercialization and "yuppification" of creative impulses which leads to this conflict and its resolution as the peaceful, but individualistic, coexistence of utilitarianism and expressivism.

A theory founded in the creativity of action leads to three fundamental requirements in the social-psychological analysis of the present. First, the potential for "integrated creativity" must be identified. This would be something like a morally non-repressive autonomy. It thereby becomes important to study the recruitment of social movements as well as general participation in the organizations and institutions of democratic politics and culture. The second focus should be on the phenomenon of unauthentic, narrowed creativity and expressivity in the individual. From Marcuse's notion of "repressive desublimation" to Foucault's interpretation of sexual liberation as a strategy of power, we have a wide variety of theoretical endeavors in this area, the character of which are largely different from the approach taken here. The third task lies in the analysis of blocked creativity and expressivity. This concerns above all the role of spontaneous violence, individual and collective, in present-day societies.

In its search for a concept of "integrated creativity" this theory might bear some resemblance to the critique of rationalistic universalism propagated by the "postmodern" movement.[24] Unlike these postmodernists, however, this theory emphasizes the dangers of moral regression arising alongside the sensitizing effects of the dissolution of concrete communities. A reflection on the creativity of action leads to the prospect of new opportunities in determining the meaning of progress and the possibilities posed today by the democratization of differentiation.

Notes

1. Max Weber "Roscher and Knies: the logical problems of historical economics," in M. Weber (1975) *Gesammelte Aufsätze zur Wissenschaftslehre* (New York: Free Press: 229, n. 81).
2. I try to develop this thesis in my (1988) essay "Das Problem der Entstehung neuer Moral und neuer Institutionen bei Durkheim" (The problem of the genesis of a new morality and new institutions in Durkheim). (Unpublished manuscript.)
3. John Dewey "Progress," in J. Dewey (1929) *Characters and Events*, Vol. II (New York: Octagon: 820).
4. The most energetic plea for the centrality of these questions is Jeffrey Alexander (1982) *Positivism, Presuppositions, and Current Controversies*. Vol. 1 of *Theoretical Logic in Sociology* (London: Routledge & Kegan Paul). For a discussion cf. Hans Joas (1988) "The Antimonies of neofunctionalism: a critical essay on J. Alexander," *Inquiry* 31: 471–94.
5. Abraham Maslow (1968) *Toward a Psychology of Being* (Princeton: Van Nostrand).
6. Maslow, ibid., p. 143.
7. Cf. John Dewey (1934) *Art as Experience* (New York: Perigore) and John Dewey (1934) *A Common Faith* (New Haven: Yale University Press).
8. Morris Janowitz (1975/6) "Sociological theory and social control," *Journal of Sociology* 81: 82–108; Hans Joas (1987) "Symbolic interactionism," in A. Giddens and J. Turner (eds) *Social Theory Today* (Cambridge: Polity: 82–115).
9. Edward Tiryakian (1985) "On the significance of de-differentiation," in S. N. Eisenstadt and J. Helle (eds) *Macrosociological Theory Perspectives on Sociological Theory*, Vol. 1 (London: Sage: 118–34). Jürgen Habermas (1984, 1987) *Theory of Communicative Action*, 2 vols (Boston: Beacon).

10. Robert Park and Ernest Burgess (1921) *Introduction to the Science of Sociology* (Chicago: University of Chicago Press).
11. Cf. Jeffrey Alexander and Paul Colomy (1988) "Social differentiation and collective behavior," in J. Alexander *Action and Its Environments* (New York: Columbia University Press: 193–221). Uwe Schimank (1985) "Der mangelnde Akteurbezug systemtheoretischer Erklärungen gesellschaftlicher Differenzierung," *Zeitschrift für Soziologie*, 14: 421–34.
12. This is the title of my (1988) critique of Habermas, in *Praxis International*: 34–51.
13. Cornelius Castoriadis (1987) *The Imaginary Institution of Society* (Cambridge: Polity). On Castoriadis cf. my essay (1988/9) "Institutionalization as a creative process," *American Journal of Sociology*, 94: 1184–99.
14. ibid.: 114.
15. Alain Touraine (1988) *The Return of the Actor* (Minneapolis: University of Minnesota Press: xxiv).
16. Michael Walzer (1983) *Spheres of Justice. A Defense of Pluralism and Equality* (New York: Basic Books).
17. Alain Touraine (1986) "Krise und Wandel des sozialen Denkens," in J. Berger (ed.) *Die Moderne – Kontinuitäten und Zäsuren. Sonderband der "Sozialen Welt"*: 35.
18. Karl-Werner Brand, Detlef Busser, and Dieter Rucht (1986) *Aufbruch in eine andere Gesellschaft. Neue soziale Bewegungen in der Bundesrepublik* (Frankfurt: Campus: 277). Ulrich Beck (1986) *Risikogesellschaft. Auf dem Weg in eine andere Moderne* (Frankfurt: Suhrkamp). Ulrich Beck (1988) *Gegengifte. Die organisierte Unverantwortlichkeit* (Frankfurt: Suhrkamp).
19. Niklas Luhmann (1986) *Okologische Kommunikation* (Opladen: 227).
20. ibid.: 229.
21. ibid.: p. 234.
22. ibid.: p. 236.
23. Beck, *Gegengifte*: 162.
24. Scott Lash and John Urry (1987) "Postmodern culture and disorganized capitalism," in Scott Lash (ed.) *The End of Organized Capitalism* (Cambridge: Polity: 285–313).

10

The relative autonomy of élites: the absorption of protest and social progress in western democracies

EVA ETZIONI-HALEVY

Introduction

The main purpose of this essay is to make the case for the analysis of change and progress in western democracies in the framework of the democratic élite, or what I prefer to term the demo-élite theory, a well established but recently neglected theory in the social sciences. This theory is not concerned with the analysis of all aspects of society, but only with the analysis of power and the processes and phenomena related to it. It is also not concerned with the analysis of such processes and phenomena in all societies, but only with those of western-style democracies. As such, it is not a global theory, but a middle-ranging theory in the Mertonian sense. But this paper is designed to show that it may make a distinct contribution to the analysis of how the machinations of power in such a democracy – and in particular those between established élites and non-established élites of social movements – are connected to social change, and of how they may therefore work for social progress.

The term social progress evidently implies a value judgment, and this may well have deterred many contemporary sociologists from using it as a manifest element of their analytical apparatus, even when the conception of progress is implicit in their analyses. As is now becoming more widely accepted, however, sociological theories contain, if not straightforward, at least implied value judgments. It therefore seems preferable to bring hidden value judgments out into the open, so that theories may be appraised *inter alia* with respect to those values. Hence there now seems to be no valid reason to refrain from using this term.

The term social progress is also evidently complex, and there probably are as many conceptions of it as there are scholars who use it. Kumar (1978:

202

14) has defined it as change in a desirable direction and, as a follow-up on this, here social progress (to be distinguished from other, e.g. scientific progress) will be conceived of as entailing – at the minimum – change towards greater freedom and lesser inequity and inequality.

To some critics a theory of élites in a democracy must favor the rule of élites, hence is conservative, has no interest in change towards greater freedom and equality, and thereby is inimical to social progress. But I will endeavor to show that – in its present version – the demo-élite theory is not open to such criticism, as it is not designed to endorse or legitimize élite rule, but rather to expose and analyze the manner in which it is exercised in a democracy. Consequently, it is no less concerned with progress than are theories that deliberately present themselves as progressive – and whose progressive self-presentation is generally accepted – such as the Marxist theories. Contrary to Marxist class theory which includes the belief that classes may be abolished, the demo-élite theory does not hold out the hope that élites may be done away with. But it works on the assumption that by leading to a better understanding of the élites' strategies in gaining, exercising, and maintaining power, it may help identify the mechanisms through which the power of élites can be checked, curbed, and curtailed or, in other words, the mechanisms through which change towards greater freedom and lesser inequality (here identified with progress) can come about.

A preview of the argument

Within the framework of the demo-élite theory it will be argued here that western-style democracies – with all their deficiencies – carry some seeds of social progress within them, and that these seeds, though contained *inter alia* in their electoral processes, are not comprised only, or perhaps even chiefly, in the direct influence of the public on policy outcomes afforded by these and other democratic processes. Rather, the potential for social progress is contained in large part in one of the most distinctive features of the constellation of power in western democracies: the relative autonomy of the other élites from the ruling, or state élites, and particularly from the elected, governing élite. It will be argued that this relative autonomy of élites – which has developed as part and parcel of the development of democracy – has made it increasingly difficult for ruling élites, and especially for governing élites, to suppress and repress other élites, including non-established, counter-élites of social and protest movements. Hence it has become necessary for governing élites to apply certain different – rather distinctive – controls on other élites in order to stabilize the system, and their own power within it. These strategies of control, when applied to the relative autonomous non-established élites of social and protest movements – are here referred to as strategies for the absorption of protest. It has thus been necessary for the ruling élites in western democracies to shift gradually from the repression of protest, to the absorption of protest, and it will be argued that the strategies for the absorption of protest are directly – though paradoxically – related to change and the possibility of progress.

It will thus be seen that the relative autonomy of the non-established élites of social movements is of prime importance in western democracies not because in itself it can bring about change and progress, but because it forces the governing élites to exert controls which are aimed at stability, yet in the very process of stabilizing the system – lead to change and possibly progressive change. The relative autonomy of non-established élites in western democracies thus signifies that the very exertion of ruling and governing élite power also opens up prospects for change and progress.

Why yet another theory of democracy

This argument, I hold, can be developed and presented only within the demo-élite theory. For, although several prominent theories have been concerned with the analysis of power in a democracy, and although they all have made important contributions to its analysis, they also have had some severe deficiencies. Elsewhere (Etzione-Halevy 1985, 1989a and b), I have presented critiques of these theories at greater length, and there would be little point in reiterating them here. Suffice it to say that older pluralist theories of democracy (e.g. Dahl 1956; Riesman 1961; Dahl and Lindblom 1953), neo-pluralist theories of democracy (e.g. Polsby 1985), and even pluralist élitist theories of democracy (e.g. Sartori 1962, 1987; Keller 1963, Dahl 1967, 1970, 1971, 1982; Truman 1971) have all over-emphasized the dispersion of power and the multiplicity of competing groups or élites in a democracy. Conversely élites (see e.g. Domhoff – who may be classified as an élitist with Marxist affinities – 1967, 1978, 1983; Field and Higley 1980; Dye 1983, 1985; Dye and Zeigler 1987; Useem 1984) and Marxists (e.g. Mandel 1975; Miliband 1977; Parenti 1980; Poulantzas 1978, amongst many others) in their different ways, have gone to the other extreme, overemphasizing the concerted nature of power, and the interlocking or consensual unity of élites in western, democratic regimes. And, partly as a consequence of this, they have failed to bring into relief what is distinctive in the manner in which power is exercised in a democracy.

It may now be added that, partly as a consequence of this, these schools of thought have also failed to come forward with realistic analyses of the manner in which the exercise of power in democratic regimes may lead to change and progress. Pluralist theories, by emphasizing the balance of power between a multiplicity of groups, convey the picture of an equilibrium, and fail to identify the mechanisms which may lead this equilibrium to change. They also take an overly complacent, self-satisfied, view of the democratic system as it exists today, and thereby the impetus to search for mechanisms leading to social progress is largely removed from the scene. Elitist theories, by emphasizing the concerted or consensually unified power of élites in a democracy, and by seeing the public largely as a passive receptacle of élite power, do not provide a handle which could help us come to grips with processes of change and progress. Also worth mentioning are participatory theories of democracy (e.g. Pateman 1970; Barber 1984; Wilson 1984); these provide us with a vision of how democracy ought to look in the future, but they, too, fail to identify the mechanisms which could lead us from here to there, and thus fail to identify the mechanisms of change and progress.

Strange as it may sound, even Marxist theories, although they are basically theories of conflict and change, have not made an important contribution to the analysis of change and progress in western democracies. For by setting their sight exclusively on revolution – which even by the admission of several of their numbers has no realistic chance of coming about in capitalist regimes in the foreseeable future – they have neglected the analysis of smaller, less significant, but by no means totally insignificant progressive changes in western democracies. In particular, they have shown a singular ineptitude in analyzing social – and even more so recent – social movements, and the contributions these have made and are capable of making to social change. In the words of Carl Boggs (1986: 57–8):

> Marxism presents the image of a bipolar world characterized by epochal struggles between . . . wage labor and capital . . . Economic crisis leading to revolutionary transformation is the projected outcome of this dialectical confrontation. Such a polarized conflict . . . was expected to produce a relatively homogeneous working class community, permeated with anti-capitalist consciousness. However appropriate this scenario might have looked in earlier phases of competitive capitalism . . . it now seems quite outdated in the more complex and fragmented world inhabited by the new movements. . . . To retain a conventional Marxian framework . . . in the face of this fundamentally new historical reality is to reduce theory to a dogmatic, reified enterprise no longer capable of grasping social change.

And theories that cannot adequately analyze social change are evidently also ill-equipped to deal with social progress.

Marxist analyses of politics face an additional problem. By following Marx's basic tenet that political power is an offshoot of economic power, and that political power holders (or the state apparatus) serve basically the interests of the economic power holders (or the ruling class), they have come to be locked into a rather narrow and simplistic view of power which has made it impossible for them to come to grips with the complexity of the phenomenon of power in general, and that of power in western democratic society in particular. Marxist theories have presented the argument of the "relative autonomy" of the state apparatus from the ruling class. But if political power is based on and derived from economic power, it is not at all clear from where this "relative autonomy" derives (see e.g. Hindess 1980; Pierson 1984).

Some Marx-inspired writers (e.g. Skocpol 1979; Giddens 1982; Evans *et al.* 1985; Block 1987) have gone further than Marxists proper in separating political power from economic power. They have offered valuable insights in that they have been able to advance beyond the reductionist approach of the Marxists proper (Mann 1984: 187). But even these scholars still couch their analysis broadly in terms of the parameters set out by Marx, for they still view the problem of political power in terms of the degree of autonomy of the state from the economy, capitalism, or civil society, even though they may regard the state as potentially, largely, or substantially autonomous from these. Here, however, it is queried whether this is indeed the most fruitful way of presenting the problem.

Moreover, some élitists as well as Marxists have belittled the importance of the principle of competitive elections and the other principles of western democracy, regarding them chiefly as rituals designed to give the people a sense of political equality where, in fact, inequality persists, and a sense of power, with little power in actual practice. Thereby, they have brought out only half of the truth, and by neglecting the other half, they have failed to bring into relief what is distinctive about the manner in which élites exert power in western democracies.

The demo-élite perspective

Like élitist theories and unlike Marxist theories the demo-élite perspective contains the argument that power may have a variety of bases, and that, therefore, economic power is not the basis of all other power. It further contains the argument that, in contemporary society, the state acts as the main center of power, that the ruling élites, that is, the élites which have direct control of the state are thus formidable, if not the most formidable élites in contemporary societies, and that they do not necessarily promote the interests of the economic élites. However, it also contains the argument that in western-style democracies the other élites are neither as interlocking with the state élites as élitists have claimed them to be, nor as independent from, as competitive with them, and as dispersed in their power as pluralists have made them out to be, that instead there is a relative autonomy of the non-state élites from the state élites and of the other élites from the elected, governing élite, which – sustained and legitimized by the principles of western democracy – is one of its most distinctive features.

Thus, while Marxists argue for the primacy of what they refer to as the ruling class (which is here referred to as the economic élite) and for the relative autonomy of the state apparatus (which is here referred to as the ruling or state élites) from that ruling class, here this argument is turned on its head, if it is more appropriate to speak of the relative autonomy of the other élites from the ruling or state élites, and of the relative autonomy of the non elected élites from the elected governing political élite in western democracies. But while Marxists have not furnished an adequate explanation for the alleged relative autonomy of the state élites from the ruling class, here, an attempt is made to explicate the relative autonomy of élites, as will be seen below.

Unlike Marxists and élitists who have belittled the electoral principle and other principles of democracy, the demo-élite perspective contains the argument that these principles (irrespective of whether the degree of actual power and influence they accord to the public is great or small) are important because they sustain and legitimize what is here referred to as the relative autonomy of élites which – as noted – is precisely what makes western democracy distinctive, and opens prospects for change and progress within it.

In making these claims, the present version of the demo-élite perspective has its antecedents in the theories of Max Weber (1947, 1968); Gaetano Mosca (1939); Joseph Schumpeter (1962); and Raymond Aron (1968, 1978). Unlike Marxists, and like élitists, these theorists have recognized that economic power was not all-pervasive and that political power had to be reckoned with as an independent factor, that the élites that controlled the state were formidable, if not the most formidable élites in contemporary societies. But they differed from both Marxists and élitists in their recognition that elections and other democratic processes created a unique interplay among élites and between élites and the public, which distinguished western democracies from other regimes. Like pluralists, they recognized that élites did not form a unified "ruling class" or "power élite," and that there was a complex maneuvering among them. But they differed from pluralists in their recognition that this maneuvering was based not on a multiplicity of power centers, but on a precarious balance of power between a few major élites which was both an outgrowth of, and a basic (though imperfect) factor sustaining democracy.

Thus, Weber saw this balance as one in which democratically elected leaders (though they did not necessarily cede much power to the public) countered the menace of the growing power of the bureaucratic élite. Mosca and Schumpeter, for their part, emphasized the importance of the balance created by, on the one hand, an elected governing élite and, on the other, an independent bureaucratic élite that countered its power and its excesses in the form of corruption. And Schumpeter, as well as Aron, also highlighted the importance of the relative autonomy of a small number of other major élites in countervailing the power of the elected governing élite, and in stemming its abuses of power in a democracy. The present version of the democratic-élite (or the demo-élite) perspective accepts and follows these theories, but endeavors to amplify them.

The control of resources and the primacy of state élites

This amplification can best proceed on the basis of some elementary assumptions pertaining to power and élites. The first of these is that power is based on the control of, or having at one's disposal, resources on which others are dependent, of which they have a need, or which may otherwise affect their lives. Resources, in turn, are here conceived of broadly, not merely in a material or economic sense, as including all (scarce) entities that may impinge on people's lives. Élites are simply those people or groups of people who hold power and influence, i.e. have disproportionate control of resources in a given sociopolitical system.

It is here assumed that in contemporary society the major resources are generated in, or accumulated and controlled by, organizations. Hence it is also assumed (in similarity to C. Wright Mills' theory) that there are certain, structured, institutional positions in such organizations which lend their incumbents the ability to dispose of resources, or lend them power, and thus turn them into members of institutionalized, or established élites. At the same time not all resources are monopolized by organizations, and thus some people may gain control of resources without the benefit of formal organizational positions. At times, too, some people may gain control of resources accumulated in (relatively uninstitutionalized) social movements. These latter persons may be characterized as non-established or counter-élites.

Since resources are accumulated in, and controlled mainly by organizations, this leads to an additional assumption. As should be obvious (but has not been admitted by Marxists), while economic élites control major organizations, nevertheless – in contemporary society – the biggest and most formidabie organization, the main accumulator and controller of resources is the state, and thus the élites that together have charge of the state, have control of the greatest chunk of contemporary societies' (largely interrelated) resources.

For any orderly, contemporary, state controls the main means or resources of coercion, which in turn lends it the ability to control a great variety of other resources, whether or not it exercises this control in actual practice. No less important is the fact that the state and its élites also command resources of "pure" power. Such power is backed up by coercion when all else fails. Or as Lenski (1986: 243) saw it, coercion "constitutes the final court of appeal" in human affairs. But this "pure" power is not straightforward coercion. More immediately, it is based on the control of structures engaged in regulatory and co-ordinatory activities, such as policy making, legislation, adjudication, administration, and defense. It thus entails control of a variety of power structures, and these lend the state élites the ability to affect and constrain the lives of the entire population. Simultaneously such power structures, ranging from major administrative departments, through the military and the police to the post-office, also act as employers for large proportions of the population. Power is thus a resource in its own right, which is the basis of, and has the capacity to generate, more power (see Lasswell and Kaplan 1950, as cited in Dahl 1986: 44).

In addition, and in close relationship to this, any contemporary western state controls major economic or material resources. The economic power based on these resources is also ultimately backed up by coercion but, more immediately, is based on control of structures concerned with accumulation, regulation, and distribution of material goods and services. Thus the state accumulates material resources through taxation and through government-owned or partly-owned enterprises. The state and its élites also control economic resources by exerting more general controls over the economy via monetary and fiscal intervention, and via general economic policies.

On the basis of its control of the state's power structures, and on the basis of the charisma of office, the state and its élites also gain control of a variety of symbolic resources, which endows them with the ability to create ideologies and define the situation for the public (Edelman 1971). The state and state élites also have control of symbolic resources in the form of prestige and honors that can be awarded at their discretion.

Thus, the élites that derive their power from the control of the state – here referred to as the state, or ruling élites (including the governing political élite, the bureaucratic élite, the judicial élite, and the élites of the security services) – have more power than and, indeed, have a degree of power over, the other élites – here referred to as non-ruling élites – including the élite that derives its power from the control of economic enterprises. For the latter is generally dependent on the former for various resources which it requires in order to sustain its élite positions. These include congenial economic policies, subsidies, and tax exemptions, as well as contracts for a variety of goods and services, and other forms of patronage. In addition, other non-ruling élites (for instance, the élites of trade unions and of the media) also depend on the state élites for a variety of benefits, including, for instance, favorable policies, patronage, and even positions of power within the establishment itself.

Of course, the dependence of the economic élite on the ruling élites is neither total, nor completely one-sided. For the well-being of the state, of which the ruling élites have charge, depends on the well-being of the economy of which the economic élite has charge – and vice versa. To a certain extent, the dependence of these élites is thus mutual, as each depends on the well-being of the other. But if the previous assumptions are correct, the élites that control the state, having control of both coercive and economic resources, generally have an edge of power over the élites that controls economic (capitalist) enterprises, and thus enjoy economic power only; the state élites also have an edge of power over the other élites, even though (for reasons that should become clear below) in practice they do not always exert their full coercive power.

The relative autonomy of élites in a western democracy

This is not to say, however, that the ruling élites totally dominate the economic or capitalist and other élites in a democracy. Indeed, it is a central argument of this analysis that despite a certain dependence of the economic and other élites on the ruling or state élites, and a (somewhat lesser) dependence of the state élites on the other major élites, *in a democracy, the basis of the control of resources of the different élites differs to a greater extent than in other contemporary regimes. Hence, the sources of power of the major but non-ruling élites differ from those of the ruling élites, and those of the other major élites differ from those of the governing political élite to a greater extent, and they are more independent from it, than is the case in other regimes, and through this relative autonomy and other élites are able to countervail the power of the governing élite, at least in part.*

Historically, this partial, or relative autonomy, was achieved through the struggles of élites for power and the control of resources. These struggles of initially non-established élites – which were protracted over several centuries but culminated in the nineteenth century – also formed the essence of the development of democracy. At times the élites that conducted those struggles led social movements representing the interests of certain classes or other social groups from which they themselves originated; at times they led movements that represented the interests of classes other than their own (Perkin 1969), and at times they represented no one in particular but themselves. Whether or not they spearheaded social movements, in any case the successive élites fought for, and managed to gain a share of power for themselves. This resulted in a dual process: the incorporation of successive élites into existing power structures (or political establishments) on the one hand, and the granting of increased autonomy to successive élites – from or within those structures – on the other.

210

Thus, the political élites of the aristocracy – which in the old regime mostly monopolized political power – were confronted by, and forced to accept into the establishment, first the political élites of the large bourgeoisie, then those of the middle class, and finally those of the working class. Simultaneously, these élites also gained increased autonomy within those establishments. This increased autonomy took the form of the gradual development of freedom of association, the related development of political parties, of relatively independent parliamentary oppositions, of trade unions – and all these associations' élites, the development of a relatively free enterprise economy and its élites, and the development of relatively autonomous bureaucratic organizations and judiciary systems and their élites (see Etzioni-Halevy 1989b: Chs 3 and 4). The élites' struggles for power thus were also aimed at, and led to, the relative autonomy of élites as it exists today.

In the process of struggling for, and gaining power and autonomy within or from the existing establishments, some of the élites genuinely also struggled for, and achieved certain benefits for the classes or groups whose interests they represented, and by which they were supported, including certain social and political reforms. Mostly they did so only as long as the interests of those classes or groups coincided with their own; in some cases they subsequently abandoned or partly abandoned the interests of those classes or groups. Moreover, the reforms they helped bring about came slowly and belatedly; they were piecemeal and hesitant. Thus, the achievements they "delivered" to those groups were frequently much smaller than was initially expected. Yet, eventually, the élites' struggles led to the reshaping of the existing political and social structures in a more egalitarian fashion (though not, of course, to the abolition of inequalities), and to the gradual development of the principles of democracy as (with all its deficiencies) they exist today.

In short, *the struggles of successive élites for a share of power, their incorporation into the establishment on the one hand, their autonomization, or the development of the relative (though incomplete) autonomy of élites on the other, and their delivering of (even limited) achievements to certain classes or groups whom they initially represented, were all inextricably interlinked with, and manifested in the development of the principles of western democracy, and their results were then enshrined in those principles.*

Consequently, the principles of democracy, as we know them today and as (though imperfectly) implemented in western democratic regimes, are also principles that legitimize and safeguard the relative autonomy of élites. The élites whose relative autonomy is now legitimized by those principles also have an interest in their perpetuation, and thus continue to sustain them. But, by the same token, the principles also sustain, constantly regenerate, and safeguard that autonomy. *Thereby, they also protect the ability of those élites to countervail, or partly countervail, and thus to limit the power of the governing élite.*

The principles of democracy: the electoral principle, the principles of freedom of association (or organization) and of speech, and the principle of the separation of powers within the state, serve to legitimize and protect the relative autonomy of élites both in themselves, and in their various combinations. Thus, the electoral principle, in conjunction with the principles of freedom of organization and speech, confront the governing political élite with a recurring, institutionalized, threat of replacement, and thereby provide the rationale, and make possible the organization and activity of its potential replacer. They thus provide a mechanism which underpins and legitimizes the existence and the relative autonomy of another part of the political élite: the opposition, or the parties not currently in power.

The latter two principles, both separately and in conjunction with each other, also protect and legitimize the relative independence of the media élite which, together with the opposition, serves as a watchdog curbing the governing élite's uses and abuses of power. The principle of the separation of powers between the legislature, the executive, and the judiciary and, within the executive, between the elected government and the appointed bureaucratic élite (however imperfectly implemented) have an equivalent effect. They legitimize and safeguard the relative autonomy of the judicial and bureaucratic élites respectively, which at times (though by no means always) also has had a certain effectiveness in countervailing and limiting the power and the abuses of power of the governing political élite.

Organizations, we have said, are accumulators of resources. The principle of freedom of association or organization thus also spells freedom to amass resources, including economic resources that are, to a certain extent, exempt from state control. Freedom of organization thus entails, *inter alia*, economic organizations (albeit not necessarily capitalist ones) that have at least a partial immunity from state intervention. The principle of freedom of association or organization also protects the relative autonomy of a variety of other élites. Where there is freedom of association, and where the society is heterogeneous, actual, relatively autonomous, groups, associations, and organizations designed to promote class, group, or other sectorial interests (including, for instance the labor movement or trade unions and social protest movements) – with their own élites – are apt to arise.

The élites of social and protest movements

Of special importance for the present analysis are the non-established or counter-élites of social movements. For, while the established élites have an interest in the maintenance of the status quo, these non-established, élites obviously have an unmistakable interest in change; indeed, their very essence lies in their clamor for change. By western values, the means of coercion (or violence) are legitimately monopolized by the state. But as long as such movements and their élites remain clearly non-violent, they find their legitimation in, and are also protected by, the principles of freedom of association, of assembly, and of speech. These principles, which legitimize and protect the relative autonomy of all élites, and thus also serve the interests of established élites, cannot be easily abrogated by the state or ruling élites – and particularly by the governing élite – when they confront non-establishing élites, without thereby incurring the wrath of the public and of other established élites, such as the opposition and the media.

Several consequences flow from this. Firstly, while social and protest movements may pose a potential threat to the state and governing élites' bases of power, the development of such movements cannot be prevented or suppressed, and there is a greater chance for social movements arising and proliferating in western democracies as compared to other regimes. In the last few decades (particularly from the 1960s and onwards) such movements have, in fact, proliferated in the west. Apart from the still persisting older labor and trade union movement, they have, of course, included the students' movement in several western countries, the interrelated civil rights and black power movements as well as the anti-Vietnam War movement particularly in the United States, the women's and homosexual liberation movements, the environmental, anti-nuclear, and peace movements, and a variety of related movements all over the western world. Thus, in West Germany alone there have recently been an estimated 38,000 citizen action groups, backed by two to three million members, supporters, and sympathizers (Mushaben 1985). And the situation is not much different in several other western countries.

Secondly – as even Marxists (including e.g. Miliband 1977 and Therborn 1977) admit – once such movements have arisen, state élites, although they may have wished to do so, have been limited in the extent to which they could repress non-violent movements. By repression I refer to a combination of two elements:

(1) The use of coercion of the threat of coercion;
(2) With the aim of making the movement disappear, or in order to prevent it from acting, or in order to alter its nature to such an extent that it no longer remains the same movement.

Thus, the previously established movements – such as the labor and trade union movement – and the new movements could not be eliminated by the state. This is not to say that no coercive repression has ever been or can be applied. For instance, particularly before the First World War in Britain, and before 1935–7 in the United States, the labor movement was

213

confronted by certain strategies of coercive repression applied by the state and/or capitalist élites (Barbalet forthcoming). But, on the whole, such measures have diminished from the last part of the nineteenth century and throughout the first half of the twentieth century, as part of the previously mentioned process of the relative autonomization of élites, which was also manifested as a process in the development of relative freedom of association. And although there has recently been a weakening in trade unionism in several western countries (Kettler and Volker 1988), this process cannot be traced back to coercive repression by the state. Indeed, at present, western state élites are restricted in the use of such repression by both the actual laws, and the norms and conventions that support and legitimize freedom of association. Therefore, while never social movements' élites have occasionally been harassed (Bottomore 1979), mostly they are allowed to express their grievances through a variety of protest activities.

Thirdly, freedom of association or organization (which also implies freedom to amass resources) sustains the relative autonomy of non-established élites in additional ways: protected by this principle, the members of such élites usually have sources of livelihood that are not dependent on, or controlled by, the state. With some exceptions, their movements have been allowed to accumulate resources that are relatively free from state control. Their own élite positions are accorded to them by these movements, so for these, too, they are not dependent on the state, or the governing élite. On the other hand, again, the state, and the governing élite, have resources that may affect social movements in a variety of ways: for instance, in order to maintain their élite positions, the élites of social movements must be able to "deliver" at least some achievements to their supporters. And for such achievements they frequently are dependent on the governing élite. In addition, while they may have independent sources of livelihood, their personal rewards may be greatly enhanced by the governing élite. Thus, their independence from the governing élite is always relative; never complete.

Fourthly, all this makes it both necessary and possible for the state élites, and especially for the governing élite, to devise various alternative strategies – not directly based on coercion – for coping with social movements; and indeed, there has been a transition towards greater emphasis on such strategies. These strategies are necessarily based on the utilization of the (non-coercive) state resources, of which the ruling élites, and to a certain extent the governing élite, have control. As noted before, these include a variety of symbolic, power, and material (economic) resources. These form the basis of the state and governing élites' own power, and many of these also can be – and are – used by the governing élite in strategies of control, to avert threats to its power, including threats of destabilization posed by social movements.

These strategies of control differ from straightforward repression of movements in two ways:

(1) They do not involve coercion directly. While coercion is always there in the background and available as a last resort, the actual strategies of control are a step removed from coercion;

(2) The aim and/or result is not to eliminate the movement and its activities, or even to alter it completely, but rather to let it persist while dissipating its threat; to let it express itself, yet without jeopardizing the system; to eliminate not the movement itself, but its destabilizing potential.

Overall, then, with respect to the governing élites' confrontation of the counter-élites of social and protest movements, *the process of the autonomization of élites that took place with the development of democracy entailed a gradual shift from coercive repression to non-coercive strategies of control, here collectively referred to as strategies for the absorption of protest.*[1]

The élites of movements and the absorption of protest

The governing élite applies these strategies of control – or the absorption of protest – by using the (non-coercive) state resources of which they have charge as either negative sanctions (curbs) or positive sanctions (inducements) or both, following the stick-and-carrot principle (on this see also Parsons 1986: 104). Thus, it may use state resources as negative sanctions to curb and penalize movements and their élites when they get out of hand, that is, for non compliance, opposition, or "radicalism." And it may use state resources as positive sanctions or inducements, to reward moderation, that is, by handing them out to the movements' leaders, their potential leaders, their members, or all three, in exchange for support to its own rule or acquiescence in the status quo.

Such strategies for the absorption of protest include, firstly, sanctions, drawing on symbolic resources. For instance, on the negative side, they may take the form of denigration, discreditation, and delegitimation of radical, extremist, or otherwise threatening movements. On the positive side, they may take the form of symbolic reassurances, such as politicians' expressions of support for the movements' causes and demands. Apart from such soothing statements, symbolic reassurances may take the form of the establishment of commissions of inquiry to investigate the movement's complaints and demands, and the publication of their reports. Prominent cases in point would be the commissions of inquiry into the conditions of blacks and women set up in the wake of the civil rights movement and the women's movement, and the publication of their reports in the United States and some other western countries.

Strategies for the absorption of protest include, secondly, power devices. On the negative side they entail utilization of the state's power structures (to the extent that they are controlled by the governing élite) to curb social movements. This may take the form of restrictive legislation. A case in point would be the manner in which the Wagner Act (1935) and the Taft-Hartley Act (1947) institutionalized, protected, but also regulated, and thus restricted, the activities of trade unions in the United States (Barbalet forthcoming). Another example would be legislation imposing a ban on secondary boycotts by trade unions, or on strikes in (at times broadly defined) essential services, over and against the opposition of trade unions and their supporters, in various western countries. A recent case in point would be the Essential Services legislation recently introduced in Australia by the government of New South Wales, and which threatens to embroil it in a constitutional brawl with the federal government. Yet another example would be the use of military or police forces to protect strike-breakers, particularly in recent years in Britain. An example with respect to other movements would be legislation passed in the late 1970s in Australia by the government of Queensland placing restrictions on street marches and demonstrations, in defiance of widespread media and public opposition.

On the positive side, power devices (also known as co-optation) entail letting movements' leaders or potential leaders gain a certain share of power in the establishment, or the incorporation of the movements and/or their leaders or potential leaders into existing power structures, in return for acceptance of those structures. Cases in point would include the incorporation of trade union leaders into decision and policy-making processes in several western countries, particularly through tripartite agreements in which business leaders are included as well; the incorporation of increasing numbers of blacks into political structures in the United States (Berns 1984); and the incorporation of environmental and nuclear movements and their leaders into the parliamentary and electoral structures in several western – especially European – countries (with the greens in West Germany as a prominent example).

Strategies of protest absorption include, thirdly, material devices. On the negative side, they may take the form of depriving certain movements or their élites of monetary resources accruing to other movements and élites. For instance, in Israel's pre-state era, the semi-autonomous Jewish National Authorities – established under British Mandatory rule – used to allocate funds derived from the World Zionist Organization only to those parties and movements that accepted their authority, and to deny such funds to the more "extremist" or "radical" movements (Horowitz and Lissak 1971). This practice has been perpetuated into the post-state era as well, despite widespread opposition to it. On the positive side material devices may take the form of policies entailing acceptance of some of the movements' demands for the reallocation of material resources. For instance, in some western countries governing élites have responded to the women's movement with legislation and policies leading to decreases in the earning differentials between men and women (Costain and Costain 1985; Jones 1983, 1984).

In addition there are, of course, combined or mixed devices. Thus, during the McCarthy era in the United States, state élites attempted to put drastic curbs on (without coercively eliminating) communist and related organizations and movements, by restricting their members' and sympathizers' access to power structures and employment, and by discrediting them in the eyes of the public.

I would argue (although I cannot provide quantitative proof for this) that the strategies devised by the governing élites for the purpose of coping with the recent or new social protest movements, in the last few decades, have been most prominently those that employ positive rather than negative sanctions. *Thus, the shift has been not only from coercive repression to other strategies of control, but also towards positive rather than negative sanctions, inducements rather than curbs.* And amongst the positive devices, the most prominent has been that of co-optation, of incorporating élites of social movements into existing power structures, in exchange for moderation. It has been argued – quite plausibly – that this "generous" approach, so to speak, by governing élites took shape in the framework of the complacency of established élites generated by the growing affluence of western societies particularly in the postwar era, and that graver economic downturns than those experienced since the early 1970s might well have led to a more restrictive approach on the part of the governing élites, one in which curbs might well have outweighed inducements in the controls applied to social and protest movements.

Be this as it may, it is noteworthy that even as it is, the inducements that have been offered to movements and their élites have not been such as to allow them to cause fundamental changes in the power structures and patterns of resource allocations in western societies. There is, of course, no generally accepted yardstick to indicate where a limited change ends and a fundamental change begins. But three criteria have been applied here: firstly, nowhere in recent decades have the movements' leaders been allowed to become major power holders within existing establishments. Secondly, wherever changes in the power structures and allocation of resources have occurred, they have not measured up to the movements' demands. Thirdly, where the movements' demands have resulted in some reallocations of resources in favour of disadvantaged groups, these reallocations have not abolished those disadvantages, and have not gone as far as to put those disadvantaged groups on a par with the more advantaged groups in society. For instance, environmental and anti-nuclear movements' leaders have not become major components of western governing élites, and despite a decrease in the differentials between men and women's earnings, average women's pay for full-time year-round work is still only between two-thirds and three-quarters of that of men's pay in the various countries of the western world (Etzioni-Halevy 1989b: Ch. 7).

The élites of movements and social progress

In a way, the strategies of using inducements derived from state resources for the absorption of protest in western democracies, and particularly co-optation, have commonly been crowned with success. That is to say, like their predecessors, several (though certainly not all) of the movements' leaders or potential leaders have, in fact, let themselves be co-opted into the existing establishments, as illustrated by the previous examples. This seems to have been the case partly because of the personal rewards involved, and partly because without such co-optation the achievements the leaders can deliver to their supporters are usually even smaller. As Robert Michels (1915) clarified long ago, when the then non-established élites of labor unions and parties came to share power within the existing establishment the very establishments they had previously undertaken to transform – their revolutionary zeal abated, and they became increasingly willing to accept the status quo. And the same is still true today; as Mann (1983) has indicated, this is one of the major reasons why western capitalist democracies have not been riddled by major revolts or rebellions.

But while Michels was correct in his factual analysis, he nevertheless missed an important point which now, with the hindsight of almost a century, has become much clearer. The point being that, while they were incorporated into the establishment, in the process of becoming incorporated, or after incorporation, the élites of the labor movement at the time have still managed to achieve certain changes in the allocation of resources in favor of their supporters; and the same is true with respect to the leaders of more recent social movements: *it is precisely before, in the process of, or after being co-opted, that the élites of social movements have achieved some of the changes favored by their supporters.* While these achievements, where they occurred, have been of a limited nature, this is not to say that they have not been valuable, or that no real and substantial changes may result from them. For, in the first place, it is possible that without the movements' intervention the situation against which they have protested might have deteriorated even further. In the second place, even small achievements may be incremental and add up to more significant achievements in the long run.

Thus, the *inducements employed by the governing élite as part of their strategies for the absorption of the protest of certain movements and*

218

élites and, in particular, co-optation have still spelled certain achievements for those social and protest movements and their élites. Co-optation (and the other strategies of the absorption of protest) thus entails a two-sided process. Co-optation is one of the major processes responsible for the dissipation of the threat of rebellion. Co-optation has a prominent share in the "domestication," so to speak, or the moderation, of potentially radical movements. Because co-optation is successful, the élites of social movements generally settle for much less than they had initially demanded. But co-optation may also prevent ossification of the system. Because there is co-optation there have not been major rebellions, and hence no far-reaching changes. But because there is co-optation there is also *some* (albeit limited) change.

In western-style democracies non-established élites of social movements have frequently (though not always) been élites which – whatever their own socio-economic position – have championed the interests of some disadvantaged classes or groups in society. And since the interests of the disadvantaged lie in change towards a more egalitarian distribution of political power and material resources, and since the non-established élites of social movements can maintain their positions only if they deliver at least some achievements to their supporters, there is always a certain likelihood that non-established élites will push for a more egalitarian distribution of resources or, in other words, for social progress.

As was seen before, it was precisely the struggles of non-established élites which mediated the manner in which a variety of socio-economic reforms towards a lessening of inequalities in the distribution of resources was achieved, and in which western democracy came into being and developed in the first place. By the same token, there is no reason to surmise that more recent, present, and future confrontations between established and non-established élites, may not be capable of leading to further changes towards lesser inequalities in the power structures and in the allocation of resources in western, democratic, regimes.

It is true that recently the distributive achievements of social movements have been less impressive than those of movements in the past, particularly towards the end of the nineteenth and the beginning of the twentieth centuries. This is because several of the most recent movements have borne the characteristic features of "postmodernism" (Luhmann 1982; Lyotard 1984, cited in Holton 1988); they have been fragmented (Boggs 1986) and have championed "post-materialist" values (Inglehart 1981). Consequently many of them and their élites have not been representing the particular interests of the most disadvantaged classes, and have not been concerned chiefly with inequality, exploitation, and the redistribution of resources in a more egalitarian fashion between different social classes (Offe 1985; Holton 1988). But, this is not to say that no movement has been concerned with inequalities, and that no redistributions of resources at all have resulted from its activities, as indicated before. Furthermore, recent movements have been concerned particularly with struggles for a more participatory style of politics, for greater democratization (Boggs 1986: Chs 2 and 6; Desai 1985), and for increased autonomous rights for groups and individuals (Feher and Heller, 1984, cited in Holton 1988). That is to say, they have been concerned with a more egalitarian distribution of power, and it is in this area that they have the greatest potential for affecting western societies (see e.g. Rueschemeyer and Rueschemeyer 1988).

If, as has been argued before, the changes brought about by social movements' élites have occurred precisely in the process of their conflict and protest being absorbed by the established élites, and in particular before, during the process, or after, they were themselves co-opted into the establishment, and if several of these changes have been towards greater redistributions of material and/or power resources, then it must be concluded that *in western democracies co-optation of non-established élites is a major process through which redistributive changes, i.e. social progress, occurs.* The élites who have let themselves be co-opted by the establishment have frequently been accused by their supporters of betrayal, and in many cases those accusations were eminently justifiable. None the less it was in the very process of betrayal that non-established élites have been a force of (albeit hesitant) progress in democratic societies.

Like past and present élites, the élites of whatever new movements for greater equality may come upon the scene in the future, may well be co-opted, may betray their supporters, and may eventually become staunch defenders of the status quo. But it is precisely through their co-optation that changes towards greater equality, or further progress, may occur. And if, or when, they get co-opted, others may well come to take their place.

Conclusion and discussion

In western democracies important redistributive changes come about through the relative autonomy and countervailing power of élites and especially of the non-established, or counter-élites of social movements. However, they tend to come about not directly through those élites' activities and achievements as such, but rather through the ruling and especially the governing élites' strategies for the absorption of the counter-élites' protest, and most prominently through the co-optation of such counter-élites and their incorporation into the establishment. The relative autonomy of élites is thus important not because it leads to change in a straightforward manner, just because it leads to strategies of control and stabilization which – paradoxically – also lead to change.

Even in non-western regimes, where there is no relative autonomy, or much less autonomy of élites, than in western regimes, people with the potential for destabilizing the system are frequently co-opted into the establishment and bought off through a variety of personal rewards. But in western democracies, where there exists such relative autonomy of élites, and where non-established élites attain and hold their positions on the basis of relatively independent resources accumulated in and by social movements, the co-optation of such élites entails an additional price: certain concessions to the movements on which the counter-élites' resources are based. And the concessions aimed at placating these movements, in turn, form an important mechanism through which social change and progress may make inroads into western democracies.

Even in non-western regimes, a social movement, if it arises at all, may leave behind a certain social legacy, including some reforms and a greater commitment to reforms than previously existed. But there the price may well be the crushing, or defeat of the movement (Sztompka 1988) and the occurrence itself would be rather exceptional (although this may, of course, change at some stage). But in western democracies concessions to movements through, or in conjunction with the co-optation, or the co-optation of their élites, resulting in the "domestication" rather than the defeat of the movements are now made on a routine basis, and – particularly in recent years – have become part and parcel of the manner in which the machinations of power work to preserve the system.

In other words, in western democracies the relative autonomy of élites, the recurring cycles of the generation of relatively autonomous movements and their élites – some of which champion the interests of the disadvantaged – the absorption of their protest entailing *inter alia* co-optation, the according of some concessions to them before, in the process of, or after they are being co-opted, without repressing them but also without letting them effect major transformations in existing structures of power and resource allocation, their consequent acceptance of the status quo, and finally the generation of yet other relatively autonomous counter-élites to take their place, may be seen as a major pattern in which change in the allocation of resources in western democracies takes place, and through which they may become more democratic and equitable democracies in the future.

The reallocation of resources that takes place through this pattern at any particular point in time may not be large or impressive; indeed, at times it may stop altogether, and at other times it may well proceed at a snail's pace. But looked at over longer time spans, the changes that do occur may be seen to be incremental and cumulative. This pattern of change has already involved major reallocations and redistributions of resources over the last centuries, and although the redistribution may have been less impressive in recent years, and although great inequalities still remain, it is not inconceivable that greater redistributions may occur in the future. Thus, the relative autonomy of élites, particularly of the élites of social movements, although it brings about only limited achievements at any given time, still turns democracy into a more dynamic and progressive system than would otherwise be the case.

Note

1. The term "absorption of protest" has been used by Leeds (1964) in organizational analysis, but it seems to me that the term may be profitably employed in the area of social and protest movements as well.

Acknowledgments

This is a revised version of a paper presented to the International Conference on "Social Progress and Sociological Theory," Krakow, June 1988. I am grateful to the participants of the conference for several incisive and constructive comments. A previous version of this paper was presented at a seminar in the Department of Sociology, the Faculties, the Australian National University, June 1988. I am also greatly indebted to the participants of the seminar, and in particular to Dr J. Barbalet, Professor B. Hindess, Dr A. Hopkins, and Dr A. Klovdahl for their most helpful comments.

Bibliography

Aron, Raymond (1968) *Progress and Disillusion* (London: Pall Mall Press).
Aron, Raymond (1978) *Politics and History* (trans. by M. Bernheim-Conant) (New York: Free Press).
Bachrach, Peter (1967) *The Theory of Democratic Elitism: A Critique* (Boston: Little Brown).
Barbalet, J. M. (forthcoming) "Social movements and the state" in *Politics of the Future*, edited by C. Jennett and R. Stewart (Sydney: Macmillan).
Barbalet, J. M. (forthcoming) "Social organization and group processes in power relations."
Barber, Benjamin R. (1984) *Strong Democracy* (Berkeley: University of California Press).
Berns, Walter (1984) *In Defense of Liberal Democracy* (Chicago: Gateway Editions).
Block, Felix (1987) *Revising State Theory* (Philadelphia: Temple University Press).
Boggs, Carl (1986) *Social Movements and Political Power* (Philadelphia: Temple University Press).
Bottomore, Tom (1979) *Political Sociology* (London: Hutchinson).
Costain, A. N. and Costain, W. D. (1985) "Movements and gatekeepers," *Congress and the Presidency*, 12: 21–42.

Dahl, R. A. (1956) *A Preface to Democratic Theory* (Chicago: University of Chicago Press).

Dahl, R. A. (1967) *Pluralist Democracy in the United States* (Chicago: Rand McNally).

Dahl, R. A. (1969) "Stability and change in the democratic creed" in *Empirical Democratic Theory*, edited by C. F. Cnudde and D. E. Neubauer (Chicago: Markham: 253–67).

Dahl, R. A. (1970) *Modern Political Analysis* (2nd edn) (Englewood Cliffs, NJ: Prentice Hall).

Dahl, R. A. (1971) *Polyarchy* (New Haven: Yale University Press).

Dahl, R. A. (1982) *Dilemmas of Pluralist Democracy* (New Haven: Yale University Press).

Dahl, R. A. (1986) "Power as the control of behaviour," in S. Lukes (ed.) *Power* (Oxford: Basil Blackwell: 37–58).

Dahl, R. A. and Lindblom, C. E. (1953) *Politics, Economics and Welfare* (New York: Harper).

Desai, Uday (1985) "Citizen participation and environmental policy implementation," Paper prepared for the XIII World Congress of the International Political Science Association, Paris, July.

Domhoff, G. William (1967) *Who Rules America?* (Englewood Cliffs, NJ: Prentice Hall).

Domhoff, G. W. (1978) *The Powers that Be* (New York: Random House).

Domhoff, G. W. (1983) *Who Rules America Now?* (Englewood Cliffs, NJ: Prentice Hall).

Dye, Thomas R. (1983) *Who's Running America? The Reagan Years* (Englewood Cliffs, NJ: Prentice Hall).

Dye, T. R. (1985) *Who's Running America? The Conservative Years* (Englewood Cliffs, NJ: Prentice Hall).

Dye, T. R. and Zeigler, L. H. (1987) *The Irony of Democracy* (7th edn) (Monterey, CA: Brooks Cole Publishing).

Edelman, Murray J. (1971) *Politics as Symbolic Action* (New York: Academic Press).

Etzioni-Halevy, Eva (1985) *Bureaucracy and Democracy: A Political Dilemma* (revised edn) (London: Routledge & Kegan Paul).

Etzioni-Halevy, Eva (1989a) "The contradiction of power, conflict, and change in a democracy: a demo-élitist perspective," *Current Perspectives in Social Theory, an Annual*, 9.

Etzioni-Halevy, Eva (1989b) *Fragile Democracy* (New Brunswick, NJ: Transaction Books).

Evans, Peter D, Rueschemeyer, Dietrich and Skocpol, Theda (1985) *Bringing the State Back In* (Cambridge: Cambridge University Press).

Feher, Ferenc and Heller, Agnes (1984) "From red to green," *Telos*, 59: 35–44.

Field, G. Lowell and Higley, John (1980) *Elitism* (London: Routledge & Kegan Paul).

Giddens, Anthony (1982) *Profiles and Critiques in Social Theory* (London: Macmillan).

Hindess, B. (1980) "Marxism and parliamentary democracy," in A. Hunt (ed.) *Marxism and Democracy* (London: Lawrence & Wishart: 21–54).

Holton, Robert (1988) "Problems of crisis and normalcy in the contemporary world," paper delivered to the International Conference on "Social Progress and Sociological Theory," Krakow, June.

Horowitz, David and Lissak, Moshe (1971) "Authority without sovereignty," in M. Lissak and E. Gutman (eds) *Political Institutions and Processes in Israel* (Jerusalem: Akademon).

223

Inglehart, R. (1981) "Post-materialism in an environment of insecurity," *The American Political Science Review*, 75: 880–900.

Jones, F. L. (1983) "Sources of gender inequality," *Social Forces*, 12: 134–52.

Jones, F. L. (1984) "Income inequality," in D. H. Broom (ed.) *Unfinished Business: Social Justice for Women* (Sydney: George Allen & Unwin).

Keller, Suzanne (1963) *Beyond the Ruling Class* (New York: Random House).

Kettler, David and Meja, Volker (1988) "The end of trade unionism in the west? social change after the age of social democracy," paper presented to the International Conference on "Social Progress and Sociological Theory," Krakow, June.

Kumar, Krishna (1978) *Prophecy and Progress* (London: Allen Lane).

Lasswell, Harold D. and Kaplan, Abraham (1950) *Power and Society. Yale Law School Studies*, Vol. 2 (New Haven: Yale University Press).

Leeds, Ruth (1964) "The absorption of protest: a working paper," in W. W. Cooper *et al.* (eds) *New Perspectives in Organizational Research* (New York: 115–35).

Lenski, Gerhard (1986) "Power and privilege," in S. Lukes (ed.) *Power* (Oxford: Basil Blackwell: 243–52).

Luhmann, Niklas (1982) *The Differentiation of Society* (New York: Columbia University Press).

Lyotard, Jean-François (1984) *The Post Modern Condition* (Manchester: Manchester University Press).

Mandel, Ernest (1975) *Late Capitalism* (trans. by J. de Pres) (London: New Left Books).

Mann, Michael (1983) "The social cohesion of liberal democracy," in A. Giddens and D. Held (eds) *Classes, Power, and Conflict* (Berkeley: University of California Press: 373–95).

Mann, Michael (1984) "The autonomous power of the state," *Archives Européennes de Sociologie*, 25: 185–213.

Michels, Robert (1915) *Political Parties* (trans. by E. and C. Paul) (London: Jarrold & Sons).

Miliband, R. (1977) *Marxism and Politics* (Oxford: Oxford University Press).

Mosca, Gaetano (1939) *The Ruling Class* (trans. by H. D. Kahn) (New York: McGraw Hill).

Mushaben, J. M. (1985) "Cycles of peace protest in West Germany," *West European Politics*, 8: 24–40.

Offe, Claus (1985) "New social movements," *Social Research*, 52: 817–68.

Parenti, Michael (1980) *Democracy for the Few* (New York: St. Martin's Press).

Parsons, Talcott (1986) "Power and the social system," in S. Lukes (ed.) *Power* (Oxford: Basil Blackwell: 94–143).

Pateman, Carole (1970) *Participation and Democratic Theory* (Cambridge: Cambridge University Press).

Perkin, H. (1969) *The Origins of British Society 1780–1880* (London: Routledge & Kegan Paul).

Pierson, C. (1984) "New theories of the state and civil society: recent developments in post Marxist analysis of the state," *Sociology*, 18: 5063–71.

Polsby, Nelson W. (1985) "Prospects for pluralism," *Society*, 22: 30–4.

Poulantzas, Nicos (1978) *State, Power, Socialism* (trans. by P. Camiller) (London: New Left Books).

Riesman, David (1961) *The Lonely Crowd* (New Haven: Yale University Press).

Rueschemeyer, Dietrich and Rueschemeyer, Marilyn (1988) "Progress in the distribution of power: gender relations and feminism as a source of change," paper presented at the conference on "Social Progress and Sociological Theory," Krakow, June.

Sartori, Giovanni (1962) *Democratic Theory* (Detroit: Wayne State University Press).

Sartori, Giovanni (1987) *The Theory of Democracy Revisited* (Chatham, NJ: Chatham House Publishers).

Schumpeter, Joseph A. (1962) *Capitalism, Socialism and Democracy* (3rd edn) (New York: Harper & Row).

Skocpol, Theda (1979) *States and Social Revolutions* (Cambridge: Cambridge University Press).

Sztompka, Piotr (1988) "The social functions of defeat," *Research in Social Movements, Conflict and Change*, 10: 183–92.

Therborn, Goeran (1977) "The rule of capital and the rise of democracy," *New Left Review*, 103: 3–41.

Truman, David (1971) *The Governmental Process* (2nd edn) (New York: Knopf).

Useem, Michael (1984) *The Inner Circle* (New York: Oxford University Press).

Weber, Max (1947) *The Theory of Social and Economic Organization* (trans. by A. M. Henderson and T. Parsons) (New York: Free Press).

Weber, Max (1968) *Economy and Society* (trans. by G. Roth and L. Wittich) (New York: Bedminster Press).

Wilson, H. T. (1984) *Political Management* (Berlin: Walter de Gruyter).

PART IV

New concepts of progress

11

Models of directional change and human values: the theory of progress as an applied social science

STEFAN NOWAK

Social progress as positively evaluated social change

When I mentioned to one of my colleagues, that I was preparing a paper for a conference on theoretical aspects of social progress, he gave me a long look and then said "You can't be serious, of course!." This colleague of mine was expressing a widespread skepticism in the social sciences with the notion of "progress," both with the empirical validity of ideas which have been associated with it in the course of the history of the social sciences, and with its usefulness in social analysis. I share the first of these doubts, nevertheless I think, that the notion of "progress" and some of its derivatives like "regress," as well as some other concepts of the same logical category, can be quite useful, provided that both their meaning and the domain of their useful applicability be properly specified. This essay will try to specify both of these.

Before doing that, however, I want to present my own methodological and philosophical position with respect to the "problem of progress." But, instead of formulating my own views, I will take a quotation from one of my Polish colleagues, since he expressed the view, to which I also adhere, in such a clear and precise form, that it would be redundant to try to formulate it in my own words. The quotation comes from a paper entitled "The idea of progress from the perspective of our time" presented at the Annual Meeting of the Polish Sociological Association held in Warsaw in March 1985 by the historian and sociologist, Jerzy Jedlicki.

Jedlicki reviews in his paper various notions and theories of progress found in the social sciences, and demonstrates, that their common denominator is the conviction of the author of each notion or theory, that history is on his side and working for the implementation of his vision of the desired future of mankind. Then at the end of his paper he comes to the following conclusions:

> Progress is a great myth if we treat it as a law of history, as a historical necessity for all times and cultures.
>
> Progress is a utopia, if we treat it as an infallible road to a millennium, to some final state of a united mankind, free of poverty, fear, oppression, fights, and of all other dramas of human destiny.
>
> Progress is neither myth nor utopy, if we treat it as a choice of values and as a task for the creative mind and human activity, operating in this zone of human possibilities, which expands between illusory demiurgic feelings of omnipotence and the despair caused by feelings of helplessness in the face of blind forces of history.
>
> Such progress is empirical possibility, not a necessity. The future is always unknown and is not guaranteed in any way. When working for progress we are guided by ideals, but we do not expect their perfect implementation; in a similar way science does not expect, that one day everything will be known, discovered, or solved. (Jedlicki 1985: 28)

Since I agree with the above view, I will simply pass from the analysis of some methodological aspects and theoretical consequences of applications of such a use of the notion of "social progress," to the analysis of social reality, which would be in agreement with the view presented above.

Therefore progress in general I understand to be such directional changes of a certain object, a class of objects, or a domain of reality which, with respect to some of their characteristics, are important to the observer, and at the same time receive positive evaluations, evaluation criteria or evaluation standards are applied to them. With respect to the social domain, the assessment of "progress" involves both the assessment of the directional change of some "social objects" with respect to certain characteristics, and the positive evaluation of these directional changes.

Study of social progress as a subdomain of applied social studies

The perception of difficulties involving the existence of some evaluative components in the notion of "progress" seems now to be pretty general, and this is true even for evolutionary biology, where at first the notion of "evolutionary progress" seemed to be so deeply rooted in the "natural mechanisms of transformation of the species," that it was not easy to see the evaluative component in it. A similar opinion about the "natural" character of social progress can be found in the period when many theoreticians or philosophers believed strongly in the "iron necessity" of the laws of social evolution. Now we can see both the empirical and evaluative aspects of changes regarded previously as going "unquestionably" in the progressive direction. What we can assess from a strictly empirical point of view is that these changes are directional; whether a certain change so assessed is additionally progressive or constitutes a case of social regress, or is from this point of view neutral, depends on the values of those who evaluate these changes. And here, depending on the similarities or differences of their value systems, two researchers may differ in such evaluations, even if they agree on the direction and speed of the given change from a strictly empirical point of view.

The fact that the evaluative component of the notion of progress comes from the value system of the researcher does not mean, of course, that "we are not allowed" to use this concept in scientific studies. But it means, that when we are doing this in the way described above, i.e. when we are using our evaluation standards as a necessary tool of social analysis, we enter the domain of applied social studies (see Nowak 1976).

As is well known, in any social study the "extrascientific" (e.g. moral or social) values of the researcher may – justifiably – play a lesser or greater role (together with some intrascientific: cognitive or methodological premises) at the stage of formulation of the problem of his study. But these values may also be quite absent at this stage and the researcher may be guided in his choice of research problem only by some strictly "intrascientific" premises and standards (e.g. by the existence of the "white spots" on the map of social facts or by the contradictions between different, accepted theories). The evaluations involving extrascientific standards may also occur at the final stage of the study, when the scientist comes to the conclusion that, from the point of view of his extrascientific (e.g. social or moral) values, he likes or does not like the facts or regularities discovered in social reality. But here again, the researcher may remain evaluatively neutral, "strictly descriptive," with respect to these findings. The same may also happen in the case of a study which is oriented towards the assessment of a dynamic process, or towards the discovery of causes and theoretical mechanisms, determining such processes, or finally towards the empirical test of a more general social theory.

But evaluating the assessed facts should be one of the goals of an applied study. This makes the values applied by the researcher to the established facts and changes a necessary "research tool." We are then looking empirically at some parts or aspects of changing social reality and at the same time we ask: how does the past, present, or future (expected) shape of social reality or the course of transformations satisfy our evaluation standards? Moreover, if the expected course of social transformations does not seem satisfactory to us, another question may then arise: what actions could we – as social scientists – recommend, in order to increase the probability, that the future course of changes will be more satisfying to us.

Such a study may be synchronic, undertaken with the intention to assess or describe the studied fragment of social reality in a certain cross-section of time, and then to state, whether it is in a "satisfactory shape." Then the notion of "progress" or some of its equivalents do not apply to the evaluative assessment of the results of such cross-sectional studies. But only if the study deals with dynamic aspects of reality and finds in them some directional changes, then the notion of progress (or regress – depending on the outcome of evaluation) may be applied.

When dealing with the future course of such transformations, we might decide to use our scientific competence in order to formulate recommendations for proper, efficient actions promoting social progress in the given domain. Here we are in another subdomain of applied studies which is sometimes called "socio-technical studies," as Adam Podgórecki proposed to call "social engineering."

It is fairly obvious why we should regard such descriptive-evaluative statements about present or future courses of social changes as part of applied social sciences. But, as we know, many questions and statements about progress deal with past social transformations of societies and of mankind. We can even say that the entire notion of progress was born from misinformed and simplified generalizations about our social history and from unjustified extrapolations of these generalizations from our past to our future. If we now insist that the "study of progress" belongs to applied social science, the question arises to what degree the study of past progresses can be regarded as a part of applied social studies. Or, in other words: how can studies of the past be practically relevant?

The ancient Romans used to say *"historia est magistra vitae!,"* i.e. history is the teacher of the present life. This may mean, that we take from history the normative examples of proper ways of moral conduct, deserving to be applied in our present life, and we know that examples of old heroes were given by Roman historians to their students for just that purpose.

But the same saying may also mean something else. Tukidydes made it clear in his introductory pages to the history of the Peloponnesian War, that he was writing this book for practical use by those, who from the knowledge of past events, are willing to derive the rules of their own behavior in the future. Should similar events occur again in the future (as they probably will), the reader will know their natural course and will be able to act according to this knowledge (see Tukidydes 1957: 13).

Tukidydes' remark is for me the earliest formulation of a program of development of practically useful nomological social science and constitutes another type of meaning for the saying *"historia est magistra vitae."* This is the one I find more scientifically relevant.

When we look at the social history of mankind, thinking – without any further specifications – about the formulation of the research problems for dealing with past social changes, we see a practically unlimited range of possible formulations of research problems, since there was a practically infinite number of such changes, occurring to various social entities, with respect to their various characteristics, and each of them could become a subject of our interest.

But when we look at the past history of mankind from the point of view of the notion of progress, i.e., also from the point of view of our present values, the choice of possible objects for study becomes more limited: both the objects themselves must belong to a general class, which is also evaluatively important for us, and their tentative characteristics, deserving our attention from the point of view of their possible progress or regress, must belong to the category of variables, which is still important to us today. To be more specific, we look for such objects and their characteristics, the nomological understanding of the changes of which could turn out, directly or indirectly, to be important for our understanding of the functioning or change of analogous important objects and processes in our present or future social situations.

Due to our evaluatively selective focus on the problems of past social progress and on theories explaining such changes we may begin to develop theories of high practical relevance, without losing our strictly scientific perspective.

To give an analogy: medicine is an applied biology, biochemistry, or biophysics, the application of which is determined by the values we attach to the shape and functioning of our organism. Thus, where those domains of the real world are studied by these sciences, medicine asks different questions, and has a different set of research priorities, from when these sciences are pursued "for their own sake," i.e., when they are not guided by reference to the possible medical applicability of their results.

Medical science also can give us another analogy: this is the notion of "illness," which is simply an undesired state or undesired process in the human organism. It also has two components in its meaning: the strictly empirical, and the evaluative one. This is now clear in the field of mental illness, but becomes more and more visible in the case of other illnesses (see Sowa 1984).

In an analogous way reference to social values sets quite another set of research priorities for an applied social scientist, as it could happen in a non-applied social study, and this applies to dynamic studies of social progress as well.

Instead of the term "progress" (which – as mentioned before – is regarded, today, with some suspicion by many researchers), other terms are being used in a similar function. I would like to recall here one term, namely "development." In some cases it means simply positive directional change of a social or natural "object," and then it is just the modern equivalent for the unfashionable term: "progress." In other cases it means just a certain pattern of directional change without any evaluative meaning to it. Finally, in some other cases it refers to a "regular directional change" when "regular" means: "going on in accordance with some known regularities of transformation of the objects of the given class." In such a strictly nomological sense we may state the fact of a development of the flu in someone's body or state the development of anomie in a society in the state of deep crisis. None of the last two statements (usually) involves positive evaluation of such "normally developing" cases.

In many uses of the term "development" the descriptive, nomological, and evaluative criteria are jointly involved in the meaning of the corresponding statement. This may be the case for example when someone states that "socialist development is going on in our country." Similar sets of notions of "progress" can also be found. I would expecially like to stress that to be the case where descriptive, nomological, and evaluative components of meaning occurred jointly in some visions of the change of mankind (as in the case of many nineteenth-century sociological evolutionists) or in similar, much more comprehensive visions of the directional, teleological development of nature in general (see, for example, Thaillard de Chardin). Such visions postulated that if the (social or natural) world is moving toward a certain direction (goal), then that course is determined by some natural (or supernatural) laws, and finally that it is good by some natural (or as in the case of de Chardin – also by God's) evaluational standards. In some cases Hegelian patterns of reasoning were applied, deriving the validity of the evaluational standards applied to history from the nomological necessity of the course of their transformations.

These two aspects of questions about "progress" or "development" – empirical and evaluative – are not always distinguished clearly enough. Thus, for example, in the well-known dispute about "eurocentrism" of the idea of "modernization" it was quite often difficult to distinguish between the two types of objections. Those who challenged the applicability of the notion of "modernization" as contemporary correspondent of "social progress," to the study of contemporary transformations of developing countries, may have been challenging the empirical validity of the statement – that a certain set of directional changes, denoted by this term, really does occur, and/or it will occur in the future, and if so, how broadly, and in what kind of societies will it occur, and so forth.

Or they may have challenged the idea, that such a course of transformation, as denoted by this concept is a desirable one and should be recommended to these countries, or be used as an evaluational criterion by them, because they did not like the set of characteristics which belonged to the notion of "modernity" so defined, or at least they did not believe that this evaluational standard should have equal applicability to all countries or cultures of the world. These are of course quite different sets of questions.

Let us finally look at some habitual limits of real applications of the notion of "progress" in science and in everyday use. There is "nothing improper" from a linguistic point of view with stating in a family situation, that "Johnny has made quite some progress with maths" and to be happy with Johnny's scientific achievement. From a strictly logical point of view this is exactly the kind of empirical-evaluative statement I was characterizing above. But when people are talking about "social progress," they usually have in mind social objects that are important to a rather great number of them, and then they also apply certain evaluative criteria with respect to directional changes of such objects, on which a sufficient number of them may agree.

Such objects are, in terms of their size, usually at least their local communities, which can unify a multiplicity of people in a common perceptive and evaluative attitude. But more often they would be larger sections of a national society or, they would be the nation itself, which seem to constitute nowadays the most typical units of such cognitive-evaluative reference, as discussed above. Sometimes we refer our observations and our hopes and fears to an even higher level of aggregation of social reality and think about progress at the level of such units of social analysis as "mankind" or the "world system."

Simple and syndromatic directional changes

The notion of directional change is understood here as a "purely descriptive" term, free of any evaluative components. Its use assumes that we have formulated a diachronic statement, stating a certain temporal sequence of some different states or events, but belonging to a more general category, i.e., constituting different values of the same, qualitative or quantitative variable.

Such propositions may refer to the sequence of some qualitative attributes, as for example in "Argentina changed from a military dictatorship to democracy," or to a quantitative one, like: "GNP per capita in Poland fell in 1982 by 25%." Or such diachronic statements may refer to a longer chain of social transformations, in which we can distinguish many such temporal links, S_1, S_2, S_3, etc., and from the point of view of a certain, strongly or at least weakly quantitative variable (like, for example, rank order of several qualitatively defined attributes), and those links can be ordered with respect to the given object, so that the value of this variable is either increasing or decreasing successively from one link to another, constituting a so-called "trend."

A directional change assessed in a study may be of a simple or syndromatic character. It is a simple (uni-dimensional) change if we assess that a certain object or class of social objects change in a directional way with respect to one characteristic or variable only. Systematic, directional increases of literacy, or of GNP per capita, assessed for a nation, or for a set of nations are examples of such single changes.

Directional change is syndromatic (multi-dimensional) if it involves analogous directional change of the given object or class of such objects, with respect to a whole cluster of such characteristics. It assumes directional (in time) co-variation of a set of variables characterizing the studied objects. Such co-varying characteristics are often jointly denoted by one term: "modernization," "folk-urban-continuum," "urbanization," are the best-known examples of such syndromatic terms used in sociology for the assessment of syndromatic directional changes of certain objects (see Nowak 1977: 111–14).

With respect to a single, directional change, the crucial empirical problem is, whether and how broadly it did, does, or will really occur with respect to the class of social objects we are interested in. But then come two other equally important questions: what are the causes of such a "trend" (as such uni-dimensional changes are often called), and what are its consequences? Answering them usually involves application of our theoretical knowledge to the uni-dimensional social transformation.

When we are dealing with a syndromatic directional change, to all these questions mentioned above, we must add another: to what degree the directional co-variance (functional relation, association, correlation) of all elements of such a syndrome is a constant characteristic for the period in which the occurrence of the directional change of a set of variables was assessed; how broadly these associations do occur; and finally, to what degree can we expect that they will occur thus in the future.

Among other theoretical questions we deal here with the question about mutual feedback between various components of syndromatic change or about their origin in a deeper underlying causal process, on which all elements of the syndrome depend. In some situations we try to establish conditions in our theories, on which the joint temporal co-variation of all components of the syndromatic process depend.

Even if the statements about directional change of some objects with respect to singular dimensions of their change may have a broad range of validity, the statements about their syndromatic co-variation are usually much less generally valid, or they are not true at all. This was for example – in the final course – the fate of "folk-urban-continuum" understood as a syndromatic concept. It turned out, that in the period of fast urbanization of developing countries the components of this syndrome are not correlated in such a way, as predicted by this "continuum." So it had to be abandoned – at least in its initial syndromatic formulation.

With respect to the use of a syndromatic concept in the assessment of directional changes, if all elements of the syndrome are functionally (i.e. in a necessary manner) interrelated to each other, then we may use any one of them as a single valid indicator of the entire syndrome, or in other words (if we add our evaluational standards to such analysis) we may assess the location of the object in question on its "road to progress" by its position in one single dimension.

If their positive interrelation is statistical only, or even when these dimensions are independent, but they belong (e.g. for evaluative or for theoretical reasons) jointly to the same notion of a process, and we find out, that all those dimensions are equivalent – i.e. substitutive in indicating the entire process of the given directional change (as, for example, alternative routes or as equally important elements from the point of view of our value system), then we may construct a cumulative index, measuring the course of the given directional change and the location of particular objects in this process.

On the other hand, it may also happen, that we don't find theoretical or normative reasons for postulating equivalence of various dimensions of a non-syndromatic process (or of a process where these dimensions are only statistically associated). Then instead of locating our objects on a singular point of our index, we must locate their position in each dimension separately and then follow their movements in a multi-dimensional property space.

It may also happen, that the elements of a multi-dimensional process, as denoted jointly by a certain notion, happen to be in reality negatively interrelated, or associated. They are then "counter-syndromatic" (if one may invent a term for this situation). Just as for example in many socialist theories and ideologies it was assumed that the increase of equality would be associated with the increase of productivity in society, and these two dimensions were supposed to constitute a syndromatic measure of "socialist development" of a society, and at the same time they were constituting an evaluative standard of its social progress. Unfortunately it seems now, that equality and productivity are probably negatively correlated with each other. They are counter-syndromatic. In such cases, particular societies have to be located separately in each dimension and evaluated according to the value someone is ready to attribute to each of these characteristics taken separately. In the domain of purposeful transformation, societies and their leaders have to decide out of these two dimensions which they would rather make progress in, or in what proportions they would like to combine them being ready to pay with a slowing of progress or even with a regress in one of them for some progress in the other.

It is relatively easy to find examples in the history of mankind of simple, uni-dimensional directional changes, and quite a few of them are quite longitudinal. Development of science or technology, increase of the population of our globe etc., are examples of such processes, which when regarded in isolation from other analogous processes seem to correspond to the old beliefs in the permanence of human progress. But it is much more difficult to find equally longitudinal multi-dimensional syndromatic processes. Such more comprehensive changes – especially those corresponding to our values and deserving to be classified as examples of more comprehensive progress, are relatively rare, because each singular process has a multitude of possible consequences, manifest and latent functions and disfunctions.

In the classical period in the history of our discipline many theoreticians had the following notion: there is one underlying cause of entire social change (let us say: technology), and if this cause changes directionally in the desired direction (as it does, they believed), it causes other elements of social processes to change accordingly, also in the desired direction.

Today we know that things are much more complicated. Each of the elements of a social process, from the most "fundamental," to the most "superficial" ones, has a multitude of effects. We like some of these consequences, and we don't like others. The larger the scope of the effects of such process is taken into consideration, the greater the number of both its positive and negative effects will be also found.

Some of the negative effects of positive trends are quite spectacular. The development of science and technology has resulted – among other things – in the development of more and more powerful weapons, capable of the destruction of many people, or even of mankind in general. The development of medical sciences has, among its other effects, resulted in a demographic explosion in many developing countries, making economic development practically impossible. Such examples are multiple.

On the other hand, if there is no joint underlying common cause, or there is no direct feedback between the elements of a process, which we could advance jointly, the question arises, is it most likely that the particular dimensions of a more complex social process, corresponding to our understanding of its progress will develop (or will be regressing, or stable) independently from each other. There are no reasons why they should co-vary in a syndromatic manner, unless we introduce through our deliberate actions such factors which could produce the entire syndrome.

And here is the importance of the theory of processes of directional change, because only such a theory can tell us why certain, both simple and syndromatic processes did – or did not – occur in some time–space areas of social reality. And only such a theory can tell us what should be done in order to increase the probability of desired transformations in the future.

Evaluation standards of simple and syndromatic processes

When we look at evaluation standards which are applied to any reality (including the social one), we can classify them in two dimensions. First we should distinguish singular evaluation criteria from the whole sets of such criteria, i.e., from complex evaluation standards.

In the second category, when having a complex evaluation standard composed from a multitude of criteria, we either evaluate this object separately in each dimension and leave it at this stage. This is tantamount to locating the evaluated object at a certain point in a multi-dimensional evaluation space. We may also come to the conclusion that we may give the object its generalized value, taking into account all sets of its characteristics which are relevant from the point of view of such a complex evaluation standard, and applying an algorithm for their joint evaluation, transformable into a single overall index, measuring the "total value" of the evaluated object to us.

In another classificatory dimension we should distinguish between such evaluative standards which specify a certain state in one or many dimensions as the reference point for evaluative comparison, and such criteria which specify only certain evaluative dimensions, where particular objects may only be compared with each other. The first kind of criteria permits us to find some "absolute" values for the evaluated object (as measured by possession of the desired trait or by the distance from the criterion point). The second category only permits their relative, comparative evaluation.

There are three possible sources for the evaluation standards applied to the evaluation of such directional changes, which make them classifiable from the point of view of their progressive character. First, the researcher may build them on the basis of his own value system. Then, he may take into account the values of an individual or collective sponsor of his study. Finally, he may take into account the values of the members of the populations he studies (provided that they are somehow uniform). In any case all these standards come – more indirectly – from human biology, from human culture, and from the researcher's mind, and in each case he must define his own attitude to the biological or cultural heritage and take all responsibility for such decisions. Whatever the case, it is the scientist who must decide whether he involves this or the other value system in his study, and both the decision and the responsibility belongs to him only. And those values are of course valid only with respect to the person chosing, they are relative to the changing value of the evaluators.

These evaluation standards may nevertheless be complicated – or enriched – by our empirical knowledge as well. We evaluate certain features of the external world for their own sake, because they are in agreement with such evaluation standards, which constitute for us the ultimate values, or "autotelic" standards of evaluation. In other cases we evaluate some things in a given way, not because they have a certain shape or observable course, but because they have certain, more or less indirect consequences. They are then judged on the basis of certain "instrumental" standards, evaluating the process not so much by its visible shape at a certain moment but by its direct or indirect consequences, functions etc.

And in the assessment of these causal or functional relations the scientist has to use his empirical knowledge. Some of these consequences are quite direct and follow the evaluated events in time, when others are so indirect that they become apparent only after a certain period of historical transformation.

When adding to the known effects of certain states or transformations an additional factor shaping our criteria of instrumental evaluations, we may have certain contradictory evaluations applied to the same process: by its own shape it may deserve a negative evaluation, but when judged by some of its consequences it may receive quite a positive evaluation. Thus some brutal rulers have been later evaluated positively by historians, when it was found that their brutal rule resulted in some social changes which elsewhere were positively evaluated. Similar contradictory evaluations are possible with respect to two consequences of the same process – as in the case of science, which both permits us to better understand the world (+), and to destroy it (−). In shaping any evaluation criterion both autotelic and instrumental reasons may play a role.

When we discover that there is a syndromatic directional change going on in a certain area or domain of social reality, it does not mean that we have to use a syndromatic concept of progress in its evaluation. It may happen that from the entire co-varying syndrome the occurrence of which has been empirically assessed, we are normatively interested in only a subset of interrelated variables, or even in one particular component of this syndrome. Thus, for example, a whole complex syndrome of directional changes is going on in a young human being between birth and maturation, but only some of them are regarded as "progressive" by his or her doctors, others by his teachers, when finally many of them are not covered by any set of evaluation standards at all; they simply happen to occur in the process of biological, intellectual, or social maturation of a young person.

Applying existing theories of social change to the study of progress

When we see the occurrence of positively evaluated directional change in some objects we are interested in, and its absence in others, we ask the question "why." When we fear that a positive trend may not continue in the future, we ask the question "how," or to what kind of mechanisms did or do these processes of directional change occur in objects, and on what conditions does the action of these mechanisms depend, and often: "what could be done in order to . . ."

To explain the course of any directional change, either simple or syndromatic, either corresponding to a set of evaluation standards, or free of such evaluative reference, we need, of course, some theories. They would have to be diachronic theories, or in other terms, theories dealing with the dynamics of social transformations and longitudinal changes of some generally defined social objects (unless it is such a unique object as the "humankind" which is denoted, by definition, by a singular concept).

Fortunately quite a few social theories deal with social change, and this goes back to the origins of our discipline, as Eva and Amitai Etzioni stated many years ago: "Many of the fathers of sociology were concerned with the general trend of history and its meaning. Mostly they sought to explain the past developments and sometimes to predict its future in terms of a definite pattern" (Etzioni 1964: 3).

As we know there are a great number of such theories of various levels of generality, and approaching their explananda from the point of view of different explanatory principles (see for example Appelbaum 1970).

Unfortunately these theories are in such a shape that they can only rarely be applied for the explanation or prediction of a real course of social change, because neither the mechanisms which they postulate as their explanatory assumptions, nor the domains of applicability of particular theories, nor finally the conditions of validity of most theories usually specified with sufficient precision to make them applicable to the explanation of particular processes, for which purpose they were formulated.

Another of their weaknesses was to make a theory applicable for explanations and predictions of certain processes or events we should first prove inductively its empirical validity for the given domain and for specified conditions. Unfortunately in the social sciences explanations of certain events by the use of a theory (i.e. applications) is often tantamount to its inductive confirmation. It would be equivalent to such situations in medicine, when we use "experimentally" a new, untested drug for a concrete patient, and when the patient survives we call it inductive confirmation. The patient has no reason to be happy with such a verification of hypotheses about the efficiency of this drug. In the human sciences we are more tolerant methodologically than in medicine and tend to accept individual explanations of concrete cases as the inductive evidence for the hypothesis used in such explanations.

It would be useless to quote all those who are skeptical about the present state of social theory (see for example Turner 1978: 13). Therefore let me limit these remarks as much as possible.

In textbooks or in our readers in theory we read about "functional theories of change," about theories explaining change by "social conflict." But here we should ask, at what level of analysis do these mechanisms operate and to which social objects can they be applied, to make these theories empirically valid (and to which objects are we not allowed to apply them); then we should ask, to what range of properties of these units, can we then apply these theories. Functional or conflict theories of change apply probably to rather large "territorial societies" and to some institutional arrangements. But they probably do not apply to other social units at a lower level. And to what properties of such unspecified units may they be applied? And in which additionally specified conditions are they supposed to be valid? And in which conditions can we explain or predict change better with the use of conflict theories and when with those assuming homeostatic harmony as a tendency of the social system.

Some of these theories are "evolutionary" while others stress the role of the mechanism of "diffusion of innovation," and exactly the same questions can be asked as with respect to the two categories of theories mentioned above. And the same doubts arise about conditions and limits of their valid applicability.

Other theories are characterized by the special causes of change, they postulate. Some see them in the dynamics of more "objective" aspects of social reality, geographic environment, demography, technology, or economy of the changing society. Others see the roots of change in more "subjective" domains, in people's changing values or attitudes. And here we should ask the same questions about conditions and limits of their intended validity, as well as many other questions mentioned above. The theories are so formulated that we rarely find sufficient answers to these questions.

And when it comes to questions about the degree of inductive confirmation of particular theories, we find more often illustrations of the action of explanatory mechanisms postulated by particular theories, than systematic empirical evidence in support of them.

The reason for that is that these theories do not specify clearly the domains of their intended applicability, i.e. they do not specify either the kinds of objects to which they apply and the types of characteristics of these objects they want to explain, or the conditions of their intended validity. This makes them in principle untestable. This also makes it extremely difficult to state which of these theories is either complementary or contradictory with reference to the same class of explananda, and to which sets of different theories such questions do not apply, since these theories refer to different and not overlapping domains of social reality.

Only when we clarify the meaning of our theories of change with respect to the substantive domains and conditions of their applicability can we apply these theories to the explanation and prediction of concrete processes of directional social change.

Single theories and the multi-theoretical models of directional change

Specification of the domain and conditions of applicability of a theory of change increases – of course – its applicability to the explanation of social processes and to their prediction. But in some situations there may be a natural limit to which we can explain in a satisfactory way some – especially more complex – processes, using one theory only. In such cases we should then try to build what I propose to call a multi-theoretical model of social change, dealing with the given object in its full complexity.

When specifying the domain of applicability of the theory and its "explanandum," i.e. the set of dependent variables it tries to explain, we are often bound to define them in a rather abstract manner. On the other hand our interests (both cognitive and evaluative) often focus on some complex of the "naturally existing and social important objects." It may turn out that we were luckly and some of these objects can be explained completely by one single explanatory mechanism and a theory which uses it.

But in many other cases we may be less lucky, and some social objects, when they are socially (and evaluatively) important for the members of the given society, are not, at the same time, such "theoretical entities," explainable by one, single theoretical mechanism. Then of course we have no chance of formulating a broad adequate, verifiable theory about them, referring to all objects, belonging to such a naturally defined class, nor of explaining or predicting singular cases of processes of the given class.

The more complex the objects or phenomena we are interested in, are, and the events or processes occurring to them, and the more their notions correspond to common language categories – which usually also means that they are in all their complexity socially and evaluatively relevant for members of the society who perceive and define them in their cultural (linguistic) categories – the less likely it is that such natural social objects will be explainable by one single explanatory theory. It does not mean that they are not explainable theoretically. But it does mean it is not possible to formulate one single, consistent, and conformable theory about them.

Many real, naturally distinguishable objects, as well as the phenomena and processes occurring in them are such "multi-theoretical entities," and the mechanisms of their functioning, behavior, and change cannot then be explained by one single law or theory. It does not mean that they are "irregular," "unexplainable," etc. It means that the mechanisms governing their functioning and change should be understood as multi-theoretical vectors, composed of several more fundamental mechanisms, each of them explainable by another basic theory. More strictly they should be understood as vectors composed from a whole set of conditional laws, or law-like generalizations, belonging to different explanatory theories. Let me call such vectors or "meta-theoretical constructions," composed from propositions belonging to different theories, multi-theoretical models of complex phenomena. Such models may be synchronic, or diachronic; we are interested here in diachronic multi-theoretical models of social change.

The term "model" has a whole range of meanings in science in general and in the social sciences in particular (see for example Brodbeck 1968, or Sztompka 1968). Some of these meanings propose a normative sense of this term, when others are descriptive, illustrative, or explanatory ones. Some see models as a subclass of theories, while others see different and non-overlapping domains of applicability for these two terms. In this essay, being aware of all these proposals, I am using the term "model" in the way it is used in such sciences, which sometimes have to apply jointly many theories in order to grasp the rules of functioning and transformation of certain complex objects.

When for example an astrophysicist constructs a model of a "neutron star" he uses for that purpose all the laws of physics he may need without asking whether they belong to one theory or not. He is aware that they usually belong to many different theories, as formulated in the textbooks of physics, but he happens to need them all in one place. And to construct this model he also adds to it those initial conditions of all these laws, which they obtain in the situation existing in a neutron star, or at the stage of its formation. Finally he takes into account possible effects of joint action of all these laws, their additiveness or possible interactions.

In such a way he constructs a general theoretical model of a neutron star, the generality of which is independent from the number of real situations in which all conditions postulated by the model are satisfied. It could in reality apply to one neutron star only, or to none at all and it would still be theoretically general, since it has been from the "bricks," which in themselves are general, i.e. from particular laws of theoretical physics. In my opinion such models have to be built in all these sciences which are interested in some natural complex objects (like astronomy or biology) and where the complexity of such objects makes them unexplainable by one single abstract theory. Sociology or psychology are also such sciences.

To build such a multi-theoretical model of social change we have to:

(1) Choose the set of characteristics of the given complex object, which for cognitive or evaluative reasons are important to us, and the dynamics of which we would like to explain, or to predict;

(2) Establish which known theories (formulated in possibly the best way we can with respect to their domain and conditions of applicability) are needed to explain the whole process in its complexity; we should remember here also that there may be mutual causal feedback between particular elements of the complex syndromatic change;

(3) Find out what kind of additivity or interaction does occur, when several mechanisms, described by different theories operate jointly in one complex process and to take this into account in our model;

(4) Finally we should establish the initial conditions of each of the regularities involved, characteristic for the singular process we want to explain or for a whole class of such explananda. Then we have to "feed" these initial conditions into our model and "let the imagined process run"

through a proper number of transformations, as in the case of any other "monotheoretical" simulation of any process. When doing this we should hope that, in the final outcome of the model of our process, we will receive the dynamics of the process, the observed, empirical shapes known to us from our earlier assessments and (or) evaluations.

If we succeed in finding a sufficient approximation of the results of such a "simulated" model in the observed course of events, it means that we did explain the given process, or the general category of such complex processes. If not, it means that either some of the initial conditions of our theories were wrong, or some of the theories themselves are wrong, or finally that something is still missing in our model, which means that we should try to discover another important component mechanism of our vector, also involved in given transformations, and supplementing it by its initial conditions, add it to our model, Needless to say, we should then also formulate another abstract theory, describing this new mechanism, and add this theory to our textbooks on sociological theories.

Such multi-theoretical explanatory models will also be able to tell us why "progress," as we understand it, occurred in some cases and did not or does not occur in others. They will also be able to tell us what should be done in a particular complex social situation, to increase the probability of such a future, which would be more satisfactory to us, than the present state of affairs in our societies.

How far we are now from the possibility of constructing such comprehensive, multi-theoretical models of change of complex social situations, that is quite another story. At this moment we should probably rather work on the improvement of particular theories of social change, because at their present stage of formulation and verification they can hardly be used for the construction of such explanatory and predictive models, or even for the explanation of much more simple, uni-dimensional processes, for the explanation of which they have been formulated.

Bibliography

Appelbaum, Richard P. (1970) *Theories of Social Change* (Chicago: Markham).
Brodbeck, May (1968) "Models, meaning, and theories," in M. Brodbeck (ed.) *Readings in the Philosophy of the Social Sciences* (New York: Macmillan).
Etzioni, Eva and Amitai (eds) (1964) *Social Change; Sources, Patterns and Consequences* (New York: Basic Books).
Jedlicki, Jerzy (1985) "Idea postępu z perspektywy naszego czasu" ("The idea of progress from the perspective of our time") *Kultura i Spoleczenstwo*, XXIX (4) (Warszawa).
Nowak, Stefan (1976) "Values and knowledge in the theory of education: a paradigm for an applied social science," in S. Nowak (ed.) *Understanding and Prediction: Essays in the Methodology of Social and Behavioral Theories* (Dordrecht, Holland: D. Reidel).

Nowak, Stefan (1977) *Methodology of Sociological Research* (Dordrecht, Holland: D. Reidel).

Sowa, Julia (1984) *Kulturowe zalozenia pojęcia normalnosci w psychiatrii* (Cultural Assumptions of the Concept of Normalcy in Psychiatry) (Warszawa: Państwowe Wydawnictwo Naukowe).

Sztompka, Piotr (1968) "Pojęcie modelu w socjologii" ("The concept of model in sociology") *Studia Socjologiczne*: 1.

Tukidydes (1957) *Wojna Peloponeska* (The Peloponnesian War) (Warszawa: Państwowe Wydawnictwo Naukowe).

Turner, Jonathan (1978) *The Structure of Sociological Theory* (Chicago: Dorsey Press).

12

Agency and progress: the idea of progress and changing theories of change

PIOTR SZTOMPKA

The idea of progress and changing theories of change

From the very birth of sociology the idea of progress seemed to be inextricably linked with theories of social dynamics. Sociology's ambition was to become the science of progress. It was easy to overlook the fact that the concept of progress is necessarily, logically linked only with a rather special kind of social dynamic; it has a meaning only within a particular image of social change. Already in the nineteenth century, within its predominant organic-turned-systemic model of society, three kinds of social change had been studied. One was a normal, everyday operation of society; a set of repeatable, regular, patterned processes supporting the functioning of a social whole, without modifying its character or identity. "Operation without transformation" was to become a focus of structural-functional theories from Malinowski to Parsons, with their emphasis on equilibrium, structural continuity, self-regulation, and reproduction. Another variety of change was the cyclical processes, from the daily routine of family life, through the weekly cycle of industrial labor, the yearly work-pattern of agrarian communities, and ending with various circular transformations of wider societies – economic, political, cultural – returning to the starting point after a more or less intricate and prolonged sequence of changes. "Change without novelty" was to become a focus of various cyclical theories, from Spengler to Sorokin. But there was also a third possibility: one could treat social changes as directional, producing an orderly, patterned sequence of fundamental transformations, in which each stage is basically novel, emergent, never repeated and each next stage brings the process closer to some specified ultimate standard. "Directional transformation" was the image central for theories of social development, with evolutionism and historical materialism as their major nineteenth-century varieties.

247

The important point is that the idea of progress has its place only within the model of directional transformation, within some version of developmentalism or, more generally, transformativism, and cannot be conceived either within the organic, structural-functional theories, or cyclical theories. It is meaningless to speak of societies as progressing, that is improving, getting better, if they are seen as basically unchanging, merely reproducing themselves, or if they are seen as changing only in closed cycles. It is only together with the idea of transformation (change of, and not only change in a society), and the idea of regular pattern or directional sequence of such transformations, that the concept of progress makes any sense.

This explains why recent disenchantment and disillusionment with the idea of progress[1] is so closely interwoven with a surge of criticism directed at major varieties of traditional developmentalism. The critique of the "metaphor of growth," as underlying evolutionism, and the critique of the "iron laws of history," as proclaimed by dogmatic, orthodox versions of historical materialsim – are taken to imply the necessary rejection of the idea of progress (Popper 1945, 1957; Nisbet 1969, 1970; Tilly 1984).

But is such a conclusion really warranted? Isn't it possible to retain a concept of progress, parting with the traditional versions of developmentalism, with their unacceptable assumptions of finalism, fatalism, or determinism? I will argue precisely for such a solution, for the revindication of the idea of progress within the framework of post-developmentalist theories, new accounts of social self-transformation. By these I mean an emerging complex of theoretical ideas addressed toward the same problems as traditional developmentalism (namely the question of mechanism and the course of major social changes), but radically different in emphases and proposed solutions. This important intellectual trend brings together sociological theorists, social philosophers, and social historians under such labels as "morphogenesis," "structuration," "relational structurism," "sociological structualism," "self-production of society," "societal self-guidance" etc.[2] The central message common to most theorists of this orientation, in spite of considerable differences of individual standpoint, is the idea that social structures and historical processes are the outcome (though not necessarily intended, and sometimes even unrecognized) of everyday practices, of human actions undertaken by individuals, collectivities, groups, classes, movements etc., in the conditions produced by the earlier generations of social actors. And hence, the notion of human agency, the active, causal force of social transformations appears at the core of theoretical debate.

I will argue that the idea of progress can be reformulated in line with the general thrust of morphogenesis-structuration theories, by linking it with the notion of the agency. And I will propose a new criterion of social progress, to be found in the qualities of human agency. In this way I hope to produce a positive critique – or a dialectical *Aufhebung*, if you wish – of the traditional notion of progress, which will retain its rational core, but liberate itself from all deterministic, fatalistic, and finalistic associations.

From the "divine will" to the "cunning of reason"

Granted that the idea of progress is logically linked to the image of directional process, there are several questions to be asked about its more specific characteristics. To begin with: at which phase of the process is the concept of progress "anchored," or less metaphorically, which phase of the process is its immediate referent. Three answers are possible. The first, most common in classical sociological theory, refers progress to the final outcome, result, product of the process; defined either as a comprehensive blueprint, complex image of society-to-become (typical for social utopias), or as some specific trait of society and its constituents (e.g. wealth, health, productivity, equality, happiness). One may speak here of "progress as ideal." The second answer locates progress in the overall logic of the process, in which each stage is seen as an improvement over the earlier one, and itself further perfectible – but without any ultimate end (this would be characteristic for evolutionary notions of gradual differentiation, or adaptive upgrading). One may speak here of "progress as betterment." Finally, the third answer would relate progress to the originating mechanism of the process, emphasizing the potentiality or capacity for progress inherent in human agency. Here, not the quality of what actually becomes, but the potentiality for becoming, becomes the core meaning of progress. Not the achievement but achieving, not the attainment but striving, not the finding but quest – are the marks of progress.[3]

I am going to opt for the last solution. But before specifying it in any more detail, I wish to take up another related question about progress, this time concerning the criteria of progress and their logical status. Some would claim that the criteria, measures of progress are absolute, constant, universal. In a word – unchanging. They supposedly provide us with an external, independent scale with which to appraise the on-going process.[4] The opposite position is relativistic and historicist. It claims that standards of progress are themselves dynamic, permanently changing, constantly evolving as the process unfolds. The needs, desires, goals, values, or any other measures of progress, are held to be modified with their satisfaction or fulfilment. They are always relative to the concrete phase of the process and never reach ultimate, final embodiment. What is strived for is changeable and variable, but the striving itself is constant. There is the variability of objects of human desire, but at the same time, the permanence of desiring.[5] Thus the measure of progress is no longer external, but rather immanent to the process itself.

The next question has to do with the deontic status of progress: does it refer to necessities or possibilities? Traditional, developmentalist approaches would treat progress as inevitable, necessary, due to inexorable laws of evolution or history. More recent, post-developmentalist theories of morphogenesis-structuration would certainly opt for different, possibilistic accounts, where progress is treated as merely contingent, as an open chance for betterment which, alas, does not need to come about, and may even remain unrecognized for human actors.

And finally, one more question has to be phrased, this time about ontological substrata of progress: what is the substantive nature of this causal, generative force bringing about progress? Four typical answers may be singled out. The doctrine of providentialism, encountered in various schools of social philosophy locates the ultimate, moving force of progress – the agency – in the supernatural order, invokes the Divine Will, providence, intervention of God. The doctrine of heroism typical of traditional historiography – sociology's elder next of kin – locates the agency in the exceptional personal endowment of great men: kings, prophets, leaders, codifiers, revolutionaries, generals etc. This is already an earthly domain, but still extra-social, because dependent on the genetic, more or less accidental propensities of individual people. The doctrine of organicism introduces the social component, but in a peculiar way; it treats the causal agency as inherent in the operation of the social organism, in its in-built propensity for growth, evolution, development. The origins of progress are social, but paradoxically – extra-human. People are still absent from the picture, where self-regulating, compensatory, automatic mechanisms seem to reign independently of human efforts. If people appear at all, it is only in the capacity of fully molded marionettes, unwitting executors, carriers of the preordained verdicts of history; as embodiments of productive forces, technological tendencies, demographic trends, revolutionary élan. It is only in the doctrine of constructivism underlying post-developmentalist theories that the emphasis is turned toward real socialized individuals in their actual social and historical contexts, and the moving force of change – the agency – is located in their normal everyday social activities. Some of the resulting progress may be intended, but mostly it is conceived here as the unintended and often unrecognized result of human efforts, as the product of the "invisible hand" (Smith), or the "cunning of reason" (Hegel), or "situational logic" (Popper). The agency is finally humanized and socialized at the same time. Common people are brought back into the picture and acquire truly human size: as aware but not omniscient, powerful but not omnipotent, creative but not unconstrained, free but not unlimited. Such an account of agency is both presupposed and entailed by the morphogenesis-structuration theories.

To recapitulate, it is claimed that the new theoretical orientation of

250

post-developmentalism, and particularly of morphogenesis-structuration suggests a new approach to social progress: (1) as a potential capacity, rather than ultimate achievement, (2) as a dynamic, evolving, relative quality of a concrete process, rather than absolute, universal, external standard, (3) as a historical possibility, opportunity, open option rather than necessary, inevitable, inexorable tendency, (4) as a product – often unintended, and even unrecognized – of human pluralistic and collective actions, rather than a result of divine will, good intensions of exceptional individuals ("great men"), or operation of automatic social mechanisms. This provides a framework for a radically new notion of progress. But to grasp its full significance, the framework has to be fleshed out. Starting from the heuristic hunches provided by the theories of morphogenesis-structuration I will attempt to go beyond them and to elaborate the new, agency-focused concept of social progress, by means of a more detailed analysis.

Human agency in society and history

As a first approximation I shall define agency as the immanent potentiality of society causally responsible for its self-transformation, or in other words, an inherent capacity for self-transcendence. Agency so conceived is an abstract, theoretical, postulated notion, the meaning of which can only be specified contextually, by locating it within the wider model of social reality.[6] I shall construct such a model in five steps.

To start with, the model I propose rests on two oppositions: (1) of two levels of social reality; the level of individuality and the level of totality, and (2) of two aspects of social reality; the aspect of potentialities (capacities, tendencies, dispositions, propensities), and the aspect of actualities (implementing, realizing the potentialities). Combining those dichotomies we obtain four categories for describing major components of social reality: structures, transformations, actors, and actions (Fig. 12.1).

Step two attempts to bridge the gap between the level of individuality and the level of totality, which obviously cannot be treated as autonomous, separate, and unrelated. The link between ongoing transformations of

	POTENTIALITY	ACTUALITY
TOTALITY	STRUCTURE	TRANSFORMATION
INDIVIDUALITY	ACTOR	ACTION

Figure 12.1

251

society (elaboration, modification, development of structures) and the ongoing actions (practices) of individuals is rendered by the theoretical category of praxis. Hence, praxis is conceived as a complex net result of structural transformations and human actions. And in a parallel fashion, the link between structures (situations, conditions) and actors placed within them (their dispositions, motivations, reasons, intentions) is rendered by the theoretical category of the agency. Hence, the agency is conceived as a complex net result of structural conditions and actors endowment. From our earlier distinction of potentialities and actualities it follows that agency is construed as the potentiality for praxis, and praxis as the actualization of agency. It may be summarized on a diagram (Fig. 12.2), by adding vertical and horizontal links to our earlier four-fold scheme (vertical arrows signifying determination, or at least conditioning, and horizontal arrows signifying actualization, implementation).

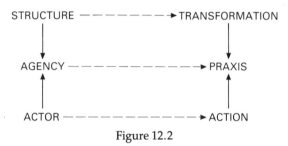

Figure 12.2

Step three introduces the natural environment; another abstract category comprising both external natural conditions and internal natural (biological, hereditary) endowment of human individuals. The society operates within the natural environment (external and internal); it is immersed in nature or permeated with nature. To some extent nature provides parametric conditions (constraining and facilitating) for the operation of society, and to some extent nature is shaped and changed by society (civilized, humanized, harnessed, conquered). There is an interactive mutual co-determination and not one-sided conditioning between society and nature. In our schematic representation (Fig. 12.3) the model is enriched by encircling all intrasocietal components with nature (remember that nature is also "inside" human actors).

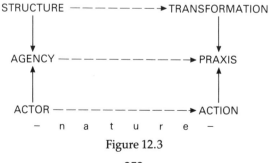

Figure 12.3

Step four puts the society in motion; introduces the dimension of time. The praxis at any given time produces consequences (intended and unintended, recognized and unrecognized) at the level of totality, modifying structures, as well as at the level of individuality, changing people. As a result, a changed agency emerges and is implemented (via changed practices and transformed structures) in a new praxis at any later time. This process is continuous and cumulative, and represents in terms of our model what is normally referred to as history. Any existing state of society is therefore only a phase of a process; a product of past operation (accumulated historical tradition) and a precondition for future operation. Figure 12.4 represents this most complex, historical dimension in a schematic form.

The final, fifth step in the construction of a model recognizes a crucial fact that the ultimate constituents of society – human individuals – are reflective and self-conscious. They do not only experience the operation of society, the impact of historical tradition, and the emergence of the future; they also reflect about all that, exercise their judgment, imagination, hopes, formulate accounts, predictions, draw images. This capacity for self-awareness is crucially important because, by way of various feedbacks, it enters as an immanent, interacting factor into the operation of society.

Having constructed the model, let me return now to the central notion of the agency. This potentiality for social self-transformation is now seen as a result of multiple lines of conditioning (variable constraining and enabling influences). First, it is conditioned by the existing structures (e.g. norms, values, rules, roles, institutions, ideas, beliefs, knowledge, communication channels, patterns of inequality, etc.). Second, it is conditioned by the endowment of actors (e.g. their skills, commitments, imagination, expertise, capabilities, etc.). Both structures and actors are shaped by the accumulated historical heritage; they are the cumulative result of earlier actualizations of agency via praxis. Thus, the third conditioning influence on the agency – mediated by structures and actors – is the historical tradition, the "push of the past." The fourth influence may be called the "pull of the future"; the future as encoded in existing structures ("socially expected durations"[7]), or as envisioned in the imagination of actors – "the images of the future" (Bell and Mau 1970). Finally, the fifth conditioning influence (both constraining and enabling) comes from the natural environment in which the agency operates (e.g. the ecological constraints, scarcity of resources – limiting the variety of possible structures; or biological, genetic constraints – limiting the scope of possible actions).

As if the model were not complex enough, there is an additional complication that has to be taken into account. Namely, all those influences are themselves pluralistic, heterogenous, often ambivalent and contradictory.

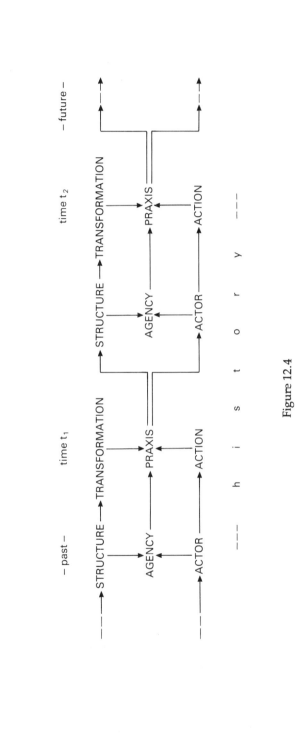

Figure 12.4

And this is because the empirical embodiments of the agency in every society are multiple and variable. There are individuals in socially influential roles, there are collectivities, classes, groups, movements etc. For each of these kinds of actors – individual and collective – their respective structural constraints and facilitations may differ; and similarly, they may encounter quite different natural conditions (e.g. occupy distinct "ecological niches"). They may also inherit different traditions and expect different futures. Often, those influences will not only be multiple and differentiated, but contradictory. Thus, the agency emerges as the extremely complex, synthetic product, a combined net-outcome of those cross-cutting determinations, and often as the result of social conflicts and struggles. Old Auguste Comte had a point when he was speaking of the "*complication supérieure*" of social reality.

The plausibility of the presented model and its central notion of agency is of course an open question, to be resolved only in view of its fruitfulness for interpretation and explanation of social phenomena. At this moment I wish only to invoke a prima facie meta-theoretical argument in its favor. Namely, it seems to bridge at least three pervasive and misleading polarities of sociological theorizing. First, the agency is here conceived as neither individualistic, nor collectivistic, but rather as a product of both actors and structures, some synthetic "third level" of social reality. Second, the agency is here conceived neither in idealist nor materialist terms, but rather it links structural and natural (material) resources with human knowledge, beliefs, reasons, imagination, expectations (ideal aspects). Third, the agency bridges the dichotomy of social stability and social dynamics; it is seen as a condensed product of the past operation of society, of earlier phases of a historical process, and at the same time a potentiality for further, future phases of the process. To put it a little metaphorically, the agency lives in the present but is looking toward the future and is shaped by the past. It is just a link stretching between the push of the past and the pull of the future. Its every static state is only a passing phase of a dynamic process.

Progress-conducive agency: an ideal type

Having sketched the model of social reality informed – at least in a general, indirect way – by the post-developmentalist tradition (theories of morphogenesis-structuration), and having elaborated the notion of the agency, by locating it in the context of the model – I must now link this discussion with the idea of progress by asking a question central to this paper: when may an agency be said to be progressive?

From the point of view of progress *any* agency certainly seems better than the lack of agency. Clearly, in order to have progress, we must have directional change, and if we conceive directional change as produced by human beings, then some human agency is an obvious prerequisite of progress. But its operation is only a necessary condition, and by no means a sufficient one for progress to ensue. Do not forget that directional change may also be in a backward direction; produce regress rather than progress. Thus, it is only a specifically constituted agency, a particular kind of agency which presents a potentiality for progress.

Which traits of the agency are especially relevant in this connection? First, of course, the characteristics of actors. Here, I would emphasize several oppositions which allow of gradations and all intermediate forms. Thus, actors may be creative, innovative, achievement-oriented; or passive, conservative, reconciled with ascribed positions. They may emphasize autonomy, independence, personal integrity; or exhibit conformity, adaptation, dependence. They may have adequate self-awareness of their social situation, or be completely ignorant, trapped in mythology or false consciousness. Which is the case for the majority of actors – or especially influential kinds of actors – will decisively shape the quality of the agency.

Second, the characteristics of structures are equally significant. They may be rich in options; pluralistic, heterogenous, complex, or just the opposite – they may be poor in options; limited, homogenous and simple. And they may be open, flexible, tolerant, allowing for large scope of variety, or rather closed, rigid, dogmatic, effectively eliminating novelty. Again, which kinds of structures surround the majority of actors, or especially influential actors – will be reflected in the quality of the agency.

Third, the characteristics of natural environment in which a society is placed exert their impact at two levels: via objective conditions and via subjective attitudes. The natural conditions may be benign, rich in resources, malleable, or harsh, poor, and forbidding. And people may attempt to harness, mold, master nature, to adapt it to their needs and aspirations, or they may wish merely to adapt themselves to nature, remain in the state of subjugation and passivity.

Fourth, keeping in mind the irreducible historical dimension of society, one must emphasize the characteristics of tradition; again at the objective and subjective level. Objectively, it seems to matter whether the tradition is marked by continuity, consistency, long duration, or rather by disruptions, discontinuities, ambiguities. Subjectively, the attitude of pride, respect, rootedness in tradition, may be opposed to presentism and uncritical rejection of the past (so typical of the "now generation"). Finally, the characteristics of the expected future may vary significantly, too. The attitude of optimism and hope is opposed to pessimism, catastrophism, and despair. The belief that the future is contingent, allows of alternative scenarios dependent on human efforts, is opposed to all brands of fatalism and finalism. And long-range image or strategic plan for the future is

256

something quite different from the short-range, immediate expectations or opportunistic, tactical scheming.

If we look again at the full list of twelve variable characteristics of the agency, it will be seen that they fall into two groups. Some determine whether people will want to act toward the transformation of their society; those variables shape action-oriented motivations. Others determine whether people will be able to act; those variables shape action-conducive opportunities. The agency may be thought of as progressive only if it brings together those two prerequisites – motivations and opportunities; only if people want to act, and can act accordingly.

I would suppose that such a situation is approximated by the conjunction of conditions at the initial poles of each dichotomy, that is by a combination of: (1) creative, autonomous, and self-aware actors, (2) rich and flexible structures, (3) benign and actively confronted natural environment, (4) continuous and proudly affirmed tradition, and (5) optimistic, long-range anticipating and planning of the future. This is an ideal type of an active society generating progress-oriented agency; a society on the course of progressive self-transformations.

One can easily construct a correlative ideal type of a passive society, generating regress-oriented agency. It would be made up of all conditions at the opposite poles of each dichotomy. Thus, it would be a society with (1) passive, conformist, and ignorant members, (2) simple and rigid structures, (3) harsh and passively encountered natural environment, (4) broken, fractured, and despised historical heritage, (5) pessimistic and fatalistic perspectives for the future. The agency in the sense of the potentiality for self-transformation is clearly absent here.

Of course, both are ideal types and actual empirical phenomena are never that simple. There will be all sorts of mixed cases and in between two polar types there will be found various modalities of crippled agency: (1) the cases where people want but cannot act (strong motivation and massive mobilization get blocked by inflexible or repressive institutions), and (2) the cases where people can but do not want to act (the opening up and liberalizing of structures do not release popular enthusiasm or immediate willingness to act[8]). Progressive self-transformation of society will not ensue in either of these cases.

Freedom and self-transcendence; the core of progress

So far we have been characterizing the agency from the external perspective, looking at it from the outside. The properties of the progress-oriented agency were reduced to the nature of conditioning, determining factors impinging upon it from without. Now I wish to take the internal perspective and focus on the operation of the progress-oriented agency, so to speak, from within. The question is: what is the *modus operandi* of the agency placed within the set of conditions and influences – structural, personal, natural, and historical – grasped by our ideal type.

I will describe it by two comprehensive, synthetic notions: freedom and self-transcendence. Thus, the viable, progress–oriented agency is to some extent free. It is free in the sense of negative freedom ("freedom from"), that is to say it commands certain levels of autonomy, independence from constraints; it operates within some open field of options, opportunities, chances. And it is free in the sense of positive freedom ("freedom to"), that is to say the capacity to influence, modify, reshape constraints, and enhance facilitations; it has some degree of power and control over circumstances.[9]

But its crucial, most important feature is the tendency toward self-transcendence; going beyond itself, overcoming limitations, breaking through constraints, crossing "frontiers." To stick with the latter metaphor, self-transcendence occurs at three "frontiers" of the human condition: transcending nature by harnessing it, controlling, regulating through work; transcending social structures by means of evasions, deviations, reforms, and revolutions; and last but not least transcending themselves as human actors through learning, training, self-control, achieving, advancing, extending their limited human powers by technology, etc. This propensity may be explained as an outgrowth of two fundamental traits of the human world: the creativity (innovativeness) of actors producing original and novel objects, ideas, institutions, and the cumulative character of constantly expanded and enriched human experience; individually learned in biographical span, and socially (culturally) transmitted in historical span. Thus, ultimately the mainspring of progress is found in the irreducible and principally unlimited creativity and educability of human beings, able to conceive novelty and to inherit as well as to pass on innovations; permanently enlarging their common pool of knowledge, skills, strategies, techniques, etc.[10]

If exercised in conditions described in the ideal type of progress-conducive agency, those human propensities and abilities safeguard self-transcendence, constant progress of humankind. Let me strongly underline this "if." There is no necessity of progress, because it is not pre-ordained that people will be willing and able to exercise their creative capacity. The constraining natural, structural, or historical conditions, or the suppressed motivations for activism (e.g. affected by socialization for passivity or by lessons, "scars" from past failures[11]) may prevent creativity from flourishing. And similarly, the process of cumulation, passing on of tradition may get disrupted, both at the biographical and at the historical level (the quality of family, school, church, media, and other institutions will be decisive here). In such cases, stagnation or regress rather than progress will be a likely result.

The self-transcendence of society in which agency participates as an ultimate causal force, feeds back on the agency itself, resulting in its own self-transcedence. The actualization of potentialities of the agency via praxis enlarges those very potentialities. Emancipation of the agency through its operation in time results in enlarged freedom and stronger tendencies toward self-transcedence. The ultimate progressiveness of the agency is found in the fact that it not only stimulates progress, but actually progresses itself. It is a cumulative historical outcome of its own operation.

The idea of progress as progressive itself

How one could go about defending, justifying the proposed idea of progress? Let us be clear about its logical status. Because in fact it is only an extended, contextual definition, a concept and not a proposition, a model and not a theory – it cannot be tested or verified by any straightforward confrontation with empirical facts. The criterion of truth or falsity simply does not apply. The idea is formulated in order to grasp, interpret, sort out, understand certain aspects of social reality somewhat more effectively than by means of alternative definitions. Therefore, the only valid empirical criterion is how it helps to achieve this goal, or to put it otherwise – what is its fruitfulness. This is the first possible line of defense.

To follow it would mean to examine wide historical evidence and to see if our concept of progress allows us to identify, delimit significant historical epochs, important periods of transformation, and whether such delimitation agrees, at least to some extent, with common intuitions associated with the idea of progress. More specifically, two questions would have to be posed; whether the periods selected by means of our definition would normally be thought of as progressive, and whether the periods normally thought of as progressive exhibit those constitutive traits which are emphasized by our definition (and particularly, those core qualities of the agency which we labelled as freedom and self-transcendence). This would be a formidable task, and I certainly don't feel competent to take it up. But at first sight, the concept seems to work well enough. The rhythm of human history is certainly uneven. There are prolonged periods of stagnation, inertia, slow movement, minor changes. And from time to time those eruptions of sudden transformation, thresholds between epochs. Just think of those exceptional periods marked by acceleration of changes which are later called the miracles of progress: Athens of the fifth century BC, Imperial Rome, Aztek, and Maya Empires, European Renaissance, China of Deng Siao Ping, Soviet *perestroika* – to mention just a few. Didn't they (or don't they) exhibit the relatively unbridled operation of the human agency, didn't they open up multiple avenues of human creativity, didn't they burst with wide-ranging activism, didn't they release large layers of optimism and hope? To put it succinctly: isn't it the case that some combination of self-transcending, creative personalities with permissive structural context produces this unique explosive force allowing human history to jump forward? Or let us think of the overall tendency to be discovered in the large spans of human history; doesn't it on the whole, in spite of many reversals, bring about growing awareness, knowledge, control over environment – natural and social; does it not typically leave more autonomy, independence to human actors *vis-à-vis* nature and society; does it not, as a rule, constantly accelerate the transformations of social structures? In short: don't we witness the gradual emancipation of human agency?[12]

But let us leave it at that inconclusive level of hunches, as I wish to move on to the second line of defense – purely theoretical, kept within the confines of "theoretical logic" (Alexander 1982, 1987). There are two arguments to be invoked at this level. Remember that the agency-focused concept of progress was inferred from the post-developmentalist theories of social change, and particularly the morphogenesis-structuration approach. It was formulated as the only idea of progress which makes sense within the account of social change as cumulative and continuous construction and reconstruction of social structures and of human actors themselves, by their own actions. Thus, if the logical link between proposed concept and this brand of theory is granted, then the concept inherits or shares in the plausibility of theory. It is indirectly corroborated in so far as the theory which informs it is found to be valid. And clearly, the evidence supporting morphogenesis-structuration theory is quite considerable and growing. This is the first, indirect theoretical argument. In a way it is like hiding behind the backs of the powerful, post-developmentalist theoretical movement.

The second argument rests on the epistemological notion of reflexivity. It has been observed that social ideas are not only about society, but in society; they become a significant part of the reality they account for, they enter the social causal nexus as important factors *per se*, by changing the conditions of human action – the knowledge and preferences of actors. In one apt formulation "among the ideas which move people are the ideas about what moves them" (Hollis 1987: 13). Ideas, concepts, theories of progress are not exempt from this reflexive mechanism. But there are striking differences among them concerning the direction of that reflexive impact. Developmentalism with its idea of necessary, inexorable progress, due either to supernatural or extra-social, or superhuman tendencies does not contribute as an additional intellectual factor to the achievement of the very final state it defines as progress. Its message for human actors is passivistic; prey and obey, or wait and see, depending on the version of developmentalism – sacred or secular. Human actors are seen as irrelevant to the generating of progress, and therefore the theory of progress cannot enter as a factor of progress. After all, its only conceivable entrance-point is through the human consciousness; motivations and consequent actions.

But the picture gets radically different when we move to the post-developmentalist theories of morphogenesis-structuration, and toward related concepts of progress as the self-transcending potentiality of the agency. Here, obviously, human consciousness, reasons, motivations, and actions become crucial for the realization of progress. Within the framework of the theory itself, the impress of the idea of progress on the progress-conducive capacity of the agency can be recognized as one of the central causal mechanisms. And the direction of that impact is clearly progressive, in terms of this very idea. The message of the proposed concept of progress for human actors is activistic; it calls for awareness, responsibility, realistic optimism, commitment, and action. It says simply: hope and strive. And hoping and striving is precisely what progress means here, just a different working of the core ideas of freedom and self-transcendence. Thus the idea of progress as the potentiality of the agency contributes itself to the emancipation of the agency. It is self-fulfilling, and hence progressive. It is the truly progressive concept of progress.

Notes

1. It must be borne in mind that disillusionment with progress is not the same as disillusionment with the idea (concept, notion, theory) of progress. The earlier is the state of mass consciousness, marked by the disappointment of unachieved promises, unfulfilled aspirations, frustrated dreams. The latter is the state of theoretical consciousness, characterizing social scientists, and marked by the critique or downright rejection of the concept itself – as meaningless, misleading, non-scientific etc. In this essay I deal with the second aspect only, even though both are certainly interrelated; the new theoretical consciousness emerges, at least partly, as a response to the "malaise" of social consciousness, and may feedback on the social consciousness aggravating its uneasiness.

2. As milestones marking this rich theoretical movement one may mention the following works: Buckley's book on morphogenesis in functional systems (1967), Etzioni's analysis of active society (1968), Touraine's study of class action via social movements (1977), Elias's idea of "figurations" (1978a and b and 1982), Crozier and Friedberg's organizational theory (1977), Giddens's numerous contributions to "structuration theory" (e.g. 1979, 1984), Burns' and H. Flam's evolving "rule-systems theory" (1987), Archer's enriched and rejuvenated "theory of morphogenesis" (1985, 1988). From the disciplinary sidelines, some historians applaud and formulate a similar framework for historical sociology and social history (Abrams 1982, Lloyd 1986).

3. Such an approach seems to bring a bonus, by bridling the ethnocentric biases so common in the theories of progress, e.g. in the theories of "modernization," or of the "stages of growth," or of other developmental schemes. Instead of comparing some actual, absolute levels of achievement (say GNP,

or number of cars, or longevity, or literacy etc.), what really counts here is the differentiated potential for achievement. Rich but stagnant societies may turn out to be less progressive in this sense than dynamic but (as yet) poor, or "underdeveloped" ones.

4. A sort of Galilean lever with which to move the Earth from a support in space.
5. There are several pervasive intellectual themes, both in social science and common sense which seem to reflect this property of the human condition: the idea of a permanent gap between aspirations and achievements, goals and realizations; the concept of secondary, contrived needs; the Faustian quest for never fully attainable knowledge; the vanishing point of human desires etc.
6. Ontologically, it has what is called a "virtual existence," that is to say it exists only in and through its actualizations – real practice, actions of people, individuals, and collectivities of all sorts.
7. This insightful concept introduced by R. K. Merton signifies the important fact that some structural arrangements have variable, expected durations in-built into them, irrespective of any subjective predictions. Examples: marriage, terms of office, deadlines etc. See Merton 1982, 1984.
8. This may be due to the unfortunate record of failed or suppressed activism on earlier occasions, encoded in the social consciousness. It may also be due to a kind of "trained incapacity" for mobilization and activism, resulting from prolonged socialization for passivity and obedience.
9. The idea of freedom, both negative and positive, is one of the most pervasive leitmotifs in the discussion about progress. But note that it acquires a new meaning in our proposal. Normally it refers to the state to be achieved, it is treated as the wished-for result of progress. In our model it describes a pre-requisite for progress. Freedom is understood here as the precondition of the agency's striving for progress, rather than the eventual culmination of progress. To put it otherwise, freedom acquires instrumental rather than autotelic value.
10. It can be seen that some notion of "human nature" is inescapable. Note that in our case this notion was inferred from the model of social reality, by "thinking back" toward the necessary prerequisites of the model's operation. The concept of human nature preserves the relativistic quality of the model, namely what is posited as constant is described only as a capacity, potentiality of human beings (creativity and educability), and not as any actual product. The capacity for creativity and educability may result (and in fact results) in an immense variety of outcomes.
11. A concrete historical illustration of this condition is described in my essay as "The social functions of defeat" (Sztompka 1988).
12. The intuitive recognition of this tendency is reflected in such formulations as "the move from the kingdom of necessity to the kingdom of freedom," or the emergence of "humanistic history" from "naturalistic history."

Bibliography

Abrams, Philip (1982) *Historical Sociology* (Ithaca: Cornell University Press).

Alexander, Jeffrey C. (1982) *Theoretical Logic in Sociology*, Vol. I (London: Routledge & Kegan Paul).

Alexander, Jeffrey C. (1987) *Twenty Lectures; Sociological Theory Since World War II* (New York: Columbia University Press).

Archer, Margaret (1982) "Structuration vs. morphogenesis," in S. N. Eisenstadt and H. J. Helle (eds) *Macro-Sociological Theory*, Vol. I (London: Sage: 58–88).

Archer, Margaret (1988) *Culture and Agency* (Cambridge: Cambridge University Press).

Bell, W. and Mau, James A. (1970) "Images of the future," in John C. McKinney and Edward A. Tiryakian (eds) *Theoretical Sociology* (New York: Appleton Century Crofts: 205–34).

Buckley, Walter (1967) *Sociology and Modern Systems Theory* (Englewood Cliffs, NJ: Prentice Hall).

Burns, Tom and Flam, Helena (1987) *The Shaping of Social Organization* (London: Sage).

Crozier, Michael and Friedberg, Erhard (1977) *L'acteur et le système* (Paris: Editions du Seuil).

Elias, Norbert (1978a) *The Civilizing Process*, Vol. I (Oxford: Basil Blackwell).

Elias, N. (1978b) *What is Sociology* (London: Hutchinson).

Elias, N. (1982) *The Civilizing Process*, Vol. II (Oxford: Basil Blackwell).

Etzioni, Amitai (1968) *The Active Society* (New York: Free Press).

Giddens, Anthony (1979) *Central Problems in Social Theory* (London: Macmillan).

Giddens, Anthony (1984) *The Constitution of Society* (Cambridge: Polity Press).

Hollis, Martin (1987) *The Cunning of Reason* (Cambridge: Cambridge University Press).

Lloyd, Christopher (1986) *Explanation in Social History* (Oxford: Basil Blackwell).

Merton, Eobert K. (1982) "Socially expected durations: a temporal component of social structure," paper delivered at the ASA Convention, San Francisco.

Merton, Robert K. (1982) "Socially expected durations: a temporal component of social structure," paper delivered at the ASA Convention, San Francisco. *Consensus: A Festschrift for Lewis A. Coser* (New York: Free Press: 262–83).

Nisbet, Robert A. (1969) *Social Change and History* (New York: Oxford University Press).

Nisbet, Robert A. (1970) "Developmentalism: a critical analysis," in J. C. McKinney and E. A. Tiryakian (eds) *Theoretical Sociology* (New York: Appleton Century Crofts: 167–204).

Popper, Karl R. (1945) *The Open Society and its Enemies*, Vol. II (London: Routledge & Kegan Paul).

Popper, Karl R. (1957) *The Poverty of Historicism* (London: Routledge & Kegan Paul).

Sztompka, Piotr (1988) "The social functions of defeat," in L. Kriesberg and B. Misztal (eds) Social Movements as a Factor of Change in the Contemporary World (Vol. 10 of *Research in Social Movements, Conflicts and Change*) (Greenwich, CT: JAI Press: 183–92).

Tilly, Charles (1984) *Big Structures, Large Processes, Huge Comparisons* (New York: Russell Sage Foundation).

Touraine, Alain (1977) *The Self-Production of Society* (Chicago: University of Chicago Press).

Index